Emotions, the social bond, and human reality

STUDIES IN EMOTION AND SOCIAL INTERACTION

Second Series

Series Editors

Keith Oatley
University of Toronto

Antony Manstead
University of Amsterdam

This series is jointly published by the Cambridge University Press and the Editions de la Maison des Sciences de l'Homme, as part of the joint publishing agreement established in 1977 between the Fondation de la Maison des Sciences de l'Homme and the Syndics of the Cambridge University Press.

Cette collection est publiée co-édition par Cambridge University Press et les Editions de la Maison des Sciences de l'Homme. Elle s'intègre dans le programme de co-édition établi en 1977 par la Fondation de la Maison des Sciences de l'Homme et les Syndics de Cambridge University Press.

The first title in the series is

The psychology of facial expression
Edited by James A. Russell and José Miguel Fernández-Dois

For a list of titles in the First Series of Studies in Emotion and Social Interaction, see the page following the index.

Emotions, the social bond, and human reality

Part/whole analysis

Thomas J. Scheff
University of California, Santa Barbara

CAMBRIDGE
UNIVERSITY PRESS

& Editions de la Maison des Sciences de l'Homme
Paris

PUBLISHED BY THE PRESS SYNDICATE OF THE UNIVERSITY OF CAMBRIDGE
The Pitt Building, Trumpington Street, Cambridge CB2 1RP, United Kingdom

EDITIONS DE LA MAISON DES SCIENCES DE L'HOMME
54 Boulevard Raspail, 75270 Paris Cedex 06, France

CAMBRIDGE UNIVERSITY PRESS
The Edinburgh Building, Cambridge CB2 2RU, United Kingdom
40 West 20th Street, New York, NY 10011–4211, USA
10 Stamford Road, Oakleigh, Melbourne 3166, Australia

© Thomas J. Scheff 1997

First published 1997

Printed in the United Kingdom at the University Press, Cambridge

Typeset in Palatino 10/12 pt.

A catalogue record for this book is available from the British Library

Library of Congress cataloging in publication data

Scheff, Thomas J.
Emotions, the social bond, and human reality: part/whole
analysis / Thomas J. Scheff.
    p.   cm. – (Studies in emotion and social interaction. Second series)
Includes bibliographical references and index.
ISBN 0 521 58491 4 (hc). – ISBN 0 521 58545 7 (pbk.)
1. Emotions – Social aspects. 2. Interpersonal relations.
3. Psychology – Research – Methodology.
4. Social psychology – Research – Methodology.
I. Title. II. Series.
BF531.S35 1997
302–dc21 96–51847 CIP

ISBN 0 521 58491 4 hardback
ISBN 0 521 58545 7 paperback
ISBN 2–7351 0736–1 hardback (France only)
ISBN 2–7351 0735–3 paperback (France only)

CE

Contents

Figures

Acknowledgments

This book has benefited from comments on earlier drafts by Walter Buckely, Aaron Cicourel, Keith Oatley, and Suzanne Retzinger. Keith Oatley's comments were particularly helpful in organizing and ordering the many strands.

Introduction

This book outlines and gives examples of a new approach to research in the human sciences. It puts into practice the recommendation of C. Wright Mills, for what he called the exercise of the sociological imagination. But I would call it instead the interdisciplinary, human imagination. Here I develop and elaborate ideas that were proposed in an early form in my *Microsociology* (1990) and in Suzanne Retzinger's *Violent Emotions* (1991). These books focused on a substantive topic: emotions and social bonds in their interrelationship. This book continues with that topic, but codifies the methodological dimension.

My goal is to describe an approach to all human research that allows the interpenetration of theory, method, and data in such a way that each equally casts light on the other, generating a theory that is based directly on observations of actual human behavior, both inner experience and outer conduct. This introduction and the first two chapters emphasize methodology, of relating the smallest parts to the largest wholes. The later chapters apply this approach to verbatim human expressions.

When part/whole methods are applied to verbatim texts, the intricate filigree of even the simplest human transactions are revealed. Inevitably, crucial aspects of this filigree are emotions and bond-oriented behavior. One important goal of the substantive chapters is to show that understanding the intricacy of human expressions is not a luxury, but an elementary requirement of human science. It is clear that societies (and the human relationships which constitute them) ride upon extraordinarily complex processes. Because emotional transactions are a vital part of human existence, and are usually omitted, the substantive chapters emphasize them, and their relation to behavior which is oriented toward maintaining the social bond. The part/whole method helps us to understand the relationship between human experience and the largest social structures.

At the heart of my method is what I call part/whole morphology. I borrow the idea of morphology from botany, where it has long formed

1

the intrinsic method of that discipline. In botanical research, the study of single cases (single specimens of plants) is just as important as making comparisons between plants. Morphology is based equally on single cases and comparative study. By microscopic study of the smallest details of a single plant, the botanist learns how it works as a system, even if no other specimens are available. To the extent that other specimens are available, microanalysis and comparative study can be interwoven, each illuminating the other. Botany is the study of both individual and groups of plants.

Although not discussed as such, botanical morphology employs what I call part/whole analysis, since it is concerned with relating the *least parts*, the tiniest details of an individual plant, with the *greatest wholes*, the structure and process of plant communities, and their relationship to their environment. The phrase "least parts and greatest wholes" is due to the philosopher Spinoza, who proposed that human understanding requires relating the least parts to the greatest wholes (Sacksteder 1991). Spinoza's proposition forms the basis of this book. As Spinoza implied and as recent research demonstrates, human beings and human relationships are so complex as to require part/whole analysis, even in cases of simple, everyday interaction.

One area in which the many-layered complexity of human activities has become quite clear is ordinary language. The failure of automated computer translation of foreign languages, and of paraphrasing meaning within a language, has strong implications for the human sciences. Typically a computer program will offer fifty to a hundred paraphrases of the meaning of a sentence, none of which is correct, and many of which are ludicrous. For example, a computer program failed to provide a correct paraphrase of the aphorism "Time flies like an arrow." One of the many paraphrases produced was "Time flies (insects) as you would an arrow." Understandably, the program mistook a noun (time) for a verb, and a verb (flies) for a noun.

From a logical point of view, an ordinary language is a mess, since its main terms, the most frequently used words, always have a multitude of meanings. How do human beings ever interpret the meaning of a text or an utterance correctly (i.e. consensually)? The implication is that humans have within them computing equipment infinitely more sophisticated than the most sophisticated computers. To correctly understand ordinary language, humans must have access to part/whole algorithms that allow them to understand the particular meanings of words (and when face to face, of gestures) in *context*: that is, the meaning of an expression produced by a particular person in a particular dialogue, in a particular relationship, in a particular culture, at a particular time in history. All understanding requires a high order of what George Steiner (1975) called "interpretive decipherment." Like the Rosetta Stone, ordinary language is always a problem of creative cryptography, needing vastly more intelligence than the solution of intricate puzzles like the Rubik Cube.

The extraordinary intelligence that humans show in deciphering language and other cultural puzzles occurs with lightning-like rapidity and effortlessness, and often, but not always, accuracy. Even a five-year old can do it, but makes more errors than adults. (When she was five, my daughter dragged her feet about visiting my friend Dennis because she thought he would examine her teeth.) Adults also make errors, but much of the time their interpretations are consensual, or else society would be impossible. Loan companies survive when most of the understandings they enter into with their customers are mutually understood.

The rapidity and effortlessness with which people sometimes understand each other pose a profound problem for the human sciences, because it has come to be taken for granted, not only by the participants, but also by researchers. The design of most studies of human beings assumes that the words and sentences used by the researchers and their subjects are largely unambiguous, and also assumes that their subjects' intelligence is not extraordinary. This assumption is particularly marked in the construction of scales, but is also central to all experiments and most interviews. Even qualitative studies make this assumption, if somewhat more cautiously.

The problem is that humans are capable of not understanding or misunderstanding standardized research situations, or of using them to their own ends, concealment, getting the researcher's sympathy, etc. Similarly, it is all too easy for the researcher to misunderstand or not understand their subjects' responses. Understanding the meaning of human expressions is a complex and intricate process, but it can be understood if part/whole methods are applied. The nearer we take as our data *verbatim* records of human expressions, the closer we can come to understanding our subjects. Verbatim records include transcriptions based on mechanical recording of interaction and all written materials.

It is now taken for granted that the "two cultures" of science and humane letters are so separated that there is no way of connecting them. This assumption pervades both cultures. Here is an example from psychology (Maher 1991, p. 72):

> [One approach to psychology] is to assert that individual behavior cannot be predicted, but only "understood" after it occurs. This solution puts [psychology] firmly into the area of hermeneutics, i.e. the humane study of texts . . . Close examination shows us clearly

that *this approach is indistinguishable from that of the biographer writing as a contributor to nonfiction literature* . . . (emphasis added)

The purpose of this book is to show that it is possible to integrate hermeneutics with prediction, that they need not be mutually exclusive. Part/whole morphology, as outlined here, combines the interpretation of texts with the use of explicit theory and method. Contrary to what Maher said, this method is quite distinguishable from the current beliefs and practices in both the scientific and humanistic camps.

There is a powerful claim that science and humanistic interpretation can be combined in an extraordinary work of the literary imagination by Nuttall (1983). He distinguishes between two types of interpretation of texts. The first he calls "opaque," which involves the separation of the interpreter from the characters represented in the text: "In the opening of *King Lear* folk-tale elements proper to narrative are infiltrated by a finer-grained dramatic mode" (p. 80). In the second mode, which Nuttall calls "transparent,", the interpreter projects life into the characters: "Cordelia cannot bear to have her love for her father made the subject of a partly mercenary game" (p. 80). Nuttall has two complaints about the formalized interpretations in the "opaque mode" which parallel my discussion here. Firstly, no matter how formalized, opaque language must smuggle in transparent interpretations, otherwise it would be meaningless (pp. 84–87). This is an extraordinarily important point, as much for the quantitative social scientist as for the literary critic. There is no way that we can *not* endow survey subjects or literary characters with life, if we are to understand the meaning of their expressions. Otherwise, the ambiguity of human expressions would not allow *any* interpretation of meaning. Secondly, opaque interpretation is necessarily narrow and partial, since it rules out the other mode. On the other hand, transparent language does not rule out formal analysis, but can easily include both. This latter point that Nuttall made is quite parallel to my assertion that science and hermeneutics can be combined.

The intensive study of single cases, when accompanied by comparative study of cases, enables the researcher to understand human behavior in all of its complexity. When Durkheim, the founder of modern sociology, borrowed what he thought was the morphological method from botany, he left out exactly half of it, the systematic study of single cases. Seeking to demonstrate that social processes exert an autonomous influence on human actions, he focused entirely on the comparative part of morphology, shearing away a vital part of an organic approach to knowledge and discovery. The division between sociology and psychology that Durkheim proposed in his early work is leading to impasse. This division, which was necessary in order to found sociology, has frozen into rigid separation, with tragic consequences for both disciplines.

One of the signal weaknesses of Durkheim's comparative approach, which continues to haunt modern social science, is the lack of temporal data showing the time order of events, and therefore the possibility of infering causation. In his powerful study comparing suicide rates in different societies and in different social strata, Durkheim was forced to speculate on the causation of suicide, since he had no data which showed the temporal development of behavior. This is the key weakness of all "structural" analyses: the absence of process data.

The combination of single case and comparative study in botanical morphology enabled researchers to understand both structure and process, by observing both the single plant as a system, and also the system of many plants as a functioning community. The most important aspect of this approach is more subtle, however: one understands the single plant in the *context* of knowing a great deal about the plant community, and the plant community in the context of knowing a great deal about the single specimen. Morphology offers a methodological solution to the most intractable problem in the human sciences, the relationship between the individual and the group. In this book I use discourse analysis to explore single cases of social interaction, and show how it may be used in conjunction with social system analysis to understand these cases in the context of other similar cases.

I use the term discourse in an extremely broad way, to include not only spoken language, the usual sense of the word, but also any record of communicative expressions. I resort to this unusual definition to avoid ponderous terms like communication or social interaction. The reader should keep in mind the broad way that I use discourse, which includes written texts of any kind. My emphasis on verbatim discourse proposes that we allow the actual voices of our subjects to be heard in our studies, voices which have almost disappeared from the human sciences.

In my approach to morphology, I suggest that the basic molecule of social behavior is what I call the *exchange*: one action (usually discourse) by one person, and the response of another person. In much of social interaction, such exchanges are usually quite brief, as little as one transcripted line for each participant. Exchanges are small systems made up of least parts and larger wholes, at various levels.

We can think of each exchange as involving a part/whole ladder of levels. An exchange between a particular mother and daughter, for example, is made up of still smaller parts: the words and gestures (level 1) of each of the component expressions. And each exchange (level 2) is also itself a part of still larger wholes: the conversation (level 3) of which the exchange is but a part; all conversations between the two participants (their whole relationship, level 4), all relationships of their social type (the mother–daughter relationship in that particular society, level 5) etc.

By taking into account the parts and wholes of specific episodes of discourse, and the relation of those episodes to the larger social and cultural wholes of which they are a part, many of the most recalcitrant problems that face the human sciences may be confronted directly. My approach combines elements that are usually pursued separately, attempting to present human experience as a whole rather than as separated parts (such as data) and separated wholes (such as theory).

Basing this approach on the exchange does not eliminate levels of subjective experience which underlie outer behavior. In order to understand the meaning of an exchange, a researcher must make inferences about the motives, intentions, and feelings of the participants, as they themselves do, because they too are parts of the whole, even though only inferential. In this respect the researcher has a great advantage over the participants; he or she has the time and inclination to subject the exchange to microscopic examination. Because of many years of such minute examination of verbatim excerpts of dialogue, it seems to me that most human interaction is so complex that its participants understand only a tiny fraction of their own motives, intentions and feelings. In an earlier publication (Scheff 1990, 100) I referred to both inner and outer levels of dialogue as the "message stack":

1. Words
2. Gestures
3. Implicature (Unstated implications of words and gestures).
4. Feelings.

All interpretations of meaning require analysis of these four levels, but usually leave out explicit references to the lower three levels, depending almost entirely on the verbal components. Even studies which include nonverbal gestures seldom explicitly refer to the lower two levels. Part/whole morphology of discourse integrates inner experience with outer conduct.

The new approach subsumes and clarifies knotty theoretical problems. Many critics have complained that Parsonian theory over-emphasizes social control as a determinant of behavior, the hypothetical grid of norms and sanctions which actors take into account in constructing their behavior. In the abbreviated part/whole ladder implied above, Level 5 implicates such a grid, but only as one part of complex structure in which the exchange is embedded. Part/whole analysis assimilates most of the current theoretical proposals in the human sciences, theories like social control and rational choice, but locates them within a much larger matrix. Of course actors sometimes deliberately or even rationally compare their options in coming to a decision, as rational choice theory would have it. But sometimes they don't. Both alternatives can easily be included in part/whole analysis.

In terms of methodology, the approach outlined here is addressed first to what Denzin and Lincoln (1994) call the "dual crisis" in qualitative methods, a crisis of *representation* and a crisis of *legitimation*. The crisis in representation involves the tangle of thorny issues that have arisen in the last twenty years about how to portray the Other in our research, another person, race, gender, or class than one's own. This issue has surfaced with intense criticism of conventional descriptions of the Other in anthropological writing, and also in postmodernist approaches. The issue is related to a classic tradition in philosophy, the problem of Other Minds. How can we be sure that we understand the thoughts and feelings of a person other than ourselves? The first crisis in qualitative methods concerns the formats we use to depict the minds and behavior of our subjects.

Denzin and Lincoln specify the problem of representation in terms of production and ordering of text and context (578): ". . . (ethnographers) must take steps to ensure that the words they put in subjects' mouths were in fact spoken by those subjects . . . But more important, the ethnographer must take care when changing contexts and reordering events . . ."

The crisis of legitimation, as Denzin and Lincoln present it, overlaps with the crisis of representation, in that both involve the truth of our representations of the other, but the crisis of representation goes further, by referring to: ". . . the claim any text makes to being accurate, true, and complete. Is a text, that is, faithful to the context and the individuals it is supposed to represent?" (578)

Although Denzin and Lincoln do not use these terms, probably because they equate them with positivism, the crisis of representation appears to be closely related to the issue of validity, and the crisis of legitimation to the issue of reliability. What is the most valid method of representing our subjects, and how can we demonstrate that the results of this method are reliable? The present volume outlines an approach to this exact problem, reporting and relating text and context in a way that offers a measure of both validity and reliability.

The crisis of representation can be confronted by reporting verbatim the exact dialogue of the participants in a specific encounter. Where possible the dialogue should be a transcript based on mechanical recording on audiotape or film. In this way, one can be sure that the actual words and gestures are being represented. This method is also applicable to written texts, such as the telegrams (chapter 5) between the heads of state immediately prior to the onset of the First World War. Written texts omit nonverbal components, but if sufficient attention is paid to both text and context, one can understand both surface and subsurface meanings in dialogue. Since the researcher is presenting the raw data and the method of analysis, the reader is empowered to confirm or criticize the interpretation, giving rise to a measure of reliability.

This method can also be used with dialogue as remembered by a participant or researcher. With this type of data, of course, the warrant of validity and reliability is less certain, since discourse that is filtered through the memory and perceptions of the reporter is subject to many kinds of distortion. Nevertheless, since this approach injects the remembered voices of named persons into an investigation, it offers an approximation of the least parts of a relationship. I have found this method to be of great help in teaching; many of my courses on social relationships begin with role-playing of dialogue as remembered by the students.

The analysis of a specific exchange (for example, the quarrels with parents, in chapter 8) usually catches the student's attention, since it suggests new features of which the student was unaware. It would not be an exaggeration to say that many students are astounded when they discover their own contributions to the problems they have with parents and lovers. In the context of similar exchanges of other students in quarrels with their parents, each single case takes on a heightened interest. By using both a single case and a comparative approach, the morphological method, each student can better understand her own quarrel in the context of the other students' quarrels, and vice versa (for example, those students who found new awareness through analysis of their own quarrel usually showed more sympathy with other students' parental quarrels).

Remembered dialogue can be useful in teaching and research, but the strongest warrant for validity and reliability can be obtained through the use of verbatim reproductions of social interaction or written materials. Verbatim records catch more of the least parts than field notes or verbal transcriptions of interviews, especially the gestural parts. Giving the reader access to the raw data, the exact voices of the participants, and the theory and method being used by the researcher, the reader is empowered to test the validity and reliability of the author's interpretations of the data. Just as important, the social reality under study comes vividly alive for the reader. This method can be applied in such a way as to combine the advantages of the three most important current approaches in social science: eyewitness qualitative methods, quantitative methods, and theoretical analysis.

The introduction of the subjects' own voices as data systematically to be analyzed, directly in the final report, may overcome the relentless march of standardization, what Weber called routinization, into social science procedures. This trend has been noted in feminist scholarship (see particularly Krieger's [1991] forceful comments). Part/whole morphology incorporates the least parts, the clues to personal identity, into the ever larger wholes of sociological analysis.

Although my approach is a way of upgrading qualitative research by making it more objective and more systematic, in response to the crises of representation and legitimacy, it is also relevant to the practice of quantitative research. The success of a quantitative study does not depend entirely on technical questions such as research design, data gathering and analysis. It also depends on how accurate and how important the hypothesis that is being tested. Quantitative research is often of little importance because the hypotheses that are tested are too simple to catch human reality. They lack grounding in actual human behavior, what the French call *gout des terres*, the taste of the earth, the intricateness, ambiguity, and complexity of human experience. In these instances the skill and talent in conducting surveys or experiments is wasted, the hypotheses are too far afield to be worth testing.

The approach outlined here is one that attempts to generate increasingly accurate and general hypotheses by close examination of the actual reality of social life. By grounding investigation in examination of the "minute particulars" as Blake said, the least parts of single cases, and later in the comparison of these cases with one another in the context of larger wholes, one may generate hypotheses that are general and important. As pointed out, quantitative analysis leads to verification or disconfirmation of a hypothesis. But verification is the third step in part/whole morphology. Before taking the last step, it is usually necessary to take at least one of the earlier steps: exploration (conventional eyewitness field work using qualitative methods), and/or microanalysis of single specimens and comparison of specimens. Figure 1.1 can be used as a guide for beginning or expanding research in the human sciences.

In Elias's (1978) magisterial study of the civilizing process, he first analyzed excerpts from advice manuals from the same historical era in each of four European languages. These excerpts represent specimens from the thirteenth century through the eighteenth. He also examined excerpts in the same four languages from the nineteenth century, showing a decided change in emotional content. His method involves both single cases and comparisons of cases in different languages and historical eras. For these reasons, his results are specific, general and important. But like literary analysts, his theory and method are not made explicit. Probably for that reason, his work has failed to have the impact it should have had.

In the approach advocated here, since verbatim texts are used, the researcher (and the reader) has the advantage of direct eye-witness observation of the behavior under consideration, as in the best qualitative methods. The researcher has access to features of the text which are often ignored by the participants, and to instant replay, which is also seldom available to the participants. If as suggested in the chapters that follow, the researcher provides the reader with a comprehensive description of the methods employed, the study, like quantitative methods, offers the reader exact definitions of concepts and procedures. Finally, as in the studies to be described below, if the study is either built on or generates general theoretical propositions, then it will have the advantage of being embedded in an abstract theoretical framework, which is the strength of current social science work in theory. Drawing on the strengths of these three areas, the studies presented in this book are therefore reminiscent of current research in the human sciences, because they combine some of the strongest elements in what is currently being done.

But in another way, all of the studies presented here will seem quite different than current studies, because each of them carries out the part/whole theme. As required by the part/whole paradigm, each study is multilevel and multidisciplinary. The studies involve microscopic examination of discourse, and understanding the results of microanalysis in the context of larger wholes, social institutions and cultural systems. The analysis of various levels also involves concepts and propositions from many disciplines, with emphasis on connecting social science propositions with concepts and propositions from history, political science, anthropology, linguistics, psychology, psychiatry and psychoanalysis. The method combines, therefore, what is often separated – for example, microlinguistic analysis of discourse, on the one hand, with social system analysis, on the other.

One feature of the studies presented here which may seem particularly strange and unusual is the pervasive focus on emotional elements in social interaction. Certain emotions, such as shame, pride, and anger, will be identified in virtually all of the episodes that are discussed. This focus does not mean that I think that all behavior is determined by emotions. Rather it means that I believe that emotions, like perception and cognition, are present in most behavior. Emotions stand out as prominent features here because they are usually left out of studies in the human sciences. Even the most qualitative of studies almost always analyze the verbal part of discourse, ignoring the rich nonverbal accompaniment, like a pianist playing only the left hand. Social science studies are seldom scored for nonverbal behavior. The part/whole method includes not only many levels and disciplinary perspectives, but also all of the components of behavior, including emotions.

It has become a tradition in the human sciences to focus on cognition (as in cognitive science), behavior (as in behavioral analysis), and/or beliefs (as in most survey studies). If emotions are mentioned at all, they are given short shrift, treated as irrational elements briefly and casually. But because I analyze emotions systematically in this book does not mean that I think they are the whole story, only that they should be taken as seriously as the other components of human behavior. For example, chapter 5 suggests that unacknowledged shame, particularly the French reaction to their defeat by the Germans in 1871, was an important factor in the origins of World War I. But in suggesting that a chain of humiliated fury ran through French politics from 1871 to 1914, I am not proposing that it was the only cause of the war. The actions of the other major nations were just as important, as were other motives, such as desire for power and expansion, and perhaps fear of the other countries. I emphasize one motive, humiliated fury, because earlier explanations have left it out.

The first chapter is very dense, covering a broad spectrum of methodological issues necessary for understanding human beings. It makes the point that human understanding is far richer and more complex than had been previously thought, showing the actual processes of effective thought. The remaining chapters are more accessible, since they involve applications of the main ideas in the first chapter to concrete episodes of human behavior. The idea of parts and wholes is very powerful, but it is also quite abstract. It may be the most general framework possible. It needs to be shown how it applies to real human activity in diverse settings, fleshing it out with actual speech and gestures, as interpreted in context.

At the center of the first chapter is Spinoza's insight that human understanding requires knowledge of the "least parts and the greatest wholes" and the relationship between them. This idea leads to the very heart of human reflexiveness: when we are thinking clearly, we carefully relate ourselves to both the microcosm and the macrocosm.

This movement clarifies what it is that we are doing, it makes contact with efforts of others, and makes our thoughts maximally useful. It is at the same time a declaration of both dependence and independence. To use Elias's favorite word, it is a declaration of interdependence.

This idea suggests a way of correcting for the overspecialization of knowledge in the modern world. There is a joke among academics that they either know everything about nothing or nothing about everything. As in most jokes, there is some truth to this one. There are the *parts* people, who know everything about next to nothing, and the *wholes* people, who know next to nothing about everything. By struggling to relate parts to even larger wholes (the empiricists in psychology and history, for example) and wholes to the parts of which they are to be composed (theorists in the social sciences and the humanities), perhaps some of the alienation and waste motion in our attempts to understand the human world can be overcome.

This book shows the need to include and study all of the parts of human communication: gestures and emotions are just as important as words, thoughts and actions. All of these components are equally necessary in understanding the character of the participants and the nature of their relationships. It is mainly for this reason that many studies of human beings seem thin and airless, since the various approaches typically omit one or more components. Many studies in the social sciences are based on interviews which focus solely on words. Studies in the behavior sciences usually focus only on thoughts and actions or actions alone (as in the psychology of facial expressions). Social scientists usually study minds without bodies, psychologists bodies without minds. Because of these lapses, it is rarely possible to come to valid conclusions because some of the parts of the system are missing. Although recently emotions are beginning to receive notice, they have been ignored for so long that it will take some time to catch up.

Even studies that include emotions usually leave out one particular emotion, shame. I argue, as implied in Goffman's (1967) brilliant essay on embarrassment, that shame is the master emotion, in that it is an actual part of, or more frequently, is anticipated in virtually all human contact. Several of the chapters focus on this emotion in order to show how shame, ordinarily considered at best as only a vanishingly small part of the human drama, may indeed play a major role in most human activity.

Shame is crucial in social interaction because it ties together the individual and social aspects of human activity as part and whole. As an emotion within individuals it plays a central role in consciousness of feeling and morality. But it also functions as signal of distance between persons, allowing us to regulate how close or far we are from others. Signs of shame and embarrassment make social relationships visible to participants, and are available in transcripts for the researcher, materializing an otherwise intangible but vitally important part of human affairs. This idea runs through many of the chapters; it is most elaborated in chapters 6–8. Chapters 4, 5, 6, and 8 deal both with single-case analysis and comparison of cases, more advanced part/whole morphology than the single case, but still at a low level. Advanced morphological methods requires systematic comparison of many cases, as well as single case analysis.

Needless to say, the approach outlined here will not solve all of the manifold problems of the human sciences, or come anywhere close. The basic idea, of part/whole relations as the fundamental building block of the human sciences, is still much too abstract, even given the illustrations of its use in the chapters below, to be yet easily applied to the task of rebuilding research on human beings. It will need to be further fleshed out with a much wider variety of problems and settings than I undertake in this book. Because these examples are only preliminary, I have given far more emphasis to single case analysis than to comparative analysis. Mature applications of my approach must give balanced attention to both single case and comparative analysis. The examples of applications of part/whole morphology below should be taken for what they are, preliminary and incomplete exercises, used to illustrate a new path for the future.

It will also be evident to the reader that I largely proceed from the work of others. I show how the part/whole paradigm can expand our understanding of work that has already been recognized as significant. Finally, my emphasis on the role of emotion in the chapters below is a further instance of the limitation of range. A more balanced application of the ideas outlined here would give equal attention to perception, cognition, behavior and emotions.

Theory and method

There is a marvelous passage in one of Kundera's (1995) essays on the history of the novel which exactly evokes the problem I attack here, how to access human reality:

> Try to reconstruct a dialogue from your own life, the dialogue of a quarrel or a dialogue of love. The most precious, the most important situations are utterly gone. Their abstract sense remains (I took this point of view, he took that one. I was aggressive, he was defensive), perhaps a detail or two. But the *acousticovisual concreteness* of the situation in all its continuity is lost.
>
> And not only is it lost but we do not even wonder at this loss. We are resigned to losing the concreteness of the present. We immediately transform the present moment into its abstraction. We need only recount an episode we experienced a few hours ago: the dialogue contracts to a brief summary, the setting to a few general features. This applies to even the strongest memories which affect the mind deeply like a trauma: we are so dazzled by their potency that we don't realize how schematic and meager their content is.
>
> When we study, discuss, analyze a reality, we analyze it as it appears in our mind, in our memory. We know reality only in the past tense. We do not know it as it is in the present in the moment when it's happening, when it *is*. The present moment is unlike the memory of it. Remembering is not the negative of forgetting. *Remembering is a form of forgetting.*
>
> We can assiduously keep a diary and note every event. Rereading the entries one day we will see that they cannot evoke a single concrete image. And still worse: that the imagination is unable to help our memory along and reconstruct what has been forgotten. The present – the concreteness of the present – as a phenomenon to consider, as a *structure,* is for us an unknown planet: so we can neither hold on to it in our memory nor reconstruct it through imagination. *We die without knowing what we have lived.* (Kundera 1995, 128–129, emphasis added[1])

How can a scientist or scholar capture the reality of human life, when the people whom we study usually cannot do it themselves? As Kundera suggests, only the greatest of novelists, giants such as

---

[1] Nicholas Tavuchis called this book to my attention.

Tolstoy and Proust, have even come close, by reporting the evocative details of sight, sound, and context that we usually ignore or immediately forget.

Kundera's comments clarify and extend the Proustian quest, not only for the lost past, but for the lost present. The title of Proust's masterpiece, if translated literally into English, is not *The Remembrance of Things Past*, but *The Search for Past Time*. And the title of the triumphant last chapter is "The Past Regained." A great artist, he demonstrates, can find the universal moments of childhood living within his or her memory, but hidden behind the conventional façade of everyday life.

Although most of Proust's commentary concerns the recovery of the distant past, a few passages concern a past so immediate that it edges upon the present. For example, in the section called "Within a Budding Grove," there is an incident in which the narrator, Marcel, finally gets to meet Albertine, the girl he has been yearning for (and who later becomes the love of his life). At first he is deeply disappointed with the meeting; the whole episode seems banal and empty; he and she both conventional and distant. But that evening, as he reconsiders the meeting, he begins to remember the fine details of her gestures, facial expression, and inflections. She comes to life for him, in his "darkroom," as he says, where he is able to develop the "negatives" of his impressions of her earlier in the day. By focusing on the details, he is able to regain a past so immediate that it points toward the possibility of recovering the present.

Proust is still ridiculed for his seeming preoccupation with minutiae. A favorite jest is that it takes him fifteen pages to describe turning over in bed. But Proust implies that the ability to recover even fleeting moments of the past and present are the *sine qua non* of the great artist: it is these recovered moments that breathe life into art. The main difference between art and kitsch is the abstractness of the latter. It describes not the details that make up human experience, but conventional abstractions of them, as Kundera suggests.

But why do we need the living present in the human sciences? I propose that it is needed to breathe life into our enterprise also. I suggest a method, part/whole analysis, for restoring human reality to the social sciences. This approach is a way of filling in the details of Proust's method of "developing our negatives in our darkroom." Using transcripts or verbatim texts as data, one interprets the meaning of the smallest *parts* (words and gestures) of expressions within the context of the ever greater *wholes* within which they occur: sentences, paragraphs, the whole dialogue, the whole relationship, the whole culture and social structure. A central theme in the work of Spinoza was the thought that human understanding requires relating the least parts to the greatest wholes. This book shows how this idea may be carried out in a disciplined program of inquiry.

The first chapter describes how the morphological method can be applied in the human sciences. It then develops the idea of part/ whole analysis. In order to show how important this approach is for the human sciences, the first chapter takes up the complexity of human intelligence. It slows down part/whole processes that occur in our thinking and feeling that are so fast as to be practically invisible. It shows how these processes lie at the heart of capable, despecialized problem-solving, of what is usually called common sense. It provides examples of two thinkers who made progress toward part/whole thinking, Elias and Lévi-Strauss, and the consequences for those who made little or no progress in this vital direction.

The second chapter examines the strengths and limitations of literary analysis in two studies. In the first, a study of poetic closure (B. H. Smith 1968), the author takes several steps toward locating her work on a part/whole ladder, how the issue of poetic closure and non-closure occurs in Shakespeare's sonnets, and in other poetry, literature, and art. The author takes one more step up the part/whole ladder, suggesting, in passing, that closure in poetry is one aspect of closure in language as a whole. However, she does not elaborate this idea, which could have related her study to those in linguistics which deal with the same issue: openings and closings in conversation. Such an elaboration could have enriched her study and those in linguistics, suggesting continuities and differences between poetry and ordinary language, making the study reflexive.

A more powerful literary study concerns the six heroines of Jane Austen's novels (Hardy 1984). The author shows that the romantic love relationship that can be inferred in all six cases involve what he calls the *sharing* of experience between the heroine and her prospective husband. This idea is demonstrated by close analysis of dialogue, which utilizes, by implication, what I am calling part/whole methods. His discussion of the romantic love relationship is much more convincing than anything to be found in the psychological and psychoanalytic literatures, because it is data-driven. Potentially this method could lead to consensus as to the validity of Hardy's analysis, since he presents both concepts and data for the reader's inspection. However, since he offers no exact definition of what he means by sharing, and no method for classifying hits and misses in his analysis of the data, independent agreement among readers would be unlikely.

Hardy's idea of sharing as an indication of true love comes very close to my concept of *attunement* as the mark of a secure bond, which

I develop in the next three chapters. These chapters generate and elaborate a theory of the social bond. This theory is based in part on earlier theory and findings, but it is also generated and vivified because it is driven, like the studies of Elias and Hardy, by close attention to verbatim texts. By combining the skills and sensitivities of social scientists and humanists, perhaps some progress can be made toward understanding the human condition.

In this section, I show how social structure lives in the smallest parts of discourse, when interpreted within the local and extended context. The manner of expression, particularly, carries clues to emotions and the social bond. These ideas will be applied to concrete situations in later sections of this book: The social status of Goodwin's boys and girls in chapter 4 is continually signaled and responded to in their discourse. When one black child derides another for having thick lips, he does not realize he is re-affirming the social structure of the boy's group and of the larger society at the same time. In chapter 7, by attending to the smallest parts of discourse, I show how age, gender, occupational and social class invade a psychotherapy session, all but overwhelming it. Chapter 5, on the origins of the First World War, shows how smallest parts of telegrams between heads of state signal the kind of alienation that leads to violence. The social structures that rule our lives, all but invisible to the untutored eye, are manifest in the smallest parts of discourse, when interpreted within larger contexts.

CHAPTER 1

Part/whole morphology: unifying single case and comparative methods

Here I describe the morphological method as a new stage of inquiry, between the first stage, qualitative methods, and the third, quantitative methods. The proposed second stage involves microscopic examination of single specimens, and, if more than one specimen is available, the comparisons of specimens with each other. This method is particularly useful for the objective determination of meaning, a crucial problem for the human sciences. Because the determination of meaning is complex, yet taken for granted, I describe its intricacy. The new method also can be used to generate micro–macro theories, perhaps the next stage in the development of the human sciences.

Morphology of human conduct

To form a bridge between qualitative and quantitative methods, which are increasingly separated, part/whole morphology can lead to research which is valid, reliable, and cost-efficient. Qualitative methods involve exploration, the first step in inquiry. Quantitative methods involve verification, the last step. Although preliminary exploration is usually necessary and always helpful, exploration requires verification. The weakness of verification alone is that since experiments and other standardized formats (such as the scale and the standardized interview) are narrow and rigid, one needs to have considerable knowledge before an adequate testing procedure can be designed. Qualitative methods are like wide-angled lenses with little depth; quantitative methods are as narrow as using the wrong end of a telescope.

Furthermore, since verification is costly and time-consuming, only hypotheses and theories should be tested which are not only plausible, but have been shown to be general and important. The procedure outlined here is more laborious than most qualitative studies, but it is also more cost-efficient than those which automatically seek verification.

The approach outlined here can be seen as the next step after what Giddens (1984) has called "instantiation." He asked for actual instances of the behavior described by any theory. His call, in turn, can be seen as a reiteration of Max Weber's (1947) insistence that the task of sociology is to reduce concepts about society to "understandable action, that is, without exception, to the actions of participating individual [persons]."

To summarize my approach: with or without initial exploration (Stage 1), the researcher would examine individual specimen cases (such as verbatim texts) microscopically, Stage 2. This step can lead directly to the development of a theory grounded in intimate knowledge of the specimen cases, but oriented toward placing them in the largest possible context, generating a micro–macro theory. Should such a theory appear promising, the final stage, verification (3), could follow (see figure 1.1).

The term morphology is meant in the sense that it was originally used in botany, which includes the intense microscopic investigation of single cases (in botany, a specimen plant). This is not the sense in which Durkheim (1903) used the term. In his usage, because of his bias toward comparative studies, he excluded the examination of the minutia of the single case. The same bias is found also in the otherwise admirable development of "grounded theory" by Glaser and Strauss (1967). In my usage, morphology includes intense study of *both* the single case and comparisons between cases.

The sequence in which these stages occur, except for the last, verification, need not be chronological. Investigation of a problem might as easily start with Stage 2 or 1. This point should be kept in mind in reading this chapter, because, for emphasis, I focus on the bottom-up strategy of starting with Stage 1 or 2. There is no reason that one could not start with a theory (topdown), or better yet, juggle research and theory at the same time (see my comment on abduction below).

The new stage provides the potential for squaring the circle, achieving at least a measure of *both validity and reliability.* The format for reporting morphological findings requires that the researcher spell out the concepts and methods used explicitly, and make the texts that were analyzed available to the reader. The interested reader will then be able to apply the researcher's methods to the researcher's data. Provided with the researcher's concepts, methods and raw data, this procedure allows judgment of the relevance (validity) of the concepts and methods employed, and the repeatability of the findings (reliability).

This is not to say that this approach could rapidly solve the many

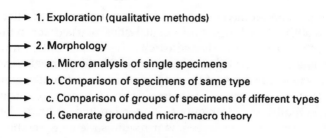

1. Exploration (qualitative methods)

2. Morphology
   a. Micro analysis of single specimens
   b. Comparison of specimens of same type
   c. Comparison of groups of specimens of different types
   d. Generate grounded micro-macro theory

3. Verification (quantitative methods)

Figure 1.1 Stages of inquiry

problems of research in the human sciences. It could bring together the necessary elements for solutions, but it is still too early to tell whether it would be practical to do so. Much of the specialization that has run riot in the human sciences, specialization by discipline, sub-discipline, levels of analysis, method and theory, has occurred for reasons that are extraneous to science. But some amount of specialization is probably necessary. In the long run it will probably be necessary to work out some compromise between the kind of de-specialization I advocate here and what Oatley (1996) has called the "social distribution of cognition," the specialized thinking (and behavior) that requires division of labor.

However, for the almost continuous determination of the meaning of human expressions that forms a major part of all social science research, it seems impractical to distribute cognition. Part/whole morphology of social interaction or written texts is particularly suited for determining the meaning of human expressions. Because the new approach uses verbatim texts or transcripts, it allows for the patient interpretation of meaning that includes the smallest details and the largest contexts. This method points toward the objective (consensual) determination of meaning.

The problem of meaning

Can the meaning of human expressions and behavior be determined? In the tradition of *verstehen* established by Weber, Dilthey, and others, meaning was the most important component of social science. To understand human behavior, we need to understand the subjective orientation of the actors. But the originators of this tradition and its followers did not consider the determination of meaning to be a technical problem, one that requires the close consideration of human actions and expressions in relationship to the context in which they occur. The technical problem of determining meaning is one that extends into the vital core of all activities of the human sciences, theory, method and empirical research.

Meaning as a technical problem is crucial in the current crisis in the human sciences because of the way in which humans in everyday life are able to exact accurate meanings from expressions that are both highly complex and ambiguous. Understanding ordinary language and other kinds of human behavior requires the consideration of the smallest parts of expressions and their relationship to the largest possible wholes (not only grammar and syntax, but biographical structures, as well as the structure of the entire language and culture). Part/whole analysis of this kind would seem to be the key component of what is called "common sense." We humans have become so adept and quick at understanding expressions by relating their least parts with the largest wholes that we do not realize the extraordinary complexity of what we do. In this chapter I slow down and therefore make explicit the bare outlines of this process.

In my view, the human sciences are becoming ever further removed from reality because they are so *specialized* that they cannot use part/whole analysis in the way that their subjects do. Understanding ordinary language and other kinds of human behavior, because of their complexity and ambiguity, requires a global, and therefore a de-specialized point of view. Fragmentation into disciplines, sub-disciplines, levels of analysis, types of method, and schools of thought has deprived the human sciences of the ability to understand human behavior even as well as their subjects do, which is not very well. The approach outlined here would enable us to at least compete with our subjects in understanding their behavior. Although ordinary people do poorly with understanding emotions and social bonds, they are probably more cunning than human scientists in using part/whole analysis to determine meaning. The method outlined here is oriented toward uncovering both overt and covert meanings. It is particularly suited toward discovering hidden emotions and bond-oriented behavior.

Hypothesis: The meaning of human expressions and behavior can be determined, but objective interpretation requires disciplined investigation of the complex three-way relationships between meaning, text and context, in the way that will be made explicit below.

Theory: Most current discussions assert that meaning is by and large a subjective matter. This position is by now so established that its adherents assume rather than investigate it. Postmodern thought, a recent development, assumes that meanings are not only subjective, but essentially undecidable. Although there is no actual evidence to support this conclusion, postmodernists postulate that poems, novels, and indeed all texts are inherently ambiguous.

The founder of the postmodern critique, Derrida, made a point which is both true and important. He and his fellow deconstructionists have popularized the point that *if taken out of context*, any text becomes ambiguous. In this light, James Thurber should be considered a deconstructionist. In his essay on his late night thoughts about the name Perth Amboy, he tells the results of repeating the name many times. After many repetitions, not only did the name begin to lose its meaning, but the very room began to whirl around his bed. Thurber had stumbled into a way of decontextualizing an expression. Words and other expressions in ordinary language are only indexical, they are ambiguous when context is removed. This idea suggests that if we are to understand how meaning can be determined, we must consider the relationship between meaning, text and context.

The only sustained consideration of this three-way relationship has been conducted by Cicourel.[1] Compared to him, I am a late arrival in this field. Although our styles of thought and investigation are different, I recognize that he was the first to realize the crucial importance of this problem, and to devote most of his time and effort in an attempt to solve it. As in my approach, Cicourel has shown repeatedly that a text can only be understood in context, necessitating a detailed ethnography of context. This chapter extends his analysis, by outlining an explicit theory and method.

In this chapter I outline a theory and method to deal with the relationship between meaning, text, and context. Certainly the deconstructionists have not seriously considered this issue.[2] In particular, they have not understood that their main point, that all texts are undecidable when removed from context, implies an equal and opposite corollary: *in context*, the meaning of a text is decidable. Postmodernists have jumped to an unwarranted conclusion that context or no, the meaning of all texts is undecidable. This chapter will argue for the importance and truth of the corollary: given sufficient investigation of a text and its context, it is possible to approach an *objective determination of meaning*.

To begin with humor, an everyday example of the issue of decidability. A joke can be lengthy and complex; "getting it" may require weaving together various relevant but conflicting threads in the narrative, ignoring extraneous details, and understanding the way the

---

[1] See Cicourel's theoretically oriented books (1964; 1974; 1981), articles (1977 1980 1981 1985), and many empirical studies.

[2] For a comprehensive critique of deconstruction, see Searle (1994) or Tallis (1988). Bert States called these studies to my attention.

punch line resolves the conflict. Grown-up humor requires a high level of sophistication, one that is absent in young children.

When a joke brings genuine laughter, its meaning was not ambiguous to the audience; they got the point. But a joke may be funny to one audience and not another. "You have to have been there." Even if the joke was told exactly as before, some element(s) could have been different in the new context. The decidability of meaning changes with context.

Empirical research: The problem of meaning is seldom discussed by empirical researchers; they usually assume that the meaning of subjects' responses is unproblematic. Although the occasional qualitative researcher may be sensitive to this problem, few studies have explored the relationship between text and context in the determination of meaning. Both in direct observation and in sophisticated techniques of measurement, researchers take much the same position as their subjects; the construction of meaning is taken for granted: it is "common sense."

Rather than explore the matter, empirical researchers have instead divided into two camps, both usually avoiding the problem of meaning. Qualitative studies use interpretation in context, quantitative studies, standardized procedures. The two approaches are exact opposites: qualitative work is unsystematic but contextual, quantitative work is systematic but acontextual.

Qualitative studies, oriented toward face validity, neglect reliability. Face validity is important; it means that an analysis of meaning can be related to ordinary language, a vast repository for understanding the complexity and subtlety of human expressions. But ordinary language is also a repository of bias, a bastion of the cultural status quo. Face validity alone, plausibility, can never be a sufficient basis for determining meaning.

Quantitative studies, oriented toward reliability, neglect validity. Reliability is also of great importance; it ensures repeatability. But erroneous procedures can be repeated as easily as correct ones. (See my discussion of standardized scales below.) Reliability alone can never be a sufficient basis for determining meaning.

Both approaches are rational, but only in part. Reliance on face validity exemplifies substantive rationality. This approach is sensitive to the particularities of situations, just as procedural rationality is attuned to their general features. Weber has warned that substantive rationality is marred by capriciousness, and procedural (formal) rationality leads to bureaucratic deadlock. A marriage seems to be needed, one which would unite substantive and procedural rationality (validity and reliability).

Several examples will suffice to illustrate the need. The capriciousness of direct observation has been demonstrated repeatedly in ethnographic studies. Oscar Lewis saw a different Tepoztlan than the one reported by Redfield, and Freeman (1983) has argued that Margaret Mead's description of adolescent sexual behavior in Samoa is entirely fictitious. Neither Lewis nor Redfield offer hard data. Freeman's critique of Mead's work is well documented, but by no means foolproof. For example, although his two visits to Samoa covered years compared to Mead's months, they took place long after Mead's visit.

Plausibility is both strength and weakness; it soothes and beguiles our judgment by "common sense" reasoning, even with claims that are false or groundless (common sense will be discussed below). Direct observation is invaluable at the beginning of an investigation, but not sufficient for the objective determination of meaning.

The widespread use of scales to measure psychological and social attitudes provides an example of the need for both validity and reliability in the determination of meaning. Although my colleagues and I (Scheff, Retzinger, and Ryan 1989) reviewed the literature only on self-esteem scales, our conclusions may also apply to all scales currently in use.

At the time we conducted the review (1988), we estimated (with the help of Morris Rosenberg) that there had been more than *ten thousand* studies using self-esteem scales. Yet despite this massive effort, no consistent findings had been reported. We found that the six comprehensive reviews of the self-esteem literature in print at the time of our article were in agreement on the absence of significant findings. The chaotic state of the field is suggested by the most recent of the reviews:

> What has emerged . . . in the self-esteem literature is a confusion of results that defies interpretation. Hypotheses have been tested about the relationships between self-esteem and hundreds of other psychological variables. Many of these variables have been supported, but most observed trends have been weak and insubstantial. There are few replications or systematic extensions, and it is difficult to know which findings are worth pursuing. Moreover, because different investigators begin with different assumptions, their findings stand in obscure relation to one another. (Jackson 1984, 2–3)

Jackson and three of the other reviews are basically critical of the whole field. On the other hand, two of the reviews are strongly positive and optimistic in their orientation. However, *all six* of the reviews are in agreement on the lack of significant findings. Indeed, the two positive reviews are the most devastating on this point. Now, some eight years and perhaps 4–5,000 studies later, the situation does not seem to have changed: deadlock.

Jackson (1984, *passim*) takes up an additional issue, one not addressed directly in the other five reviews: lack of a theory or even an abstract concept of self-esteem may be the crucial reason for the failure of the field to develop. I will return to the point below, after discussing the stages of inquiry.

Text and context

The state of the art in the detailed analysis of meaning can be found in Pittenger, Hockett, and Danehy (1967) and Labov and Fanshel (1977). Each study carefully analyzed every sound, both verbal and non-verbal, hearable in audiotaped excerpts from single psychotherapy sessions. Unlike most studies, they also reported the reasoning upon which they based their inferences about meaning.

Although the authors of these two studies were not familiar with them, both consistently used two methods which have been described abstractly in the phenomenology of meaning. The first has been called the method of *prospective–retrospective understanding* (Schutz 1962). This idea breaks down the extremely broad and abstract concept of *context* into two components, the past and the future context. One understands the meaning of an expression by placing it in context of what has happened before it occurs, and what happened afterwards. One can further subdivide into the *local* and *extended* context. That is, one understands a word or sentence in terms of the some of the text that comes before or after it (local context) or, ranging more broadly, events before and after the entire text, the extended context.

As might be expected, both Pittenger et al. and Labov and Fanshel based their inferences of the meaning of expressions on references to the local context, passages occurring before and after the expression in question, often immediately before or after. Occasionally, however, they looked further. An example in the former study is the analysis of the meaning of the patient's third utterance. When the therapist asks her why she came, near the very beginning of the session, the patient lists her symptoms in a formal, organized manner. As it turns out in the rest of the session, her report exactly summarizes her main problems. Also she uses several contractions which suggest repeated use of this form. The study's analysis is based in part on knowledge that she is a nurse, which she mentions in her sixteenth utterance. Using both the prospective and retrospective method of understanding, Pittenger et al. reason that she is enacting the role of a nurse reporting to a doctor.

Pittenger et al.'s interpretation of the patient's misunderstanding of the therapist's manner, one of the central findings of their study, is based in part on their knowledge that she has had only one prior session with a mental health professional, which she mentions only near the end of the session. (A substantial book can hardly be understood in one reading, especially if one begins at the beginning and then proceeds to read the pages in the correct order. Readers who peek ahead in order to understand what they are reading are using the method being discussed here.)

Pittenger et al. make no explicit use of historical, biographical or follow-up data: they make no references to factual events in the extended context. But Labov and Fanshel had such data; they made references to the extended context. For example, their understanding of the effects of the therapist's tactics is based in part on their knowledge of events before and after the patient's sessions with the therapist. Before psychotherapy began, the patient, who was anorexic, had starved herself to the point that her life was endangered. At follow-up, five years after the last of many sessions, the patient was reported to be symptom-free. Labov and Fanshel used this information to confirm their analysis of the meaning of the therapist's tactics in the excerpt they studied.

Hypotheticals (Counterfactuals): Even though Pittenger et al. did not use historical or biographical knowledge not contained in the actual dialogue, their analysis of meaning is based not only on the dialogue itself, but also on events that they imagine had happened before it began. In the language of phenomenology, such events are called counterfactuals. Because the usage of this term varies somewhat in philosophy and linguistics, I will use the term *hypotheticals* instead.

Much of the analysis in Pittenger et al. is based on imagined, hypothetical events. Already mentioned is their explanation of the form of the patient's report of her symptoms; the researchers imagined her making such a report in this form many times before the present instance in her capacity as a nurse reporting symptoms of a patient to the doctor.

Pittenger et al. also make more extended use of hypotheticals in understanding the patient's response to the therapist. They imagine that the patient's response to a therapist who seems to her cold and detached is much like her response to her husband, who she refers to in a way that suggests that she also sees him as distant and unsympathetic. Although Pittenger et al. never use the term, their analysis involves almost constant use of hypotheticals. They even name the method they use to understand one type of hypothetical (those that could have occurred instead of the actual utterance), the Principle of Reasonable Alternatives.

Similarly, Labov and Fanshel do not limit their search of the extended context to factual data. Much of their analysis of meaning is based on hypotheticals, such as patterns of discourse within the patient's family. On the basis of re-enactments by the patient of conversations between herself, her mother, and her aunt, Labov and Fanshel imagine patterns of highly conflictful discourse in the family. They largely understand the meaning of the patient's responses to the therapist in these terms.

This chapter suggests that the determination of meaning is neither mostly subjective, as assumed by theoretical approaches, nor objective, as assumed in most empirical research, but a varying mixture of subjective and objective. To the extent that researchers *locate all relevant context*, and to the extent that their hypotheticals are *confirmed by factual data*, their interpretation of meaning is objective.

Of course in actual practice discovery of the relevant context, and the confirmation of hypotheticals with factual data, is likely to be beyond the range of a single researcher. But it is conceivable that one or more later re-analyses could approach the objective determination of meaning, limited only by the amount of interest and resources. What kind of data could warrant such an expenditure of effort?

The parameters that determine the answer to this question would probably concern the importance of the problem, method or theory under investigation, the extent of research investment, and the promise shown by existing studies. Choosing an exemplary study from a series of important studies for a replication using part/whole morphology would be ideal. For example, the study of Expressed Emotion (EE) represents considerable investment by a wide variety of researchers in a very fundamental problem, the possible origins of mental illness in family processes.

George Brown (1972) and others have shown a promising connection between family criticism and emotional over-involvement with ex-mental patients and relapse. However, the studies are virtually atheoretical, the methods difficult and time-consuming, and the size of the relationship is only moderate. A part/whole morphological study of the audio-tapes generated in one of these studies might be of particular help in generating a theoretical framework. (For a first step in this direction, see Ryan's [1993] microanalysis of the transcription of one of the cases from an earlier EE study [Hooley 1986]. Ryan shows that the discourse between an ex-patient and his wife exactly fits the shame–anger paradigm (see part 3).

Another example of texts which might deserve subsequent reanalyses are analyzed in my study of the emotional causes of the First World War (see chapter 5). Immediately prior to the beginning of the war, there were six telegrams exchanged between the heads of state of Russia and Germany, and the Foreign Minister of England. In addition, the Kaiser's comments that he wrote on three of the telegrams he received have been preserved. Although these texts have been the subject of many prior analyses, I found them each to be incomplete, since they all focused on content, without analyzing manner.

Because of the formal and somewhat oblique language of the telegrams, a deep search of the extended context was needed to determine their meaning. The texts being brief, I feel confident of my analysis of their structure. But the twenty-five pages that I devoted to the context, political, psychological, and social, seems a mere beginning. Since the causes of this war are still a mystery and an enigma, the objective determination of the meaning of these texts might be of great import.

Even though a single researcher is unlikely to have the time, resources or patience for an objective determination of meaning, the more resources put into microanalysis, searching the context and confirming hypotheticals, the more objective the determination of meaning. Once again I turn to Pittenger et al. and Labov and Fanshel as examples. In the cases of both studies, their analysis takes up an entire volume, even though the excerpts they studied are brief (five minutes for Pittenger et al., fifteen for Labov and Fanshel). But their analysis is not complete, because of limitations in their methods and data.

In regard to *methods*, both studies determine only cognitive meanings. Though both frequently mention anger, embarrassment and other emotions, analysis is brief and casual. For that reason, their determination of emotional meanings is incomplete. In subsequent reanalyses I inferred emotional meanings omitted from the Pittenger et al. study (Scheff 1990, ch. 6); and inferred emotional meanings omitted from the Labov and Fanshel study (Scheff and Retzinger 1991, ch. 6).

In regard to *data*, Pittenger et al. were unable, as any subsequent analysts would be, to confirm the accuracy of their hypotheticals in the extended context, since they made no explicit use of historical, biographical or follow-up data. (I personally contacted the therapist in the recorded session used by Pittenger et al; he told me that he had no further information about the session or the patient). Labov and Fanshel had only a limited amount of factual data outside of the text they analyzed. For example, they had no actual verbatim dialogues from the patient's family that would confirm their hypotheticals regarding patterns of discourse there. (I also contacted both Labov and Fanshel, but neither responded.)

Although Scheff (1990), and Scheff and Retzinger (1991) removed a limitation in the methods of the original studies, they could not remove the limitations of data. Because of the lack of sufficient historical and biographical data in these four studies, their determinations of meaning are a mixture of objective and subjective elements.

An additional expenditure of effort in collecting relevant data in the extended context might have been justified. My re-analysis of the Pittenger et al. data is one of the bases of a general theory of interminable conflict. The Scheff and Retzinger (1991, ch. 7) re-analysis of the Labov and Fanshel data proposes a theory of the causation of anorexia. Although anorexia has been studied extensively, there is no successful theory of its causation. Under these conditions, further steps toward testing might have been warranted.

There is one further limitation of these two studies. Exemplary as they are, their purview is only psycholinguistic: they fail to discuss or investigate the institutional context in which their texts are embedded. For example, even a casual hearing of the recorded session will reveal that the patient in the Pittenger et al. study had a strong Boston working-class accent. (A LP record comes with Gill, Newman and Redlich 1954.) The therapist, on the other hand, has no discernible accent, strongly suggesting a difference in social class between the two subjects. The researchers do not comment on this difference, let alone investigate its implications.

Gender differences are also observable. The therapist's tactic of responding only to the informational aspects of the patient's expressions, brusquely ignoring her emotional responses, is gender related, at least in part. Since the session is an initial one, the therapist no doubt had a rationale for this tactic. But his curtness in ignoring the strong emotions expressed, and abruptness in switching back to information issues seems connected with the state of gender relationships, and perhaps class and age, in the United States in the 1960s, the era in which the session occurred.

Surprisingly absent from the excerpt is even the slightest attempt of the therapist to explain his tactics, even though they seem to confuse and irritate the patient. On the patient's part, no attempt at overt protest was made. At several points she withdraws or sulks, but she does not put into her words her feelings about the therapist's behavior toward her, which borders on being abusive. The male therapist, who is undoubtedly older and of a higher social class dominates the younger, lower-class female patient. Although she withdrew several times, the patient mostly subordinates herself to the therapist. If sufficiently analyzed, this session might tell much about the role of gender in therapist–patient contacts in that time and place.

Similarly, in the Labov and Fanshel study, although the accent of the patient suggests that she is Jewish, the researchers did not investigate this issue. They comment on it, but only in passing. Neither study develops the sociological implications of clues to the embeddedness of their data in age, class, gender, or ethnic structures. This kind of embeddedness will be a key issue in my discussion of theory, below.

The balance between text and context

Several implications relevant to the problem of meaning follow from my discussion. One is that no matter how exhaustive the analysis of a text, the determination of meaning will be incomplete, and therefore partly subjective, without referring to relevant historical and biographical knowledge. For example, the interpretation of the meaning of a poem or novel may require substantial biographical knowledge of the author and/or of the historical period in which she wrote. Although this proposition is contrary to most literary theory, it follows inevitably from my argument. Postmodern ideas distract attention from this issue.

One example of the need for supplemental factual data is provided by the study of several hundred recorded psychotherapy sessions by Helen Lewis (1971). Using a systematic procedure for coding emotions (Gottschalk and Gleser 1969), she discovered a consistent pattern of hiding virtually all of the emotion of shame and much of the anger among patients, and that the therapists ignored most of these episodes. However, lacking the methods used by Pittenger et al. and Labov and Fanshel, her analysis of cognitive meanings is incomplete.

Even Lewis's analysis of emotional meanings is incomplete, because she had no data outside of the transcripts to confirm her inferences. For example, since she could not tell from the text alone whether the patients were aware that they were hiding their shame and anger experiences, she used an ambiguous term for classifying these experiences: *unacknowledged* emotion. She was unable to distinguish, therefore, between conscious and unconscious emotion. Nor could she tell the extent that the therapists were aware of the patients' emotions, the emotions that both patients and therapists seemed to ignore. Lewis's classification of all of the shame episodes as either overt, undifferentiated or bypassed shame suggest that she assumed the patients' experiences of shame were below the level of consciousness. But without debriefing, she had no way of confirming this supposition.

The amount of supplemental data needed for the determination of meaning, the balance between *text and context*, will vary. In the case of Lewis's study, she might have been able to clear up some of the ambiguity over the patients' and therapists' awareness by reviewing a sample of the requisite episodes in their transcripts, a relatively small addition to the original analysis. This expenditure of effort would have been justified, since the existence of vast amounts of unconscious shame has been a sticking point in the acceptance of Lewis's findings.

On the other hand, a comprehensive analysis of cognitive meanings, in the manner of Pittenger et al. or Labov and Fanshel, would have made for a huge additional amount of analysis, even with only a sample of the cases. Such an expenditure of effort would have been difficult to justify. Unlike Lewis's findings on shame, her analysis of cognitive meanings did not suggest an important new direction for future research.

Parts and wholes in verbatim texts

The issues concerning the balance between text and context can be considered in a more abstract way by invoking relations between parts and wholes. The parts are words and accompanying gestures (if available), wholes the biographical, linguistic, social, cultural and other structures in which the text is embedded. This very general mode of analysis has been adumbrated in earlier discussions in social science and philosophy.

The idea of part/whole analysis is implied in the definition by C. Wright Mills (1959, p.7) of "the sociological imagination":

> the capacity to shift from one perspective to another–from the political to the psychological; from examination of a single family to comparative assessment of the national budgets of the world; from the theological school to the military establishment; from considerations of an oil industry to studies of contemporary poetry. It is the capacity to range from the most impersonal and remote transformations to the most intimate features of the human self – and to see the relations between the two.

Mills begins ("from the political to the psychological") and ends his definition with the psychological ("the most intimate features of the human self"). The latter passage implies minute psychological aspects. In the remainder of the passage, Mills ranges over social institutions of the largest magnitude. Since in several places in this book he explicitly refers to relations between parts and wholes, Mills seems to have been implying that the human sciences should study the relations between the smallest parts and the largest wholes.

The idea of relations between parts and wholes is a familiar topic in philosophy. It is particularly crucial in the work of Spinoza.[3] Although his treatment of this theme is not free of seventeenth century theology, the implication is clear: human understanding requires relating "the least parts to the greatest wholes" (Sacksteder 1991).

The idea that understanding a problem requires knowledge of its least parts, on the one hand, and the greatest wholes, on the other, may be used as a foundation for inquiry. It points to a path which could lead, potentially, to the objective determination of meaning. In following this path, the least parts–greatest wholes idea also suggests a way of connecting meaning and social structure. As discussed below, the objective determination of meaning makes explicit the micro–macro connections which arise in understanding discourse.

Although the least parts–greatest wholes paradigm provides an explicit contrast to specialized approaches, it subsumes rather than rejects them. Highly specialized knowledge is implied by under-standing least parts (e.g., empirical data) and largest wholes (e.g., abstract theory). Part/whole analysis begins where specialized approaches leave off: it relates the findings that specialized work takes as ends in themselves.

Specialized and general intelligence

The part/whole approach can serve as complement and corrective to specialization, the reigning pattern in our current quest for know-ledge. Specialization brings benefits, but also limitations. The most puzzling aspect of this irresistible tide involves narrowing of vision, not only in behavior, but also in thought. The neurosurgeon needs special skills, but need not *think* only as a neurosurgeon. Narrowing of outlook because of disciplines, theories, methods and schools of thought is creating a crisis of knowledge in our time. Given their intellectual and emotional commitments, the great majority of re-searchers seem to be entrapped within their specialty. The part/whole approach described here suggests that we need de-specialization as much as we need specialization.

Pathologies seldom occur at the time of founding a new specialty. At this point a combination of system and intuition, procedural and substantive rationality, may be a necessary condition. A clear illustra-tion of this is the birth of computer science, created largely by the

---

[3] Part/whole relations are clearly a central theme for Husserl (Lampert 1989) also, but his approach is so abstract I found it impossible to follow. For an extremely cautious modern approach to parts and wholes, see Lerner (1963).

mathematician John von Neumann. The computer is an exact embodiment of what Pascal called "the spirit of system." It is based on processes which are linear, reductive, and explicit. The language which drives a computer is so systematic that the slightest ambiguity, even a missing comma, cannot be tolerated. In this respect, program and ordinary language are exact opposites: the symbols in a program must be completely unambiguous, in ordinary language, the symbols are virtually all ambiguous.

Computers are monuments to procedural rationality. Yet von Neumann's own method of mathematical work, which triggered the birth of computers, was completely intuitive. His intimates have described his mode of operation. To begin, von Neumann would list, on separate pages, a large selection of unsolved mathematical problems. He would then turn the pages, giving each problem a glance, one by one. If he did not quickly see a plausible solution, he would go on to the next problem. When he came to the end of the set of problems, he would begin again, continuing until he either found a solution or quit.

Von Neumann seems never to have troubled grinding out analytical solutions. His method of thinking was entirely intuitive, the exact opposite of the machine he helped create. Von Neumann was an embodiment of what Pascal called "the spirit of finesse" (i.e., intuition). The subsequent development of computer science might be viewed as the routinization of Von Neumann's charisma.

It appears that specialties are effective as long as system and finesse are in balance, or near it. But as a specialty becomes institutionalized, the spirit of system (procedural rationality) increasingly prevails. Making this point exactly, the physicist Boltzman noted, with some bitterness (he was a genius unrecognized during his lifetime): when a new method yields "beautiful results," many become unconsciously wedded to it; they come "to believe that the development of science to the end of all time would consist in the systematic and unremitting application of it." Although this statement was written at the turn of the century, it exactly captures the trajectory of current science and scholarship. An imbalance has been created which seems to be leading rapidly to ineffectiveness, if indeed it has not already been reached. System alone, as Weber pointed out, creates deadlock.

Science and scholarship which overemphasize system at the expense of finesse correspond to the stage that Kuhn (1962) called "normal science." He pointed out that this stage is effective in the "mopping up operations" that are needed in the wake of a great discovery. For example, the Human Genome Project represents a vast investment in mopping up the discovery of the structure of DNA. Perhaps Kuhn was too tactful to point out, however, that normal science is completely ineffective in areas where there have been no great discoveries, as in the humanities and social sciences.

The great problem-solvers in science have usually been intuitive types like von Neumann, who corrected the over-emphasis on system with a great jolt of imagination. Kepler broke through the bizarrely complex mathematical systems of centers and epicenters that were impeding the science of astronomy. He was able to discover the orbit of Mars because he placed the sun rather than the earth at the center of the orbit, an intuitive leap.

Kepler's leap was based on a premise that was entirely irrational, both in its source and content: as a young man, he had literally dreamed a fantastic scheme of crystalline solids which were supposed to determine planetary orbits. (He thought that the orbits of planets were constructed by their enclosure in five perfect solids [a sphere, pentahedron, tetrahedron, etc].) The orbit of the earth and the other planets were determined by polyhedrons of various shapes. The orbit of Mars was determined by a sphere. (The circularity of the orbit of Mars was an assumption began by Aristotle and continued by Kepler until he finally made his discovery.)

The main features of Kepler's scheme were outrageous, but contained, unconsciously, the last step Kepler needed to break the impasse. After struggling for decades to determine the orbit of Mars on the assumption that the earth was at its center, his realization that the sun was at the center of his structure of crystalline solids was the final step that allowed a solution. He was right, but for the wrong reason.

Being right for the wrong reason is an enormous advantage that intuition provides in solving problems. Another example of this advantage in Kepler's case involves the astonishing inaccuracy of his numerical calculations. He made a multitude of errors, some quite large. Yet he correctly plotted the elliptical orbit of Mars; his errors canceled each other out. His unconscious, one might say, was working overtime.

Similarly, Einstein intuited the solution to the failure of classical physics with a stroke of imagination, a direct intuition of the nature of the physical universe. Virtually illiterate in mathematics, he first proposed the special theory of relativity as a *joke*. When David Hilbert, the great French mathematician, was asked why Einstein, rather than others (like himself or Poincaré) immeasurably better qualified, made the discovery, he responded: "Because he had learned nothing about all the philosophy and mathematics of time and space" (cited in Feuer 1982, 62).

Both in the case of Kepler and Einstein, it is clear not only that system may not solve difficult problems, it can actually stand in the way. Yet it was Brahe's systematic data which allowed Kepler to make his discovery. Einstein called upon friendly mathematicians, those hostages to system, to put his theories in their final form. Although no such credit was given, his general theory of relativity required virtual collaboration with a mathematical colleague.

Perhaps the classic case of the marriage between system and finesse in problem-solving is the discovery of the structure of DNA by Crick and Watson. Like von Neumann, Watson represented pure intuition. He was a graduate student when he and Crick made their discovery, utterly ignorant and untrained in requisite sciences. The model of DNA they developed was an assembly of the discoveries of others, but an assembly touched by imaginative genius. The scientists on whom the discovery of the structure of DNA was based each understood their own findings and fields, but misunderstood or ignored the work of the others. They had tunnel vision; they were trapped within their specialized outlook.

Like Einstein in his ignorance, Watson was a complete outsider. Being on the outside, he did not suffer from the biases and limitations of vision of the insiders, and from specialized procedures that had become more hindrance than help. Watson was something of an outlaw: he abandoned normal procedures and channels in a way that is still shocking to established scientists (Watson 1980). But Watson also needed a conventional insider, Crick, to help him put the partial discoveries together into a workable whole. Discovery of the structure of DNA, like Kepler's and Einstein's, required a partnership between system and intuition.

Intuition: its structure and function

Attempts to use computers to linguistic ends suggest that human intelligence is vast because it involves balancing system and intuition. The failure of automated translation of ordinary language posed a puzzling problem: if machines cannot understand ordinary language, how is it understood, quickly and without effort, in daily life? The solution to this problem points to the nature of general intelligence, how it requires balance between system and intuition, and the crucial role of ambiguity in human expressions.

Linguists have long known that certain types of expressions have meanings that are entirely contextual. Pronouns are an obvious example. When words like *you, he, she* or *it* are used in discourse, their meanings are blank checks, to be filled in by contextual knowledge. But the failure of automated translation has shown that *all* expressions in ordinary language are ambiguous without context. (Artificial languages, such as math and computer programs are exempt, since their symbols have singular meanings. Unlike a text in ordinary language, a file in Word can be translated quickly and exactly into Word Perfect.) In ordinary language, commonly used words have many meanings; the correct meaning can be determined only in context.

This point suggests that understanding ordinary language requires a mind that is a *general problem-solver*; it relates the smallest parts (words) and wholes (not only systems of grammar and syntax, but a vast array of cultural practices). Even before the advent of attempts at automated translation, the philosopher Wittgenstein understood this point. He proposed that understanding even a simple rule ("Stop at red lights") involved what he called "mastery of practice" (understanding an entire cultural system).

The relation of text to context in the determination of meaning can be rephrased in part/whole language. The method of prospective/retrospective understanding implies that understanding ordinary language requires search of the local and extended context. Although the local context is strictly finite, the particular text of which an expression is a part, the extended context is not. The prospective context is all that happened after the expression, the retrospective context all that happened before it.

As if two potential infinities were not enough, the necessity of using hypotheticals to infer meanings requires still another file that may be large, if not infinite: all the statements that could reasonably have been used as alternatives to the actual one. As indicated earlier, Pittenger et al. discuss this type of hypothetical under the heading "The Principle of Reasonable Alternatives." Their discussion concerns only alternatives to actual statements in the text, the local context. It is not applied to the past and future in which the text is located, as is my discussion of hypotheticals.

One component needed for understanding ordinary language is a vast file of information, which amounts to biographical knowledge of the author(s) of the text, the audience, and historical and cultural knowledge available to both authors and audience. A second component involves the pathways used in the search for understanding. Given the vastness of the context, how can one find all the information needed for an objective determination of meaning? What makes this task impossible for computers is not merely the size of the information base, but also the means for searching this base.

Computers are limited to pre-defined pathways for searching a file, and, for the most part, to strictly logical operations. These operations involve *concepts*, class names built upon similarities and differences. Although the classificatory principle is a powerful method of searching, human thought seems to involve many other kinds of paths in addition. Recent attempts to use "fuzzy logic" in computer programs represent a step away from strictly logical operations, if only a very small step. Compared with the ambiguousness of ordinary language, fuzzy logic still reflects the spirit of system.

In explaining their thought processes, chess-players and creative scientists usually refer to non-logical paths such as the "feel for the positions of the pieces on the board" in chess, and instinct or intuition in science. Ordinary language makes use of a wide variety of associations which are not logical. Puns, for example, depend on sound rather than meaning. Solving complex problems seems to need not only logical connections, but also idiosyncratic ones: emotional or biographical contiguity, for example. (One remembers the date of one's first investment because it happened the day before the death of John Kennedy.)

Pathways of creative thought involve what I call *total* association, of which logical associations are only one part. Associations which are merely contingent, such as punning, emotional or alliterative associations, etc., allow for a diversity of connective paths that may be as vast as the memory files themselves. It is the number of pathways that allows human intelligence to be an open system, a general problem-solver (Scheff 1990, 59–62).

Human intelligence is an open system because problem-solving operations need not follow pre-defined pathways. To phrase the matter under discussion here in computer language, the kind of mental processes that occur in problem-solving may be massively *parallel*, rather than *serial* in nature (Scheff 1990; 1993). Total association, much of it improvised at moment of need, allows for a vast number of pathways. Computers, no matter how large the memory and how advanced the program, are limited to pre-defined pathways using non-ambiguous information. For this reason, the number of pathways is likely to be small compared to the size of the file. And logical connections are inherently serial, since they require matching each item with each other item for similarities and differences.

The exact difference between artificial and human intelligence is that mental processes use ambiguous tokens, and proceed through improvised pathways. The ability of the mind to deal with ambiguous tokens and contingent pathways gives rise to what is called intuition, the rapid and seemingly effortless solution of complex problems.

Since words and gestures in ordinary language are only indexical, context dependent for their meaning, understanding and using ordinary language requires the analysis of smallest parts and the largest wholes, a general problem solver. It may therefore be the acquisition of ordinary language that lays down the template for human intelligence. This proposal seems to contradict the prevailing theory of language acquisition (Chomsky 1957). Chomsky proposes that language ability is an inborn drive. This idea bypasses what I consider to be the supreme importance of language learning in forming adult intelligence.

Minsky's society of mind

Minsky's (1985) theory of mind is useful for explaining intuition.[4] He argued that mind is based upon structures he called "agents," procedures that generate rapid problem-solving. In Minsky's scheme, the infant comes equipped with only a few agentic procedures, eating, sleeping, playing, smiling, crying, etc. (see figure 1.2). Very early, however, the infant begins developing learned agents, skill procedures, such as walking erect, tying shoe laces, throwing a ball (and jumping into a complex realm), speaking sentences. Adult competence depends upon developing, in Minsky's estimate (1985, 314), as many as a *billion* such agents.

Minsky is careful never to use the term self in his discussion, but his scheme suggests a theory of selfhood. He predicates a type of agent more complex than a skill sequence, capable of command and control. An infant early experiences conflicting desires, e.g. playing, eating, and sleeping. The presence of an ego or self means that the infant develops an agent to detect conflicting desires and to mediate between them by issuing commands. In this case, the control agent might command the playing and eating agents: "Stop!", the crying agent: "Cry!" and the sleeping agent "Wait!" Without a command-control agent, the neonate must respond only passively to stimuli. Self-control and thought require the regulation of conflict.

A command-control agent is complex compared to a skill sequence because the latter is fixed; it is a *constant*, one might say. Although a molecule of DNA *in situ* is extremely large and complex, it is unchanging. A command/control agent is not constant, but variable. In order to serve as mediator, it must be able not only to detect conflict, but make decisions which resolve it. It seems to follow, therefore, that self and mind arise out of conflict.

Minsky's discussion of mental processes implies a further complexity. Even in infancy, he proposes a *hierarchy* of control agents.

---

[4] The following review of Minsky is based in part on Scheff 1993.

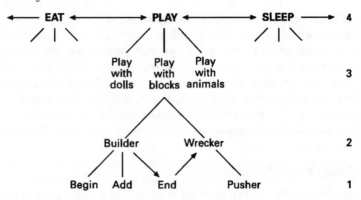

Figure 1.2 Minsky's hierarchy of control agents

Level 1, under "builder" (level 2), building with blocks, is simple and concrete, made up of discrete actions: begin, add, end. But level 2, builder, already implies control, able to choose between the impulses to begin, add, or end. The diagram also implies, but does not show, a level 5, perhaps at this age the highest level, the ego, which mediates all conflicting impulses. Given the growth of the number of agents, and the increasing complexity of the problems to be solved, more and more levels of control surely would be required.

For example, as an adult vocabulary and syntax are acquired, the language agent presupposes a structure huge both in width and height. Yet this structure must be under the control of an agent at a still higher level, the ego. Another example concerns dreams. Supposing that dreams are produced by a dream agent, the nature of dreams might give us some idea of the functions of the ego, those I assume to be unavailable during sleep.

The particular combination of coherence and incoherence typical of dreams suggest the possibility of a tripartite level of control immediately below the ego level, as it functions when one is awake: 1. Receive Information, 2. Evaluate, and 3. Remember. During the dream state, level 2, Evaluation, seems to have entirely closed shop, and level 3, Remember, functions only weakly or sporadically.

Whatever the specifics of the structure of intelligence, this discussion implies that the mind grows not only horizontally, with increasing numbers of skills, but also vertically, with an increasing number of levels of control. Although horizontal growth may occur through passive accumulation, as in memorization, vertical growth occurs *only* through conflict. The *area* (size) of intelligence, one might say, is as dependent on conflict as on breadth of learning. This proposition has so many implications for learning and for education that brevity forbids further discussion, except to say that it implies a need for conflict and discovery in education at least equal to passive acquisition.

Minsky's theory suggests an explanation of intuition. The image that he uses is that the mind is like a *society* made up of myriads of agents: intelligence involves effective cooperation between them. In Minsky's scheme, the mind is a large society; the number of agents is of the same order of magnitude as the human population of the earth. Given the importance of the differentiation of levels of agents, this model emphasizes hierarchy, as do most sociological models of society. But this is the only aspect of social organization that Minsky invokes. His discussion treats society, with this one exception, as a mass of unorganized individuals.

Minsky proposed that most of the actions of agents goes on out of awareness: "An idea will seem self-evident – once you've forgotten learning it" (1985, 128). In the predicated society, most of the activity of individual and groups of agents occurs outside of the ruler's (the ego) awareness. Minsky's model, in the context of the discussion above about parallel sequencing, suggests the way in which complex problems can be solved rapidly and with little conscious effort.

Suppose that the challenge of a complex problem triggers the actions of thousands of agentic attempts at solution *simultaneously*. There are a wide variety of logical paths to be tried. At the same time, however, many more non-logical paths, which is probably what we call *guessing*, might also be involved. If one of the paths unconsciously followed leads to a solution, we call the process intuition. The vast number of diverse paths, logical and non-logical, gives rise to a great multitude of simultaneous investigations. Intuition is constituted by this covert process.

Although the covert mental processes summarized under the heading intuition can lead to rapid solutions of novel and complex problems, this process is not infallible. Since deductions are built on past experience, they may be inadequate in situations not encountered earlier. Like any other hypotheses, intuitive insights need to be verified.

General intelligence requires both deduction and induction, a rapid movement between imagination and observation. The philosopher C. S. Peirce called this process *abduction*. He was referring not only to the scientific process, the testing of hypotheses against empirical data, but more generally any kind of movement back and forth between imagination and reality. Peirce seems to imply that the most efficient kind of problem-solving involved the rapid movement between imagination and observation by the individual thinker.[5] The approach to inquiry outlined in this book seeks to maximize the opportunities for abduction, for rapid interplay between theory and fact.

The morphological approach, when combined with explicit part/ whole analysis, can generate investigations which are both theory- and data-driven. The method of botanic morphology requires the close observation and description first of single specimens, then comparison of specimens with each other and with other plants. The study of specimen plants in botany is microscopic, the analysis of minutiae, the smallest parts. These minutiae are used for two different purposes: firstly, to understand *the way the specimen itself works as an organism*, and secondly, to differentiate specimens of a given plant from each other and from other plants, a larger whole.

The greatest triumph of the morphological method occurred not in botany but in Darwin's research. One of the crucial observations that figured in the theory of evolution was the minute differences in finches' beaks on neighboring islands. He reasoned that the birds on separate islands were beginning to differentiate because differences in their environments called forth differences in form.

The most explicit description of the morphological method, however, occurs not in Darwin but in Goethe. Although today known only as a poet and writer, Goethe was a polymath, as active a scientist as a poet (Amrine et al. 1987). In his substantial studies in botany, he proposed, contrary to Linnaeus, that the scientist should study *function* as well as *form*. This idea goes to the heart of the morphological method. One needs microscopic understanding of the details of a specimen, not only to describe it, as Linnaeus did, but also to understand how it works as a system (in the case of plants, as organisms). Goethe championed what would today be called functionalism, but as a method (in modern terms, systems analysis) rather than a theory.

Goethe proposed that specimens should be understood in terms of *gestalten*, a word with no exact equivalent in English. It roughly means patterns, but in Gothe's usage, he emphasized one connotation, *complete* patterns. Goethe meant not only the pattern within the specimen, but also in relation to its environment. Collecting a huge number of specimens of plants and of animal skeletons, and closely investigating their gestalten, form and function, Goethe came close to

---

[5] Peirce's idea of abduction is somewhat diffuse. On the one hand, some of his descriptions make it sound like a strict logical procedure, as in his example of the white beans. On the other hand, he clearly states that abduction is always guessing. "We must conquer the truth by guessing, or not at all " (Sebeok and Umiker-Sebeok 1983, 11). One example that Peirce offered, the time that he found the thief who had stolen his gold watch, involves pure intuition, with no logical steps whatsoever.

anticipating, by almost 100 years, some of the features of Darwin's theory of evolution.

Goethe's morphological method implies part/whole analysis. His use of *gestalten* as patterns of relationship within and between organisms, and with the environment, and his pursuit of the relationship between form and function both involve least part/greatest whole analysis. In order to understand the organism, he implied, although it is a system itself, one also needs to understand the host environment, and the relationship between organism and environment. Although Goethe could not know about cells, one can pursue his metaphor within the organism as well: to understand the cell, one needs to understand the host organism, and vice versa. In modern terminology his approach was to show the interrelations between systems and subsystems.

Some passages from Goethe (1790) explicitly suggest part/whole analysis:

> In every living thing what we call the parts is so inseparable from the whole that the parts can only be understood in the whole, and we can neither make the parts the measure of the whole nor the whole the measure of the parts; and this is why living creatures, even the most restricted, have something about them we cannot quite grasp and have to describe as infinite or partaking of infinity.

Goethe's idea of part/whole relations can be easily applied to Darwin's theory of evolution. He showed how all living organisms are subsystems within a larger system of organism-environment relations. Can similar concepts and methods also be applied to psychological and social systems?

Time order and causal inference

One advantage of the morphological method applied to discourse is that because the temporal sequence is unmistakable, it generates causal rather than correlational theories and evidence. In mechanical records of interaction (that have not been subject to tampering), there can never be any doubt about the time order of events.

Retzinger's (1991) study of the causes of escalation in marital quarrels was generated by Lewis's (1971) study of emotions in psychotherapy because it was causal. Lewis noted in many instances that a patient's hostility toward the therapist seemed to occur shortly after the patient showed cues to unacknowledged shame. From these instances, Lewis reasoned that the patient's hostility was caused by shame that went unacknowledged by the patient and uninterpreted by the therapist. Since Lewis had only commented, in passing, on the causal sequence leading from shame to anger, Retzinger designed her research to provide systematic support for it. Both studies were grounded in the incontrovertible time order in which anger and shame appeared in the recorded data.

Retzinger developed a causal theory of destructive conflict, and supported it with sixteen instances, all escalations of conflict in the four marital quarrels she studied. She found that although overt anger was present in all instances, cues to unacknowledged shame invariably *preceded* the indications of anger. (The coding system which Retzinger (1991; 1995) developed for identifying hidden shame and anger can be found in the appendix to this book.)

The advantage of a clear temporal order occurs in verbatim texts, but is not absolute. Although unusual, deception and mistakes are possible. For example, it is now clear that after the end of the First World War, the Russian and French governments faked documents attempting to obscure the order and completeness of mobilization of the armies of the combatants. The fact that the Russian army mobilized first and that their mobilization was complete rather than partial is a key piece of evidence in understanding the origins of the war (chapter 5). Nevertheless, the time order of most verbatim texts is establishable, as is the case with all mechanical recordings. For this reason, the generation of causal hypotheses and evidence is facilitated more than with correlational data.

Returning once more to Pittenger et al. and Labov and Fanshel, these studies can be seen as a beginning step in the morphological method. Each was a microscopic examination of a single specimen. Although not using this term, each was able to describe *gestalten*, recurring patterns within the single texts they studied. Lewis went a step further in this method, microanalyzing not only single texts, but comparing them each to the other, the second step in morphology. But she did not take the final step, the systematic comparison of the patterns of dialogue she found with types of dialogue other than psychotherapist–patient.

Perhaps because she dealt with so many cases, Lewis failed to make inferences about larger patterns beyond the subjects she studied. Analyzing only a single text, but intensively, both Pittenger et al. and Labov and Fanshel took an inferential step beyond their texts. As already described, both studies inferred relationships within their subjects' families: Pittenger et al. compared the subject's relationship with her therapist with a hypothetical relationship with her husband, and Labov and Fanshel inferred extensive hypothetical relations within the subject's family. The comparison of the Pittenger et al. and Labov and Fanshel inferences with Lewis's suggests a surprising advantage of intensive study of single cases, as against Lewis's much more extensive study of many cases. The closer the analysis of a single case, the more likely it will generate micro–macro inferences, even if they are inadvertent.

On the other hand, findings in the approach called Conversation Analysis so far seem to contradict this last proposition. CA, as it is called, is a highly developed example of the microanalysis of verbatim texts. Its analysis of the words and gestures in ordinary language is state of the art in terms of precision and rigor. This approach, however, has produced few inferences about the institutional embeddedness of their texts.

The lack of higher order inferences in CA seems to follow from its concern for objectivity. The central tactic employed to this end has been to avoid the analysis of meaning; the procedures are intended to concern behavior rather than thoughts and feelings. But the extent to which analysis of meaning is avoided is questionable. If my reasoning is correct, because of the indexicality of ordinary language, the objective determination of meaning requires least parts/greatest wholes analysis. The parts are the words and gestures, but the wholes that are needed to understand them include the thoughts, feelings, motives, intentions and institutional and historical embeddedness of the subjects who create the text. These components of social interaction seem to be implicated in CA analysis, but only covertly, as in quantitative studies, disguised as common sense.[6]

Like most other approaches, CA is highly specialized: it is tied to only the first and second steps in what I am calling morphology, the microanalysis of single specimens. Like computer science, CA was created by a highly intuitive researcher, Harvey Sacks. Like most other specialties, this one has gone the route of increasing emphasis on system at the expense of finesse. The incorporation of CA into the three stages of inquiry advocated here might be stimulating and beneficial both to CA and to human science as a whole.

Standardized scales

One last example of the potential of the part/whole approach concerns the construction of psychological scales, such as the self-esteem scales mentioned earlier. The construction of scales bypasses explicit theory by using what has become a conventional "empirical" method. Psychologists construct scales by first generating a set of scale items

---

[6] For a preliminary comparison between the methods used in CA and those used in quantitative studies, see Schegloff 1993.

intuitively (i.e. by using an implicit, unstated and therefore undiscussed theory), give these items to subjects, perform a factor analysis, and derive groups of items that correlate with each other more than with other groups, so an individual item correlates with summed scores of its group. In the case of self-esteem, the concept comes to be whatever the vernacular term means, which is assumed, without evidence or even discussion, to relate to the operational concept derived from the scale.

I will use items from a standard scale, the Coopersmith Self-Esteem Inventory (1967), to illustrate a glaring problem with this approach. My argument seems to apply equally well to all of the items that make up the scale; three were selected for brevity.

4. I can make up my mind without too much trouble.
19. If I have something to say, I usually say it.
24. Things usually don't bother me.

All three of these items are scored as positives; that is, a "yes" indicates high self-esteem. Although this may be true in some cases, it is probably false in others. Lacking an explicit theory of the relation between feelings, thoughts and behavior, the construction of the scale does not deal with the possibility that positive responses could also reflect personality *defenses*.

Although an explicit theory has never been used in the construction of scales, the procedures used imply an implicit one: other things being equal, when responding to a researcher who is a stranger to them, with little or no incentive or time for truthfulness and self-awareness, subjects usually say what they mean and mean what they say. Given the sizable literature on the contradictions between attitudes (as constructed from interviews, paper and pencil tests, etc) and behavior, the implicit use of such an obviously inaccurate theory suggests that an explicit theory is needed for the construction of any scale.

Neither these three items nor any of the others attempt to tap repressed or hidden feelings. For this reason, they could just as well indicate impulsive, repetitive, or inappropriate speech (19), or the repression of feeling (4 and 24). Indeed, all three of these items could be scored negatively on a scale designed to detect freedom from obsessive-compulsive behavior. The positive scoring of items that might equally well indicate defenses against feelings of *unworthiness* as genuine *self-confidence* may be one of the reasons for the poor performance of self-esteem scales.

How could one distinguish between self-confidence and defensive maneuvers? The morphological method, in the form of microanalysis of verbatim dialogue, might be a place to start. Suppose in a study using a self-esteem scale, one also interviewed the respondents afterwards, asking them to explain their answers to the paper and pencil test.[7] By probing for examples, one might be able to form an accurate idea of the particular meaning to the subject of the answers to these three or any other scale items for each subject. By making the transcripts of the interviews available to the reader, and by explaining one's methods, the resulting study might be both valid and reliable.

Part–whole analysis is the effective component in what is referred to as *common sense*. It is this process that enables the construction of scales (and all other reliable procedures) that the creators believe to measure self-esteem or other attribute. Yet it has become customary in the human sciences to disparage this process as "psychologizing." Unknown to the creators of scales, they also indulge in the same process, but in a covert and therefore undisciplined way.

In naming the concept purportedly measured by the scale, self-esteem in this instance, and in coding responses as positive or negative, the scale-maker is psychologizing, but in a way that is hidden and not debatable. For example, judging that a positive answer to item 4 above is an indication of high self-esteem involves inferring the meaning of the item, but in a mechanical way. The morphological method could determine the meaning of scale items for *each subject individually*, and perhaps in the long run, lead to modifications of scaling procedures that might make them more effective.

Generating theory

Although there are hints of such inferences, neither Pittenger et al. nor Labov and Fanshel took the next step beyond inferring patterns in the subject's families, which would be to infer patterns in types of families, or membership in religious or other institutions. Even if they had made such inferences, they would have been unable to confirm or modify them, since their data was limited to texts only.

Inferences concerning the social institutions within which a text is embedded provide a rich resource for generating a micro–macro theory. Such a procedure is enriching because the texts intimate, in great detail, the subjects' connections to larger institutions. Mention has already been made to institutions beyond the family within which the texts studied by Pittenger et al. and Labov and Fanshel were

---

[7] For a study in this vein, see Fearon 1994.

embedded: class, gender, ethnicity, and age. Verbatim excerpts from discourse, one might argue, are *microcosms*, they contain within them, brief as they may be, intimations of the participants' origins in and relationships to the institutions of the host society.

Perhaps the idea of functionalism could still be useful, not as a theory but as a method. The discussion of the analysis of psychological and social systems and sub-systems involves the *method* implied in functional ideas.[8] These earlier ideas about functions concerned relationships between parts and whole, but without a method or data. The method described here leads to the investigation of such relationships, rather than using them as explanations. The stages of inquiry proposed here lead from the microanalysis of single specimen texts up to the generation of theories grounded in texts.

The generation of micro–macro theories from linguistic texts is an unusual procedure, but it has been practiced by two masters. In a series of studies, Lévi-Strauss (1963) teased out cultural implications of myths that he gathered from small traditional societies. From the myths of each culture studied he deduced what he called the cognitive structure of that culture, the fundamental dimensions of thought.

Although in some ways Lévi-Strauss's approach is similar to mine, it is also quite different. Two differences are basic. Firstly, Lévi-Strauss did not use transcriptions of the myths he gathered. For this reason, he was unable to analyze what I would consider the smallest parts of the cultural systems he studied, the words and their nonverbal accompaniment. But emotions and social structure virtually always ride upon gesture. Even adroit questioning will seldom yield much reliable information about emotions. Institutional connections might be somewhat more available, but even there the descriptions are usually threadbare. Without the nonverbal components of discourse, even if he had wanted to, Lévi-Strauss would have been unable to infer much about emotions and social structure.

For example, in my re-analysis (chapter 8) of the text used by Pittenger et al., I used nonverbal elements in the recording to infer that the patient was responding to the class difference between her and the therapist. At several points, after mispronounced words or other errors, the patient not only corrected her speech, but also showed signs of embarrassment. I inferred that she was seeing her responses from the point of view of the therapist, and judging them from the point of view she attributed to him, rather than her own.

---

[8] This point was also made earlier by Turner and Maryanski (1979, 130–133). In this connection they also twice mention part/whole analysis, but only in passing.

This finding is a clear indication of dominance-subordination in the relationship.

These instances of the patient's behavior also hint at what I call *engulfment* on the patient's side, giving up parts of herself out of deference to the other person. The difference between engulfment, a form of alienation, and *isolation*, the other form of alienation, on the one hand, and solidarity, on the other, invokes fundamental structures of relationship that are just becoming available to empirical research (see chapter 4). The smallest parts, in this case the words and their accompanying emotion cues, allow inferences about the emotional meaning of the relationship to the patient, and also its social structure.

Just as Lévi-Strauss's analysis is entirely cognitive, it is also entirely psychological. He makes inferences about the mental functions of individuals; he has no categories of relationship. Except for hierarchy, Minsky's (1985) brilliant analysis of the nature of mind has a similar limitation. Just as Lévi-Strauss interprets culture in individual terms, Minsky interprets society. Neither analysis conceptualizes types of relationships, which are as much building blocks of societies as individual persons are.

Elias (1978), a second master who generated micro–macro theories from linguistic texts, conceptualized both individual and relational structures, both cognitive and emotional meanings. For these reasons, his approach is much closer to mine than Lévi-Strauss's.

Drawing upon some 500 years of European history, Elias analyzed excerpts from etiquette manuals in four languages. Closely examining advice on table manners, body functions, sexuality and anger, he showed that his excerpts suggested an explosion of shame connected with modernity.[9] His analysis of an excerpt from a nineteenth-century text advising mothers about their daughters is illustrative. The author, a male, advises fables, silence and suppression when daughters ask sexual questions, such as where babies come from.

Although working with a printed text, Elias was able to tease out the emotions implied, principally the author's intense embarrassment about sexuality, and how the behavior advised would shame the daughter into silence. Elias notes both what is stated and what is omitted, and most importantly, the manner of presentation, to infer emotional meanings.

Elias provides a very close analysis of specific texts, but he also infers emotional meanings involving social structure. In a bold and

---

[9] The following comments on Elias are a condensed version of passages in Scheff and Retzinger 1991.

provocative way, Elias linked changes in emotional expression to changes in social structure. For example, he outlined the way in which the narrowing of the control of the means of violence in a society to a small ruling elite might be related to increasing suppression of individual anger throughout a society.

Unlike Lévi-Strauss and Minsky, Elias uses relational categories as well as ones involving individuals. He criticized studies based on what he called *homo clausus*, the closed, solitary individual. In the place of this conceptualization, he proposed an incipient theory of social solidarity/alienation. He argued that social relationships can involve either independence, interdependence, or dependence. This scheme is only implied in the 1978 study, but is stated more explicitly in his later work (for instance, Elias 1987). His scheme is closely related to Durkheim's analysis of the causes of suicide, and other classic work in sociology (see chapter 4).

Elias used elements in the two stages of inquiry I am advocating, morphology and micro–macro theory, but his approach is still different from the one outlined here. The difference involves explicitness with regard to concepts and methods. Although he analyzed verbatim texts, Elias has no explicit description of his methods, nor of the concepts in the micro–macro theory he seems to generate. For this reason, it is difficult to argue with his findings, or even to state with any precision exactly what they are. This limitation, lack of explicitness about methods and concepts, may be the reason for the widely varying understandings and evaluations of his work.

Elias's study pointed the way to the approach outlined here because it combined elements of two of the three stages of inquiry. In this particular study, all of Elias's propositions about personality, social structure and social change are derived from and grounded in microanalysis of verbatim texts. The clarity and incisiveness of this study, as compared to most of his later work, are probably due in large part to this procedure. If Elias had been more explicit about his methods and concepts, perhaps the study would have been more widely accepted, and generated later attempts at verification.

Being cavalier about methods and concepts may be characteristic of discoverers. The above comments are also applicable, to a slightly lesser extent to the major work by Lewis (1971). Although she used a standard and therefore explicit method as one part of her approach to coding emotions (Gottschalk and Gleser 1969), she did not attempt to explain or even discuss the more intuitive methods that she combined it with. And although she was explicit about defining some of her concepts, there is no formal statement of theory, and no attempt to infer larger social structures.

Summary

This chapter has described a part/whole morphology of human behavior. The core of my proposal is the need for a new step of inquiry that will bridge the chasm between exploration and verification. When combined with *qualitative* methods, part/whole morphology can be used to approach seemingly intractable problems in the human world, generating comprehensive hypotheses to the point that they might be tested. When combined with *quantitative* methods, the same two steps can lead to the comprehensive testing of the hypotheses they generate.

The basic strength of this approach is that it places the researcher (and the reader) into direct contact with the raw data of human behavior, verbatim texts or mechanical records of interaction. This approach has an intensely inductive quality that is missing from conventional research designs.[10] Quantitative studies shield both researcher and reader from contact with actual events and sequences of events by cross-sectional designs and by layer on layer of paper and pencil tests, coding, scales, and numerical analysis. Qualitative studies may come closer to human reality, or plausibly appear to do so, but only as filtered through the observers' fallible memory, sensitivities, and biases. As in quantitative studies, the human reality on which studies are based is usually unrecoverable.

The approach outlined here allows for the recovery of large parts of the original events – instant replay – in a way not permitted by conventional methods. Such recovery not only allows direct falsification, it also means that data are not lost forever. It can become the grounds for subsequent advances, as I have shown with the Pittenger et al. and Labov and Fanshel studies in this chapter. Given this approach, the voices of our subjects are not silenced by our methods, but amplified and preserved for future generations.

Being exposed continually to the raw data of human interaction is particularly stimulating to a researcher. Listening to audiotapes and viewing videotapes or film come very near to being able to reproduce the original scenes at will. Exposure of this kind allows us to learn something new about the subjects and about ourselves, expanding the horizons of the study, whatever its original intent. Human voices and faces, so long absent from so much of human science, spring to life repeatedly, as they are needed as a prod to our sleepwalking through our projects.

Since the approach proposed here is synoptic, rather than special-

---

[10] Discussed at greater length in Scheff and Retzinger 1994.

ized, it might be a way to begin integrating the contributions of theory and method, and the various methods, disciplines, levels of analysis, and schools of thought in the human sciences. In this way it is possible to envision, instead of the alienation that now prevails, at least a beginning for community among those of us who try to understand the human condition.

One final implication of the approach outlined here is the need for generalists as well as specialists to solve the problems which beset our disciplines and our societies. Perhaps one direction would be to press for centers of general studies, whether programs, institutes, or departments, to deal with the masses of specialized knowledge with which we are now inundated. The fate of the interdisciplinary programs in our era has not been heartening, but our circumstances cry out for new beginnings.

This chapter has argued that part/whole morphology, by successive approximation, can generate valid micro–macro theories. Although this approach is arduous, it may provide a framework for integrating existing work in the human sciences, and goals for the future. As Blake noted, all art and science is based on "minute particulars." The approach outlined here may yield robust theories of individual and collective behavior that are deeply grounded in the minute particulars of human existence. Needless to say, there is many a slip between the cup and the lip. The chapters below show, in a halting, preliminary way, some of the results of applying the new method.

CHAPTER 2

Limitations of literary analyses of texts

This chapter provides a preliminary example of one use of part/whole thinking: the framing of a study in a way that positions it within the larger contexts of which it is a part. This is always a crucial issue for scholars both as individuals and as members of scholarly disciplines. What are the advantages of relating your own particular study to larger contexts? And to what lengths should one go in this direction? What are the advantages and disadvantages to limiting of the context to frameworks of one's own discipline? These are quite general questions that apply to all research, and raise complex issues about the costs and benefits of insularity and universality. In this chapter I illustrate the problem with two studies, each of which traverses only a few steps of the part/whole ladder.

Most studies in the human sciences concern either parts or wholes, but seldom include both. Typically, empirical studies focus on parts, theoretical discussions on wholes. There is a standard format in experimental social psychology, for example, which deals with theory only tangentially, as low-level generalizations. These generalizations are usually phrased in the vernacular, rather than in terms of concepts which are bound to some general theory. Because of this format, the same results tend to be found in different contexts, leading to senseless repetition. The Asch studies produce a flood of similar studies, finding conformity in many different settings. But since no general theory was formulated, similar findings were reported many times, with no culmination. The same could said for studies of the Prisoner's Dilemma, and most of the other topics of investigation in social psychology laboratories. Placing experiments within a framework developed from some general theory would likely make them more parsimonious and consequential.

Another implication of part/whole thinking for experimental social psychology relates to what has been called the question of ecological validity. The responses of a subject in an experiment can be seen as

The first section of this chapter revises and expands pp. 192–195 of Scheff (1990).

parts of a larger whole, that subject's behavior in everyday life. To what extent are the laboratory responses determined by the particular setting? Or do they reflect general patterns in the subject's life outside the lab? Although most studies assume the latter, they have not investigated the possibility of the former. Collecting accurate data on the subject's outside responses would be a complex and resource-consuming task. This dilemma is reflected in an academic joke. A man going to see his friend one evening finds him down on hands and knees on his porch. When asked what he is doing, the friend replies that he has been looking for his car keys for over an hour. The man asks: "Do you know where you lost them?" The friend replies, "By the car in the driveway." "Then why are you looking on the porch?" "Because the light is better up here." Part/whole reasoning leads one to follow the path most likely to lead to the lost keys, rather than the path of least resistance.

At the other end of the scholarly spectrum, theorists in the human sciences and humanities usually follow another kind of path of least resistance. Theory has currently become increasingly defined by the absence of data, or even consideration of possible data. Currently theory has come to mean considerations of concepts independently of present or future data. Just as empirical research usually means parts without wholes, theory usually means wholes without parts. This chapter provides two examples of studies which imply larger contexts within which they can be located.

In human behavior, any part implies a larger whole, which is in turn part of a still larger whole, and so on, up the ladder. Applied to discourse, this idea suggests a movement back and forth between small concrete parts, and ever larger abstract wholes.

Part/whole ladder
Concrete level
1. Single words and gestures.
2. Sentences.
3. Exchanges.
4. Conversations.
5. Relationship of the two parties (all their conversations).
6. Life histories of the two parties.

Societal level
7. All relationships of their type: i.e. therapist–patient, man–woman, etc.
8. The structure of the host society: all relationships.
9. The history and future of the host civilization.
10. The history and destiny of the human species.

Practical intelligence in the lifeworld appears to involve abduction, that is, the rapid, effortless shuttling up and down this ladder. The system can be visualized as Chinese boxes, each box containing a smaller one, and nested within a larger one. Indeed the concept of *nested contexts* is crucial for understanding discourse.

The distinction between topic and relationship hints at this larger system: the topic is at level 2, since it involves sentences, the relationship, at level 5. However, all levels are implied in the actual understanding and practice of discourse. The process is awkward to describe in explicit language, but it takes place constantly, effortlessly, and instantaneously in discourse.

Contemporary scholars and scientists seem to have difficulty visualizing part/whole relationships. In the current division of labor, the organic connection between part and whole is lost in the division of intellectual labor: theorists deal with wholes, but not parts, researchers deal with parts but not wholes. The contributors to an interdisciplinary colloquium on parts and wholes (Lerner 1963) seemed to have difficulty in even approaching the topic. Only two of the papers convey some sense of the relationship: Roman Jacobson (natural language as an organic system), and I. A. Richards (poems as organic wholes).

Even Jacobson and Richards fail to give a minimal sketch, however. Both commit what Richards refers to as "the pathetic fallacy," they locate the system in the verbal parts, rather than in the social-cultural whole. Richards discusses only the integrity of the poem, rather than its relationship to social and psychological process in creator and audience. Like the subjects in the dialogues in this book, he sticks to a topic, rather than commenting on relationships. This same difficulty continues to haunt current discussion. The structuralists have discovered the ambiguity of expressions: they show that various expressions are "undecidable," and that translations may be "indeterminate." As already indicated, when social context is shorn away, as it is in most structuralist interpretation, all expressions become ambiguous. But in context, "interpretive decipherment" (Steiner 1975) can result in consensual understanding.

A clear evocation of the contextuality of understanding can be found in Levine's examination of sociological theory (1985). By showing the contradictions which result from the attempt to eliminate ambiguity from expressions, he makes a case for the role of intuition in understanding the relationship between parts and wholes.

Goffman's technique of "frame analysis" (1974) also can be used to expand on part/whole process. The frames that he refers to can be seen as contexts in the nested context structure of thought. Goffman, however, limits himself to the analysis of the *social* aspects of framing, missing the opportunity to connect the social and the psychological. His analysis of "frame-breaking" nevertheless points toward an important issue. The framing structure itself, the particular set of Chinese boxes that is tacitly assumed in a group, however limited, takes on a sacred character. Under these conditions, frame-breaking, the use of a different part-whole structure, may be taken as an affront.

A study of poetic closure

To illustrate these abstract ideas, I call upon a part/whole analysis implied in a study of poetic form. Flexing part/whole muscles in her introductory comment, Smith outlines a structure of nested contexts (Smith 1968; the level numbers have been added by the present author):

> This study is concerned with how poems end. It grew out of an earlier one that was concerned [1] with how Shakespeare's sonnets both go and end; and although the child has consumed the parent, it testifies to its lineage throughout these pages, where sonnets, Shakespearean and other, will be rather frequently encountered. In my earlier attempts to describe and to some extent account for the strengths and weaknesses of Shakespeare's sonnet endings, I found myself involved at almost every point with more general considerations of poetic structure and with what I finally recognized as a subject in its own right, [2] poetic closure. I also found that, although literary theorists from Aristotle on have been occupied with beginnings, middles, *and* ends, there had not been (aside from a brief and somewhat whimsical essay by I. A. Richards) any treatment of this subject as such. The questions and problems that pushed outward from sonnet endings to lyric closure in general continued to move out toward even broader considerations of closure in all [3] literature, in all [4] art, and finally in all [5] experience. Having bumped into a continent, however, and even having set a flag upon the shore, I realized that I was equipped to explore and chart only a bit of the coastal area. It seemed wise, then, to hold the line at poetic closure.

Smith locates her work within a larger structure. A part/whole ladder with five levels is implied: 1. Closure in Shakespeare's sonnets. 2. In poetry. 3. In literature. 4. In art. 5. In experience. She puts her particular study at level 2, poetry, in a structure of nested contexts: it is broader than just Shakespeares sonnets (level 1) but not as broad as literature (level 3). She does, however, make a number of significant comments about levels 4 and 5. I will use one of these comments to show both the strength and limitation of her analysis.

The use of nested contexts, Chinese boxes, one within the other, involves *recursion*, as Hofstadter (1980) suggests. This kind of part/

whole structure may be a way of giving concrete meaning to the abstract concept of reflexiveness, the kind of self-referencing which gives rise to self-awareness. A discussion like Smith's is reflexive to the extent that it locates its own argument within a part/whole structure, a total rather than a special frame of reference.

Smith takes an important part/whole step on the very last page. Her main argument has established that traditional poetry depends up a large variety of techniques for closure, for establishing that the poem is ending. These techniques are mostly conventions of rhyme and syntax. She notes that most *modern* poetry involves not only closural devices, but suggestions of rebellion against these devices. That is, many modern poets seem to want their poems to appear open-ended or continuing, rather than closing with a snap. She locates this tendency not only in poetry, but also in literature and art, particularly in painting and music (e.g. John Cage, serial or random music) as a rebellion not only against closure, but against all structure. In this way, she locates her description of the conflict between poetic closure and anti-closure in a larger context, the conflict between structure and anti-structure within art as a whole.

Her analysis ends with a very brief reference to a still larger whole. In trying to make sense of the conflict over structure in art, she argues that the traditional structures of poetry, which press toward closure, have a hidden ally which give them their staying power (p. 271):

> poetry is not without a sustaining vitality continuously fed and renewed by its relation to the rather formidable institution of language itself – and that as long as we continue to speak at all, no matter what new uses are made of language, there will remain revelations and delights to be found in the old uses. Poetry ends in many ways, but poetry, I think, has not yet ended.

Her comment implies conflict between social institutions. In seeking freedom for new forms within the social institution of art, poets pit themselves against another institution, "the rather formidable institution of language itself". The implication is that poetry will always press toward closure because it is based on language itself, and language, that is the natural language that is used in everyday life, will always press toward closure.

Smith's discussion of poetic closure could be grounded in the studies of turn-taking in linguistics and conversation analysis, as in the many studies generated by Sacks, Schegloff, and Jefferson (1974). These studies suggest, among other points, that signaling closure is an extremely rich and complex part of ordinary conversation. Such a comparison would elaborate the continuities and differences between traditional and modern poetics, on the one hand, and ordinary language, on the other. Her comment implies the value of an additional part/whole level, higher than 4, art, but before the leap to all experience at 5, the level of social institutions.

Studies like those of Smith might be used to give new meaning to the abstract concept of *reflexivity*. Her study is reflexive in the sense that she carefully located her particular study within a broad and deep structure of nested contexts. She could have easily avoided that responsibility. Her study would have met the expectations in her genre had she made only passing reference to levels 3 and 4, and no reference at all to the level of institutions, and to level 5. Such a study would probably give the alert reader a feeling of claustrophobia, as do more conventional scholarly and scientific studies. Overspecialization means the failure to establish responsible structures of nested contexts, of not exploring the relevant part/whole ladder.

Perhaps it was tactful of Smith not to get involved in what Goffman would call "framebreaking." Had she said much more about the conflict between the institutions of art and language, most of the members of her audience, quite content with the conventions of the genre, might have been puzzled. She would have found herself in a "no-persons land" between two genres, literary interpretation, on the one hand, and sociolinguistics, on the other. Perhaps the line between intellectual creativity and responsibility, on the one hand, and deviance, on the other, is vanishingly thin.

This discussion suggests an exact definition of reflexivity; the traversing of complete part/whole structures. To the extent that thought and creative effort travels the entire part/whole ladder, it is freed of its purely local dependence and becomes optimally useful and stimulating. However, as already indicated, it also runs the risk of antagonizing the conventional structures of context, and in this way becoming puzzling and opaque.

Discussion

To understand the significance of an expression in context, the researcher as well as the participant needs to refer it to other levels. For example, to understand the meaning of her lover's farewell, a woman might observe not only the exact words and gestures at level 1, but also compare them to how other lovers might have responded, a counterfactual (level 7). The interpretive decipherment of natural language, to use Steiner's phrase, requires part/whole thinking.

Does an understanding of the micro and macro-worlds of discourse contain the seeds of liberation? Only under the condition that performance is added to interpretation. Analysis is only theoretical; it does not insure the kind of fluency needed to escape from structures of domination. To use a musical metaphor, you may be a great musical theorist, but to play Mozart, you must practice at the keyboard. Effective tactics for change in a classist, patriarchic society require understanding and practice at every level. Electing a president with vision or reforming the divorce law are small parts of a vast functioning system. These changes need to be augmented with changes at other levels, especially at the micro-level.

Because it has been neglected, understanding and practice involving the micro-world of discourse tactics may be strategic in our era. If workers, women, students and other members of dominated classes could learn new tactics, the conditions for wholesale changes in the larger systems might be prepared. One great incentive is that these tactics, if sufficiently understood and skillfully practiced, often give immediate practical returns: one's relationship with family members, boss, or subordinates improve. In interminable quarrels and impasses, improvement benefits both sides: teachers as well as students, bosses as well as workers, men as well as women. To be sure, change involves losses on both sides, but if these can be negotiated, they may not be as threatening as they seem when discussed in the abstract.

These ideas apply to researchers as well as to members of the society. In our research, we need to understand the part/whole abduction that our subjects use, practice it ourselves in conducting research, and acknowledge it openly in reporting our findings. Perhaps in this way we can escape from the prison of formal rationality, with its attendant overspecialization. If so, our work might have more immediate relevance to the struggle of our civilization to survive.

It is easy for us to recognize in nationalism a kind of runaway specialization. The citizens of each country are overspecialized, they are concerned mostly with their own country, less with the larger issues that threaten the globe. The war between Iran and Iraq did not arouse our interest the way war between California and Arizona would. Anarchy between states is not tolerated, but anarchy between nations is. The ruling majority of *every* nation is under an emotional spell, nationalism, which precludes understanding.

In the academy, disciplines and sub-disciplines have become strongholds of a similar kind of overspecialization. Knowledge has been divided up between nations, tribes, and clans, i.e. disciplines, sub-disciplines, and "schools," each ignoring or at war with the other. By basing their work on premises and methods acceptable only to their own tribe or clan, each group is contributing to the onset of stasis. As the history of science has shown repeatedly, it is the very premises that are being taken for granted in each group that need to be overthrown before advances in knowledge can occur. What can be done about this kind of nationalism?

The approach to research advocated in this book moves away from overspecialization, by applying part/whole analysis to our own work and that of others, a step toward integration of the multitudinous schools of thought and disciplines that make up the human sciences and humanities.

Love, attunement and defenses: Comments on a study of Jane Austen's heroines

It has been often noted about the novels of Jane Austen that the spell they cast is elusive. How does she do it? Virginia Woolf put it succinctly: "Of all great writers she is the most difficult to catch in the act of greatness." In the study (Hardy 1984) to be discussed here, a modern writer, in an act of homage to Austen, attempts to explain one of the qualities that makes Austen's novels so attractive. His topic is the relationship of each of Austen's heroines with their future husbands. Since all six of the novels concern the heroines' quest for a husband, Hardy has selected the central subject of Austen's work: courtship and marriage.

I have chosen to discuss Hardy's study because it touches on several of the central themes of this book: part/whole issues of theory and method in the analysis of human conduct, the need for interdisciplinarity, and the nature of human relationships. Within the confines of his literary approach, Hardy analyzes each of six fictional romantic relationships, but his analysis may tell us something about the nature of love in general. Although there is a large literature on the nature of romantic relationships in the abstract, and also a vast number of studies of particular relationships, there has been little work which combines the two. Out of his detailed study of six cases, Hardy's study makes a real contribution to the understanding of love, a topic that has rebuffed analysis for ages. Since Hardy does not explicitly consider general issues, the study may carry implications which Hardy himself does not recognize.

Needless to say, Hardy does not refer to any of the social science literatures. Nor does he define any concepts, nor describe his method of investigation. Any of these steps would violate the code of *belles lettres*, that tacit group of assumptions which seems to govern literary criticism. In this code, one must write in the vernacular with as little theoretical elaboration as possible, and certainly with no avowed method of inquiry. Yet Hardy does use an idea that could be developed into a concept, and he has a method, although he is not explicit about it. My discussion will attempt to describe the concept and method that are only implied in the study, and tease out some of the study's larger implications.

The concept that is central in Hardy's analysis of love relationships is what he calls the "mutual sharing" of inner experience between the lovers. He proposes that Austen's lovers have "those qualities of mind and heart which enable a process of mutual sharing to occur between two people" (p. xiii). This process leads to the kind of intimacy in which the two people are able to share their private worlds with each other (p. xii). In the brief (five page) introduction, the idea of sharing is repeated five times. It is also used in the analysis of the six different romantic relationships. The idea occurs with greatest density at the end of the last chapter, the discussion of the relationship between the lovers in *Persuasion*, where it is used three times in the last paragraph. Although not named as a concept, mutual sharing is the pivotal idea in the study.

Hardy does not systematically develop his notion of sharing as a social scientist would; instead, he makes passing hints at some of its characteristics. One important comment he makes concerns the *extent* of the sharing that takes place: "What catches between the heroines and the men they come to marry is not themselves in any abstract sense, but their very beings as defined by their characters and their whole personalities" (p. xv). This is an important idea, though hardly developed: the implication is the mutual sharing in these relationships has virtually no limits, it extends into the very core of the lover's beings, into their whole selves. A second aspect is that the kind of mutual sharing Hardy describes implies absolute equality between the lovers; neither takes a privileged position with regard to the other. I will return to the concept of mutual sharing below.

What is the method that Hardy used to come to these interpretations? Although there is of course no mention of method, the procedure that he used comes close to what I have called part/whole morphology, both in his analysis of single cases, and in comparing the cases with each other. Hardy carefully examines the dialogue that takes place in each of the six relationships in a way that is similar to microanalysis of dialogue: he infers the characters' ostensible thoughts and feelings from their discourse, as in single case morphology. But he also notes similarities and differences between the six cases, a step toward comparative morphology.

As an example of Hardy's method, I will review his analysis of one part of the relationship between the heroine and her husband-to-be in *Pride and Prejudice*, the way in which Elizabeth teases Darcy. Hardy argues that the teasing in this case leads to intimacy and sharing between them. Darcy is a wealthy aristocrat whose manner is aloof and laconic to the point of rudeness. Rather than condoning or ignoring his manner like everyone else, Elizabeth attacks it, but with wit and humor.

When Darcy has made a comment at the expense of both his friend Caroline Bingley and Elizabeth, who at this point in the novel is still only an acquaintance, Caroline playfully asks Elizabeth "How should we punish him for such a speech?" (Hardy 1984, 41) Elizabeth replies that they should "teaze him – laugh at him." But Caroline replies that it would be impossible. Apparently she is so overawed by Darcy that she can not imagine teasing him. But Elizabeth can and does.

Hardy quotes the ensuing dialogue between Elizabeth and Darcy:

> "Mr. Darcy is not to be laughed at!" cried Elizabeth. "That is an uncommon advantage, and uncommon I hope it will continue, for it would be a great loss to *me* to have many such acquaintance. I dearly love a laugh."
>
> "Miss Bingley," said he, "has given me credit for more than can be. The wisest and the best of men, nay, the wisest and best of their actions, may be rendered ridiculous by a person whose first object in life is a joke."
>
> "Certainly," replied Elizabeth – "there are such people, but I hope I am not one of *them*. I hope I never ridicule what is wise or good. Follies and nonsense, whims and inconsistencies *do* divert me, I own, and I laugh at them whenever I can. – But these, I suppose, are precisely what you are without."
>
> "Perhaps that is not possible for any one. But it has been the study of my life to avoid those weaknesses which often expose a strong understanding to ridicule."
>
> "Such as vanity and pride."
>
> "Yes, vanity is a weakness indeed. But pride – where there is a real superiority of mind, pride will be always under good regulation."
>
> Elizabeth turned away to hide a smile.
>
> "Your examination of Mr. Darcy is over, I presume," said Miss Bingley; – and pray what is the result?"
>
> "I am perfectly convinced by it that Mr. Darcy has no defect. He owns it himself without disguise."
>
> "No" – said Darcy, "I have made no such pretension. I have faults enough, but they are not, I hope, of understanding. My temper I dare not vouch for. – It is I believe too little yielding – certainly too little for the convenience of the world. I cannot forget the follies and vices of others so soon as I ought, nor their offences against myself. My feelings are not puffed about with every attempt to move them. My temper would perhaps be called resentful. – My good opinion once lost is lost for ever."

Although she uses humorous exaggeration, Elizabeth has brought up to him what seems to be a central aspect of Darcy's persona, his air of arrogant superiority. Under the guise of teasing, she has challenged a central aspect of the way he presents himself to others.

Darcy responds to the challenge:

> "*That* is a failing indeed!" – cried Elizabeth. "Implacable resentment *is* a shade in a character. But you have chosen your fault well. – I really cannot *laugh* at it. You are safe from me."
> "There is, I believe, in every disposition a tendency to some particular evil, a natural defect, which not even the best education can overcome."

Once again, Elizabeth's response challenges his air of superiority, and again, in a somewhat exaggerated way: "And *your* defect is a propensity to hate everybody." Darcy quickly replies, but he is smiling: "And yours is willfully to misunderstand them." This episode is only the first of a series in which Elizabeth teases Darcy about his offensive manner.

Although other kinds of instances are not mentioned by Hardy, Elizabeth's challenge to Darcy is not limited to playful teasing. His arrogance is also a key reason she gives to him for heatedly rejecting his first marriage proposal. She found his proposal offensive because he explained at some length how his love for her had conquered the many objectionable features of such a marriage, particularly the low social rank of her and her family relative to his, and the vulgarity of the behavior of her mother and the younger of her sisters on social occasions. Darcy seemed completely unaware of how offensive such a formulation would be to her; he seemed to think that Elizabeth would be so gratified by his proposal that she would not even notice.

But Elizabeth angrily rejects his proposal. She demands equality; she wants to be treated with respect, regardless of their difference in rank and station. One implication of her demand is not taken up by Hardy, but further supports his idea of mutual sharing. Elizabeth's rejection contains two elements which are steps toward mutual sharing. Firstly, she openly expresses her feelings of insult; she does not hold them back in deference to his feelings. Secondly, and more subtly, she lets Darcy know that she expects him to be able to see the matter from her point of view, how such a proposal would affect her feelings. That is, she not only challenges his external behavior, but also his habit of not always taking into account the thoughts and feelings of others.

The aggressive insistence of Elizabeth on equality and openness is the most dramatic of the six instances, but it is not the only one. Hardy notes the mutual teasing that goes on between Emma and her husband-to-be, Knightley, which also leads toward equality, and in Emma's case, increases her knowledge of herself. Hardy makes similar analyses of the romantic relationships in the other novels as well. He notes that openness and sharing can be observed as it develops in the love relationship in all of the novels but one. The exception is *Mansfield Park*, in which Austen fails to show instances which lead to sharing between Fanny and her future husband, Edmund. The plot involves Edmund in intense infatuation with Fanny's rival Mary Crawford for virtually the entire length of the book. Austen treats Edmund's falling in love with Fanny like an afterthought. As Hardy notes, the absence of mutual sharing in this novel accentuates the extent to which it takes place in the other five.

There is one further feature of Austen's portrait of romantic relationships which Hardy emphasizes, the never-ending interest of the partners in each other: "What is involved [in the relationship between the lovers] is not merely mutual respect . . . but such mutual responsiveness as guarantees that the conversation between lovers will never have an ending" (Hardy 1984, xv) Hardy repeats this point with several of the romantic relationships, but most emphatically with respect to the lovers in *Persuasion*, Austen's last novel, the novel of her maturity (she died at the age of forty-two). In the case of Anne and Wentworth he suggests that their sharing involves not only the present, but also memories of the past and anticipations of the future: "because they engage in sharing what is so poignant and so ceaseless in interest, the reader knows what the lovers themselves so surely know – that of yesterday and today there could scarcely be an end."

This last idea, particularly, of the lovers' never-ending conversation, brings up an issue that is not taken up by Hardy. To what extent are the portraits of love in Austen's novels idealizations? Surely most romantic relationships are not like these, with complete equality and openness, mutual sharing in all aspects of the lovers' interior lives, and especially the idea of love as a never-ending conversation. Even in the best of marital relationships, surely there are times when mutual interest flags, when conversation ends, at least temporarily. Are Austen's love relationships only fantasies? This issue does not arise for Hardy because he saw his task as only to describe the quality of love relationships in Austen's writing. Following the code of belles lettres, his interest was entirely in describing concrete instances without taking the step of applying these instances to human behavior in general.

Taking a step toward generalization, I will argue that these instances are not idealizations, but can be understood as ideals of what, freed of impediments, a human relationship could be. But to make this argument, it will be necessary to do what Hardy did not do, to invoke the literatures of the human sciences. How can we relate specific romantic relationships to general aspects of the human condition?

Attunement and secure social bonds

Hardy's analysis of love reaches deep into the nature of human relationships, but it would go still deeper if it were reformulated with concepts developed in the social sciences and philosophy, where the idea of the sharing of the individual's inner life with others has a long history. (See chapter 4 on the history of the idea of solidarity/ alienation.) For my purpose here I will relate it to one particular formulation, the idea of attunement (this idea is developed in detail in chapter 7).

In my formulation, a secure bond between two persons is character- ized by substantial mutual understanding of each other's thoughts, beliefs, and feelings. That is, a secure bond exists when two persons accurately understand each other's interior life. This formulation, although somewhat more specific, is almost identical to Hardy's idea of mutual sharing . My formulation goes somewhat further, however, in also specifying that in a secure bond, the parties not only under- stand each other's interior life, but they also accept what it is they understand. The idea of mutual acceptance is implied in Hardy's treatment, since all six of his instances involve romantic love. My formulation is more general than his, since it implies to any kind of secure bond, not just romantic love.

Being more general, my framework also includes bonds that are not secure. There are two basic formats for alienated relationships: iso- lated bonds, where each party emphasizes their own point of view over that of the other, and engulfed bonds, where each party over- emphasizes the other's point of view, at the expense of their own. As already indicated, the classifications of attachments developed by Ainsworth et al. (1978) and by Mary Main et al. (1985) are quite similar; their avoidant attachment is similar to what I call an isolated bond, and their anxious-ambivalent attachment is similar to what I call an engulfed bond.

The inclusion of types of alienated relationships in my discussion of attunement points to still another parallel with Hardy's analysis. In his introductory comments (pp. xii–xiii), he exactly states the idea of a secure relationship balancing the viewpoints of self and other: "As well as remaining true to inner feelings and perceptions, they have the ability of acknowledging the legitimate claims of others." Hardy does not describe alienation: but in my framework, in engulfed relation- ships, one or both the parties overemphasize the claims of the other, at the expense of their own claims; in isolated relationships, one or both parties overemphasizes his or her own claims, at the expense of those of the other. Hardy's analysis of particular cases is compatible with my general theory of human relationships.

Openness, denial, and other psychological defenses

The use of general concepts from the social sciences takes a step toward locating the six romantic relationships in Austen's novels more generally. A further step in this direction can be taken by raising a question about their ideal quality. What keeps most lovers from the kind of mutual sharing and never-ending interest that Austen invokes for her lovers? An answer to this question may be found not in the literature of social science, but in the psychological and psychoanalytic literatures.

What one learns from a survey of psychological and psychoanalytic studies of personality and interpersonal relations is that most people are strongly defended against self-knowledge, against revealing themselves to others, and against understanding others. This idea was expressed succinctly in the mid nineteenth century by Matthew Arnold, in his poem "The Buried Life," as in this segment:

> Alas ! is even love too weak
> To unlock the heart, and let it speak?
> Are even lovers powerless to reveal
> To one another what indeed they feel?
> I knew the mass of men concealed
> Their thoughts, for fear that if revealed
> They would by other men be met
> With blank indifference, or with blame reproved;
> I knew they lived and moved
> Tricked in disguises, alien to the rest
> Of men, and alien to themselves

Arnold's poem exactly prefigures the portrait of the human condition that emerges in the clinical and linguistic work in our current era. If the psychological–psychoanalytic estimates of the defensiveness of the average mortal are correct, the open, equal, and responsive romantic relationships portrayed in Austen's novels would be extremely rare.

Of course one of the goals of psychotherapy is to free persons from the prison of their defenses. Another possibility is that a romantic relationship might be a means of personal change for one or both of the partners. This is the possibility that Austen explores in each of her novels. In the earlier novels, one partner serves as a teacher for the other. Henry Tilney (*Northanger Abbey*), Knightley (*Emma*), and

Edmund Bertram (*Mansfield Park*) are older, and except for Bertram, wiser than the heroine. The male in these three novels instructs the younger woman. Edmund's bride-to-be, Fanny Price, is young and sheltered; she knows little about the world. Edmund is glad to serve as a tutor in worldly matters.

But in terms of morality, openness, and responsiveness, Fanny is much more advanced than Edmund. She makes several attempts to reach him in these matters, but they are so gentle and subtle as to be lost on him. Knightley and Elizabeth Bennett are much more successful in this arena. Knightley's good-humored, teasing criticism of Emma's actions, along with the contretemps she causes by her inane attempts at matchmaking, have some effect on her. She undergoes a modest increase in her degree of self-knowledge as a result. Elizabeth's challenge to Darcy's arrogance strongly affects him: as he acquires knowledge of himself from Elizabeth's response to him, his whole manner, indeed his character, undergo change. He learns to respond openly to Elizabeth as she responds openly to him.

Although Elizabeth takes the lead, the changes in the relationship between Elizabeth and Darcy are not a one-way street. Just as he finds out from her that he is prideful and arrogant, by conscientiously reviewing her own behavior toward Darcy, she finds out from him that she has been prejudiced toward him. This parallel growth in self-awareness is unique among the six cases, but it suggests that a romantic relationship may result in unparalleled self-awareness on both sides.

The idea that each partner in a marriage might need to grow in awareness before being able to share with the other seems to me as important now as it was in Jane Austen's time. This idea contradicts a central tenet of the current love myth, that romance involves a quest for Mister or Miss Right, someone who is already exactly compatible with the searcher. The search under this premise is entirely on the outside, no inner search is necessary. If Jane Austen was right, those who follow this path are doomed to contribute to the already astronomical divorce rate, or at least to be disappointed with the quality of their marriage.

The idea that both lovers could grow in self-awareness to the point that they each would be at least partially liberated from their defenses explains another aspect of Austen's love relationships; the never-ending conversation. As I pointed out in the last chapter, human beings are infinitely complicated. Goethe's comment about living organisms applies especially to human beings, since we are the most complex of all creatures. But our complexity is usually covered over by layers of habits, routines, and at the deepest layers, defenses, so that our thoughts, feelings and actions usually have a repetitive, stereotyped quality. (For examples, see the descriptions of the particular relationships in the remaining chapters in this book.) For this reason, most of us, most of the time, tend to be boring and predictable, not only to others, but even to ourselves.

One implication of the discussion of human complexity in chapter 1 is that we all have the capacity to make creative responses to new situations (as in generating or understanding sentences we have never used or encountered before). Given this assumption, two persons in love who were able to help each other unlearn their defensive postures would become responsive to each other, as Hardy notes about Austen's lovers. Furthermore, as the defensive layers were removed, the creativity and complexity of each lover would continually engaged the fascinated curiosity of the other. In such a relationship the possiblity of never-ending conversations would not be merely a fantasy.

Conclusion

In this chapter, I have pointed out some of the limitations of literary analyses of verbatim texts. Smith's study of poetic closure is very effective at the lowest levels of the part/whole ladder. She shows tellingly how closure is signalled in traditional poetry, and how this convention is being challenged in modern poetry and other art forms. But her examination of the implications of her findings in terms of larger wholes, such as linguistics, is minimal. Nor has she explicated her method of investigation, nor connected her findings with general theory. For these reasons, her study failed to connect with parallel work going on in other disciplines, such as the work in linguistics and conversation analysis on turn-taking, a central feature of contemporary empirical work. Such a comparison might have led to enlightening comparisons of the languages of art and of everyday life.

The object of Hardy's study of love relationships in Austen novels is a more complex topic than Smith's, requiring part/whole analysis of social relationships in the fictional, and in the historical contexts in which they occur. Although Hardy's theory and methods are no more explicit than Smith's, his analysis of his six cases provides more even coverage of the various levels of the part/whole ladder, leading toward a substantial contribution to our understanding of love relationships. My commentary on the six cases shows how his findings can be deepened and located within our knowledge of human behavior in general.

Generating theory: the social bond

The concept of a social relationship is crucial for all of the social sciences, but somehow it has never been described in a way that captures its vast importance. The idea of relationships between persons is so primitive and fundamental that it goes without saying, both in ordinary and in social science discourse. The chapters in this section outline a model of the social bond, and a method of determining the state of the bond, through microanalysis of transcripts or verbatim texts. The three chapters in this section each illustrate an application of the basic model.

Sociologists have made a preliminary step toward defining relationships, but only in terms of conventional roles, such as the father–daughter, or employer–employee relationships. Role-relationships are considered to be made up of reciprocal rights, duties, and rules which govern interaction between persons in the respective roles. The idea of role-relationships is helpful because it establishes the contours of the kinds of behavior which are expected in a given society. We would usually find a wide consensus on these contours.

But the concept of role-relationships is of limited use in understanding an actual relationship between particular persons, since it refers to idealized, abstract expectations rather than specific behavior. Between any father and daughter or therapist and client there is an enormous variation in what actually occurs between them. Especially if we want the nuances of a relationship, types of role-relationships are of virtually no help, because they are partial, they concern only one aspect of a whole. Much is missing from such classifications, since they are only stereotypes.

It might help us visualize the problem of further defining the concept of a relationship if we imagined the opposite mode of conceptualizing, the least possible abstractness. Consider, for example, a second-by-second description of transactions between actual persons in a relationship, what was said and done by each person, and their manner. We would put the discourse that constitutes a relationship under a microscope. From such a highly particularized

69

description, we might be able to also infer the subjective side of the relationship, what each person thought and felt at each moment. We would also need to include the biography of the relationship, and the social context.

As already indicated, an approximation is offered in great novels. Tolstoy, George Eliot, Proust, and Joyce often described in detail not only the history of a given relationship, but also the words and manner in dialogue between characters, and accompanying thoughts and feelings. The novel itself provides careful delineation of the biographical background of each character and social context for each relationship. These descriptions go far beyond role-relationships, allowing us at least the illusion of understanding whole relationships, the motives, perceptions, and personalities of fictional persons.

In the social sciences, a comparable approach can be found in microlinguistic studies, beginning with the work of Pittenger *et al.* (1960) and Labov and Fanshel (1977). Although these studies deal only with parts of psychotherapy sessions, they come close to an ideal description of the complete outer behavior of persons in a transaction, the details of articulation and manner. Because they focused so intensively on brief moments in relationships, these studies were able to describe *every* sound, all verbal and nonverbal speech, that could be heard on the tapes. The richness in the resulting descriptions brings to mind Blake's poetic vision in "Auguries of Innocence":

> To see a world in a grain of sand
> And Heaven in a wild flower
> Hold infinity in the palm of your hand
> And eternity in an hour . . .

The time spans in the Pittenger and in the Labov studies are so brief (Pittenger, *et al.* is five minutes, Labov and Fanshel, fifteen minutes) that together they make up even less than Blake's eternity in an hour. (Some readers of Pittenger *et al.* complain about eternity when reading a five-page discussion of a single sentence). But the precise attention given to fine detail in these earlier studies is so great that they move toward the Proustian ideal of recapturing the present.

Microanalysis of social interaction is possible because of the existence of verbatim texts, and the invention of recording technology. Microanalysis approximates the goal of nineteenth century historians such as Ranke who wanted to describe history "wie es wirklich gewesen war" (as it actually happened). The work of microanalysts like Pittenger et al., and Labov and Fanshel on the complete verbal and nonverbal elements in communication allow us to recover sequences of past time that would otherwise be lost.

Emboldened by their deep knowledge of the brief excerpts they studied, in many instances these authors interpreted the *meaning* of events to the subjects of their study, their thoughts and feelings. These inferences are informal, however. Neither study openly acknowledges an intention to explore inner as well as outer events. Both claim as a goal only careful description of outer behavior. The method of part/ whole morphology allows us to make explicit the procedure for recapturing both internal and external moments of history; in Proust's terms, of developing "negatives in our darkroom." And it also suggests the need for an explicit theory as a guide.

As the fate of the studies by Pittenger et al. and by Labov and Fanshel indicate, precise description for its own sake, without applying it to the generation or testing of a theory, is not very useful. To this point, their methods and results have not had a large effect. Perhaps if their work had been in the service of an abstract theory, they would have sent larger ripples through the smooth surface of the social sciences.

In this part I develop a theory of the social bond, based in large part on several earlier theories and approaches. I take the term the social bond from Bowlby (1969), whose work on the life-threatening effects of insecure attachments of infants to their care-takers sounded an important note in the study of relationships. This direction was taken up by Bowen (1978) and other family systems theorists. The differentiation of insecure relationships by Bowen into two different and opposite types is central to the typology of social relationships in many earlier theories, and will also be central in mine. Bowen distinguished between relationships that are cold and distant, which he called isolated or "cut-off", and those which are too close and suffocating, which referred to as "fusion" or engulfment. I will use the terminology derived from family systems theory, distinguishing between secure bonds, and bonds which are either isolated or engulfed.

Chapter 3 provides a concrete illustration of the abstract idea of alienation, a family breakfast which was videotaped for a television program. By close analysis of the words and gesture, I show the structure of alienation in this family: the parents are engulfed with each other, and isolated from their children. The father, particularly, seems to suppress his own inclinations toward the children in deference to his wife, who takes a hard line toward them. The parents do not treat the children as "thou's" but as "its," lecturing and spanking them rather than discussing matters. The pattern that I call bimodal alienation (engulfed within groups, isolated between them) is characteristic of protracted conflict, in this case between parents and children.

Chapter 4 outlines a theory of integration in social relationships, the balance between alienation and solidarity, and illustrates its relationship to actual data. The theory combines elements from classic and current approaches to social integration. The theory is formulated in terms of an *I–We balance* (Elias 1987) which classifies relationships as predominately isolated, solidary, or engulfed. The data comes from a comprehensive study of children's discourse by Goodwin (1990). I focus, as did Goodwin, on gender differences in the children's discourse. Exploring the relationship between abstract theory and concrete data advances understanding in many ways, but particularly in showing how both theory and method can be modified and elaborated through exposure to concrete details of human interaction. This exercise illustrates how part/whole morphology suggests new directions in theory, method, and the interpretation of data.

Chapter 5 applies the idea of bimodal alienation on an extremely large scale, the causation of the First World War. I apply part/whole analysis to the telegrams exchanged between heads of state immediately before the beginning of the war, to show how they imply bimodal alienation, engulfment within the Allies and within the Central Powers, and isolation between the two blocs. This analysis also links alienation to unacknowledged shame, by focusing on the humiliation of the French in their defeat by the Germans in 1871. I show how French poetry and novels show a shame/anger spiral in the French population in the period between the two earlier wars.

This part shows how on the one hand, a theory of the social bond is closely related to sociological ideas and studies of alienation, and human development studies of attachment, and on the other, how part/whole analysis of real social transactions can flesh out the details of abstract theories of alienation and attachment. These part/whole studies also introduce a crucial connection between the state of the bond and emotions, how shame signals the state of the bond, and how unacknowledged shame explosively disrupts the bond. The relationship between bonds and emotions is further explored in the last part. The present part begins with a study of the interactions among members of a single family at a breakfast with the "Smiths." I show how the "negatives," of this transcribed episode, the words, gestures, and context, can be "developed" into an interpretation of its meaning.

CHAPTER 3

Punishment, child development and crime: the concept of the social bond

This chapter introduces the idea of the social bond by showing how it applies to an extended episode in a family. Since I borrowed the videotape of this episode from a larger study of corporal punishment in families,[1] the episode contains several such incidents. But the present study interprets corporal punishment within a general conceptual framework. The theory of social bonds proposes that personality and basic behaviors and attitudes arise from the nature of relationships with others. The theory suggests that the extent to which children become effective and responsible adults depends upon the quality of their social bonds. My analysis of the discourse in this family shows the main thrust of the idea of bonds: spanking, along with other frequent behaviors, such as parents lecturing and threatening children, can be viewed as aspects of alienation, of insecure bonds with the family. This chapter will serve to introduce the basic idea of the next chapter (on social integration) by showing concrete aspects of alienation, insecure bonds, as they can be inferred from actual events.

This chapter proposes that the state of social bonds determine wide reaches of human conduct. General theories of social relationships and their effects on behavior are very rare. The major theories focus on individuals, with little or no attention to relationships. Certainly behaviorism is completely individualistic, as is psychoanalytic theory, at least in its orthodox form. Marx's analysis of social systems allows for the importance of human relationships in theory, in its emphasis on alienation. But in Marx and the writings of his followers, alienation remains abstract and unexplicated, so that in actual applications, social relationships play little role.

The theory proposed here depicts social relationships in terms of alienation and its opposite, solidarity. It suggests that the *structure* of actual social relationships involve mixtures of alienation and soli-

---

[1] The videotape of the family breakfast and of the spanking incidents in this family was graciously loaned to me by Murray Straus.

darity, and that the exact proportion can be determined through the analysis of verbatim discourse. In the scheme to be outlined here, alienation can occur not only from others, but also from self. I argue that secure bonds in the family and in later life lead to responsible conduct. Insecure bonds, the concrete carriers of alienation, take two forms: bonds that are either too loose (isolation) or too tight (engulfment).

The *dynamics* of relationships are explained in terms of the emotion which accompanies solidarity, pride, and the one which accompanies alienation, shame. Pride signals and generates solidarity. Shame signals and generates alienation. Shame is a normal part of the process of social control; it becomes disruptive only when it is hidden or denied. Denial of shame generates self-perpetuating cycles of alienation.

Straus's theory of crime and corporal punishment

In a widely discussed paper, Straus (1991) has proposed a relationship between corporal punishment of children and their later involvement in crime as adults. I single out Straus's theory as a springboard, because it is clear, explicit and testable, and because he has conducted significant studies of corporal punishment. Since most theory is of the armchair variety, and most empirical studies eschew theory, his work stands out from the crowd.

I have two basic criticisms of Straus's theory. Focusing only on corporal punishment, it is much too narrow, ignoring a wide range of other influences on child development. It also seems to be contradicted by a substantial body of evidence.

Although the format of Straus's work is exemplary, the content is another matter. Basically, Straus's work falls within the behaviorist approach: Straus assumes that human behavior can best be understood solely in terms of rewards and punishments, like the behavior of non-human creatures. Behaviorists believe that human actions are largely generated by conditioning (by the regular schedule of rewards and punishments that follow behavior). Within this framework, corporal punishment, which Straus sees as a particularly harsh form of punishment, is envisioned as having major and longt-ime effects.

There is a vast literature supporting the behaviorist position, much of it is not quite relevant to the particular issue being considered here, the major and long-term effects of punishment on children. A considerable portion of this literature concerns animals, which has only questionable relevance to humans. A further large portion concerns only short-term effects; the typical study involves observation of small spans of time, usually minutes, occasionally hours.

The subjects are often a captive audience, such as undergraduate students in a psychology class; changes in their behavior wrought by conditioning schedules may be short-lived, since follow-ups and longitudinal studies are rare in the behavioral tradition. Finally, of the remaining studies, most concern minor behavioral effects outside of real-world environments, relative to the issues considered here, criminal vs. non-criminal behavior. These effects are seldom checked to see if they transfer to the real world.

Within the discipline of child development, however, there is a body of studies that have the characteristics that make them relevant here: they concern human children, often in their own homes; some of them employ longitudinal or follow-up designs, and they trace what are for small children major real-world behaviors, such as degree of obedience to their mother. These behaviors are checked to see if they transfer to the real world.

In an impressive critique of Straus's theory, McCord (1991) has called attention to these and other studies. Since her review is detailed and to the point, I will not repeat it here. Instead, I will summarize her major criticisms, and describe as an example one of the studies she cites, Stayton, Hogan, and Ainsworth (1971). Ainsworth has long been a contributor to attachment theory, which is closely related to the theory of social bonds that I develop here. The study by her and her colleagues will be used to represent the body of studies which seem to contradict Straus's theory.

The researchers studied twenty-five infant–mother pairs for a period of *three months* in their homes. They found that the children's obedience was unrelated to the frequency of verbal commands and physical interventions. Instead, it was highly correlated with the mother's degree of acceptance of the child (as against rejection) and the mother's sensitivity and responsiveness to the child. The authors interpret their findings to show that "obedience emerges in a responsive, accommodating social environment without extensive training, discipline, or other massive attempts to shape the infant's course of development" (Stayton, Hogan, and Ainsworth 1971, 1065).

On the basis of this and other studies, McCord argues that Straus's theory is invalid, that it does not offer an accurate account of the causes of adult criminal behavior in its relationship to childhood. As an alternative to Straus's theory, McCord offers what she calls Construct Theory. She proposes that a child's personality is formed through language. Her theory is much broader than Straus's. She locates the causes of adult behavior in the linguistic world created for a child in the family and other settings.

McCord also argues that even if one restricts oneself to the punishments that occur in the child's world, the scope of causal influences in Straus's theory is much too narrow. In addition to corporal punishment, she argues, children are also punished in many additional ways, through abuse of other kinds, neglect and rejection. Although Ayres and Braithwaite (1991) do not cite child development studies, their criticisms of rational choice theory, a form of behaviorism, are similar to McCord's. Braithwaite's (1989) image of effective family discipline, reintegrative shaming, also implies mutual understanding and acceptance between parents and children (secure bonds), as I will indicate below.

The theory I offer here, like McCord's, speaks to the formation of personality in terms of the whole world of the family, rather than a single type of reward or punishment. In terms of the scope of the theory, it falls between Straus's, which deals with an extremely narrow causal agent, and McCord's, which in its focus on language, is extremely broad. I argue that the key determinant in child development is the *structure of social bonds* in the family. To the extent the bonds in a family are weak and insecure, to that extent the children from that family may become alienated adults, which may result in various kinds of irresponsible or antisocial behavior, of which crime is one possibility. This hypothesis presents a testable alternative to both Straus's and McCord's theories.

Both McCord's and Ayres and Braithwaite's criticisms of behaviorist theories fit within a theory of social bonds, as well as the findings from the studies of child development that McCord cites. The new theory also speaks to gender differences in violence and criminality.

Social bonds

My model of the social bond is based on the concept of *attunement*, mutual identification and understanding. A secure social bond means that the individuals involved identify with and understand each other, rather than misunderstand or reject each other. I assume that in all human contact, if bonds are not being built, maintained, or repaired, they are being damaged.

That is to say that in every moment of contact, one's status relative to the other is continually being signaled, usually unintentionally. Goffman (1967, 33) made this point:

> The human tendency to use signs and symbols means that evidence of social worth and of mutual evaluations will be conveyed by very minor things, and these things will be witnessed, as will the fact that they have been witnessed. An unguarded glance, a momentary change in tone of voice, an ecological position taken or not taken, can

drench a talk with judgmental significance. Therefore, just as there is no occasion of talk in which improper impressions could not intentionally or unintentionally arise, so there is no occasion of talk so trivial as not to require each participant to show serious concerns with the way in which he handles himself and the others present.

Status-relevant verbal and nonverbal signs both signal and determine the state of the bond at any given moment. Although Goffman seemed to be thinking about interaction between adults, his formulation applies equally well to contact between adults and children: each party is supremely sensitive to signals of their standing with each other.

Threats to a secure bond can come in two different formats; either the bond is too loose or too tight. Relationships in which the bond is too loose are *isolated*: there is mutual misunderstanding or failure to understand, or mutual rejection. Relationships in which the bond is too tight are *engulfed*: at least one of the parties in the relationship, say the subordinate, understands and embraces the standpoint of the other at the expense of the subordinate's own beliefs, values or feelings. The other is accepted by rejecting parts of one's self. In engulfed families, a child can only be "good" by blind obedience and conformity, by relinquishing its curiosity, intuition, or feelings.

In such a relationship the child and parents are alienated. The child is alienated from self, because of having given up important parts of the self out of loyalty to the other, or fear of the other. The parties are also alienated from each other, since neither is aware of the parts of self that the child has rejected. The children in the Smith family, to be discussed below, seem to be in such a situation: they are still young enough to feel attached and loyal to their parents; the family world is the only one they know. In this world, however, because of the lack of relationship talk, and the frequent punishment and threats of punishment, the children also seem to be intimidated by their parents, and to fear them.

This view of alienation is congruent with, and further develops, Durkheim's theory of social integration, which he derived from his study of the causes of suicide (1905). He argued that suicidal inclinations were generated by bonds that were too loose (egoism) or too tight (altruism). My theory extends Durkheim, by describing the microscopic components of this system, and also the structure of a secure bond, which Durkheim only implies, one that is neither too loose nor too tight.

In my scheme, a secure bond involves a balance between the viewpoint of self and other. Although each party understands and accepts the viewpoint of the other, this acceptance does not go to the extreme of giving up major parts of one's own viewpoint. The behavior of the responsive mothers in the Stayton et al. study suggests this kind of relationship: the mothers seem to understand and accept the child's point of view. Although Stayton et al. are not explicit on this point, the responsive mothers would also need to stand up for their own points of view in relationship to the child, to avoid engulfment with the child.

A child in an alienated family, such as the one to be described below, is faced with the alternatives of embracing or ignoring the continual flow of instruction, command, and discipline from parents. If the child embraces parental strictures out of loyalty or to avoid punishment, it needs to give up major parts of the self, which is synonymous with engulfment. The self can only develop to the extent that its major features are accepted both by self and significant others. If the child ignores or defies parental strictures, the alternative is isolation, in which the child risks missing the beneficial parts of parental care and knowledge. The small child in such a family cannot win. Given this situation, the self may be damaged in such a way as to impede the development of adequate bonds with others as an adult.

As will be further developed in chapter 4, the theory of solidarity suggested here overlaps with earlier work by Elias (1977), Buber (1958) and Bowen (1978). The master trope in Elias's approach is *interdependency*, patterns of cooperative relationships between individuals and between groups. A close reading of his work shows that it implies three types of social relationships: dependence, interdependence, and independence. These three types correspond closely to the three levels of integration mentioned above: dependence corresponds to integration which is too tight, independence, too loose, and interdependence, a balance between the individual and the group.

I–We balance in relationships

Elias furthermore suggests a way of connecting these levels of integration to the empirical world: the concept of the *I–We balance*: independence should be marked in discourse by emphasis on the "I," dependence, on the "We," and interdependence on a balance between *I and we*. (There are hints of this direction in his *Involvement and Detachment* 1987. The actual discussion occurs in his still unpublished manuscripts. I am grateful to Stephen Mennell and Joop Goudsblom for this information.) According to Elias, the state of integration between individuals or between groups might be visible in the disposition of pronouns in their discourse. (As was shown in an earlier publication [Scheff 1994, ch. 1], the mechanical counting of pronouns is too simple for anything but a crude estimate; determining the balance between self and other may require discourse analysis because adults may manipulate pronouns in a way that disguises the state of the bond.)

The idea of the I–We balance can be elaborated by referring to ideas from Buber (1958) and from Bowen (1978). Buber distinguishes between two types of relationship: I–thou, where each person endows the other with the same humanity as self (which I call mutual identification), and I–it, in which one treats the other as an object. This is an important idea, but it is cast in categorical terms. It can be modified by restating it in terms that will admit *degrees* of connection: I–it represents the self in foreground, the other in the background. I–thou places both self and other in foreground. Other as object represents only the extreme position on a continuum of the relative emphasis on self or other.

An extension of Buber's language is also necessary if one is to consider the third state of the relationship, too much integration. In Buber's framework, this state might be represented as it—thou; one places one's self in the background, the other in the foreground. For example, in a traditional marriage, the wife was expected to subject herself to her husband. It–thou involves subjugation of self, one's own needs, feelings, and point of view, to the other person, or to the group. Blind patriotism provides another example. I–it means that one's own needs, feelings and points of view are dominant over those of the others', but in it–thou, they are swallowed out of a sense of loyalty, or because of fear.

The three-fold division discussed here is also related to family systems theory, especially as formulated by Bowen (1978). He referred to dysfunctional relationships as involving either isolation or engulfment. Isolation is marked by "cut-off," dealing with difficulties by withdrawing physically or emotionally. Engulfment, which he also referred to as fusion, by confounding one's own needs, feelings, and viewpoint with those of the other. This latter state is also discussed as a boundary problem; in an engulfed relationship, the parties have difficulty in distinguishing the boundaries of the self.

One aspect of family systems theory is particularly relevant to the present discussion: the distinction between discourse that is topic-oriented, and discourse that is relationship-oriented (Watzlawick et al. 1967). Topics involve objects in the outer world such as eating, chores, money, grades, etc. Relationships involve the thoughts and feelings that are occurring between the participants. Parents who are oriented toward command and control of children's behavior are unlikely to deal adequately with relationship issues. But secure bonds require relationship talk: the child must not only understand what is expected of it by the parents, but the parent's reasons for the expectation.

Behaviorist theories completely ignore this point. In its most common form, behaviorism proposes that child-rearing is merely a matter of shaping outer behavior. This perspective allows no room for relationships or for feelings. It is completely oriented toward topics. From the point of view of this book, behaviorism both expresses and generates alienation.

Corporal punishment can be used as an example of the importance of the distinction between topic and relationship. Punishment is both a topic, an action in the outer world, but it is also accompanied by attitudes and feelings. Striking a child in anger, without warning or explanation, implies a relationship issue, the status of the child relative to the parent.

Being struck without warning would be experienced as especially intimidating, giving rise to terror on the child's part. Another implication is equally important: that the status of the child is so low that it warrants no respect at all. A child that can be hit in anger, with no warning, or neglected, verbally abused or rejected, is likely to grow up with little sense of self, lacking the skill and inclination to develop secure bonds with others. Within this framework it is conceivable that if spanking were administered in a way that allowed the child foreknowledge and dignity, it might do less damage to the bond than non-physical abuse, such as neglect or rejection.

The theory of the social bond provides a framework for organizing the critiques by McCord and by Braithwaite, and the findings in child development studies. In particular, the characteristics of the effective mothers (accepting and responsive) found in the studies by Stayton, Hogan, and Ainsworth (1971) (and in other studies with similar findings, such as Parpal and Maccoby 1985) are exactly those predicted by the social bond theory.

The ineffectiveness of training and discipline, as reported in these studies, is also congruent with social bond theory. Discipline and training are usually oriented to behavior rather than to inner thoughts and feelings, and to topics rather than relationships. Over-emphasis on behavior and topics, according to the theory, would be expected to damage, rather than build or repair bonds. The mothers who were responsive and accepting, on the other hand, would be building and repairing bonds, according to the theory. Similarly, McCord's complaint that Straus ignores other significant punishments such as neglect and rejection fits within a theory of the social bond.

The proposed theory also speaks to gender differences in child-rearing and in personality. In modern societies, males have been raised to be independent in order to find work roles or careers. By the same token, females, until quite recently, have been raised to be oriented toward families rather than work. Since these influences begin in early childhood and persist throughout the person's lifetime, it would not be surprising to find that personalities and relationships would be strongly gender related. There is a preliminary discussion of this issue in Braithwaite's (1989) masterful theory of crime causation. His discussion is only preliminary since he does not go into the details of shame dynamics, as I will do in a later section.

A series of studies initiated by Helen Lewis (1971 1977) concerned the distinction between "field dependence" and "field independence," whether a person is primarily oriented toward others' viewpoints or one's own. Lewis's studies and those of others following from hers show that women tend toward field dependence (engulfment), men toward field independence (isolation). Lewis's studies also showed a correlation between field dependence and shame format: she found that women tend towards expressing the overt, undifferentiated type of shame, men toward the bypassed type. That is, women tend to manifest shame and embarrassment more overtly than do men. Men's shame and embarrassment is likely to be disguised and denied. In a later section I will relate this difference to differences in male and female crime rates.

The Smith family

As a part of a television broadcast on corporal punishment of children on the program 20/20, the producer recruited four families who volunteered to allow filming of punishment in their homes. A cameraperson spent ten or so hours in each of the homes, focusing on episodes of punishment. In the context of studies of corporal punishment, these films are a valuable adjunct to statistical studies, since they allow us to view naturally occurring behavior in the home. Unlike experiments, surveys, and interviews, the sources of most data in current social science, these videos show moment-by-moment details of interaction in the family.

For this discussion I will use all of the scenes that were filmed showing the Smith (pseudonym) family, from two different sources, the broadcast itself, and the out-takes (extra scenes not used on the 20/20 program.) The broadcast showed spanking episodes, interviews with the parents, and a panel discussion with all of the families and the sociologists Straus and Favarro. The out-takes showed spanking and the breakfast scene which I comment on at length.

For my discussion I have chosen the Smith family because they punished their children most of the four families, and also were clearly the most resistant to advice that would change their disciplinary practices. In the panel discussion, the other three sets of parents seemed to be responsive to the advice offered, but not the Smiths, who were defiant. They represent an extreme case for the problem of changing family behavior in this area.

The rate of punishment in this family seems extremely high, relative to survey results. I counted twenty-four spanking and slapping episodes, fourteen by the Mom, ten by the Dad. I also noted several instances of threats of punishment which were only verbal. If the filming took place over ten hours, that would be a rate of more than two episodes per hour in the family, which would mean slightly less than one per child (only the three older children were spanked). On the other hand, since most of the episodes are quite brief, considerably under a minute, most of the interaction between parents and children does not involve punishment.

Although I will comment on all of the episodes of punishment observable in the Smith family, I will emphasize one episode, a five-minute breakfast scene. The camera-person included it because it contains four spanking incidents, but it is unique among the others in that it shows many other kinds of family interaction. While it offers a window into the nature of the whole network of relationships between the members of this family, as well as instances of punishment, it also reveals the poverty of communication within the family. There is dialogue only between husband and wife. Speech directed toward children involves only commands and instructions. There is virtually no interchange between parents and children that is not related to discipline.

A family breakfast

There are four children in the Smith Family. Ashley and Jordan appear to be identical twins about four years old, Cindy is about three. The infant appears to be less than one year old. The mother is sitting at one end of a round table, Dad at the other. Ashley is next to Mom on her left side, Cindy on Mom's other side. Jordan is next to Ashley, on Dad's right side. The infant is away from the table, to Mom's right in a high chair, off camera most of the time. The parents seem to be in their early thirties. Both are short and stocky, with Mom somewhat overweight.

The scene might have been filmed late in the 1980s. The economic standing of the family seems low. Assuming the filming occurred on a weekday, the presence of both mother and father all day suggests that one or both might work a late shift, or less likely, that one or both are out of work. The house is always in disorder in every scene, even though the parents are present.

The table setting points to their life style: they are using paper plates for breakfast, and are drinking Sunny Delight (orange juice flavored punch) instead of orange juice. The only indication of prosperity is the presence in one of the rooms of a new and elaborate climbing toy. The home's exterior has chipped paint and is in need of repair, in what appears to be a low-rent area. The family automobile is a stationwagon from the seventies.

The transcript of the breakfast episode, which lasts slightly less than five minutes, can be found in appendix I. Appendix II is a transcript of the components of the 20/20 broadcast which involved the family.

One obvious feature of the breakfast scene is that with exception of Mom and the infant, the parents show little interest in and affection toward their children. Mom, much more than Dad, seems interested in and proud of the infant, as clearly indicated in lines 63–68. But neither parent shows any pride, interest or patience with the other children. Both parents seem embattled. The father is more polite than the mother, who yells and hits. But both usually are exasperated by the children's behavior.

The primary emotion the parents show toward the children is self-righteous, indignant anger, both in the breakfast and in many of the spanking scenes: *"How many times do i have to tell you?" (As is the convention in linguistics, the asterisk * signifies a "hypothetical," a statement not actually made, but that summarizes many actual statements.) The implication of their attitude is that the children are either stupid or intentionally defiant. The mother seems much more out of control than the father, but both seem stressed. Several of the spankings concern the children not paying attention to the parent. The parents in these instances seem particularly angry and indignant.

The mother states during the broadcast panel that she and her husband always count ten before spanking. Actually, more than half of the spankings on the tapes involve no hesitation whatsoever. They look impetuous. Moreover, using Retzinger's (see Appendix) scheme for coding overt and covert anger, almost all of the scenes show the parents angry. The Mom's anger is often overt; her movements are abrupt, her utterances have a loud, staccato quality, and her facial expression shows the characteristic muscular configuration of anger: eyes narrowed, cheek muscles taut, teeth clenched. The Dad's anger is usually more covert, except when he spanks because the children are ignoring him. In these situations, his anger is overt like Mom's.

From the point of view of a theory of the social bond, the key feature of the breakfast scene is the character of the bond between Mom and Dad. Mom is loud and active, Dad soft-spoken and withdrawn to the point that many of his remarks are inaudible. The contrast between the actions of Mom and Dad at breakfast is striking: the father speaks briefly and infrequently; his principal activity is eating. The mother, however, eats nothing at all; she only plays with her food. She does nothing at the table but talk and spank. At several points she seems exasperated not only with the children, but with her husband, culminating in the sarcastic remark about his intelligence (line 51).

The pattern of interaction in this scene is common in dysfunctional marital relationships: one partner is passive and withdrawn, the other angry and aggressive. These patterns are usually reciprocally related and self-perpetuating: the more the one withdraws, the more angry and aggressive the other, and vice versa. Both sides feel rejected and insulted by the other, but neither expresses these intense feelings openly. In this family, the husband's response to rejection is to withdraw, which causes more anger in the wife. The wife's response to rejection is to become angry and aggressive, which causes more withdrawal in the husband. These parents seem to be equally and jointly entrapped in their emotions and silence.

This pattern is subtly pervasive throughout the entire breakfast scene. The mother is much more vigilant of the children's behavior than the father. This difference is quite blatant. The mother's resentment of the father's withdrawal from child care is implied in some of her words and gestures, but it is explicit in lines 45–51.

According to earlier studies, the passivity of the husband is somewhat more common, but reverse gender roles also occur, with the husband the active, aggressive one, the wife withdrawn or passive. This dynamic has been documented many times in the family interaction literature. It has also been described in detail in Retzinger's (1991) study of marital quarrels.

It should be noted that the Mom's behavior during the broadcast panel discussion on 20/20 is not consistent with her behavior in the breakfast scene. During the panel discussion, except for one episode, in which she interrupts him, the Mom defers to her husband. He is also different in this public situation than in the private one. He is not passive and withdrawn during the panel; instead, he manifests what comes near to being arrogant self-confidence. Perhaps under what they perceive to be an attack on their child-rearing practices from the interviewer and from the two sociologists, they temporarily band together to resist the common enemy.

I will assume that the breakfast scene is much closer to their customary behavior in their home than during the broadcast panel.

The usual way in which psychologists have described this dynamic is in terms of "unmet dependency needs." Which is to say, in my language, that the bond between the parents is insecure. For most people in our society, the marriage bond is by far the most important. Deprived of the emotional support of a secure bond even in their marriage, the parents *misperceive their children's age-specific normal behavior* as signs of rejection. They take everything the children do personally. A child's show of independence, particularly, is perceived as rejection. For this reason, a dysfunctional relationship develops between parent and child similar to that between the parents. One is angry and aggressive, the other passive and withdrawn.

With very young children, as in the case of the Smith family, it is almost always the parent who takes the active-aggressive role, the child the passive-withdrawn one. As the children grow older, however, the roles may be reversed: the child becomes angry and aggressive, the parent passive and withdrawn. This analysis suggests a model of the way insecure bonds in a child's family of origin may lead to juvenile delinquency and to crime, violence or irresponsibility as an adult. In this model, corporal punishment plays only minor role in the causal sequence. It is only one of many indicators of alienation in the family.

One final feature of some of the spanking scenes shows the parents, particularly the mother, insisting that the child who has been punished embrace and kiss the parent. This practice may be fraught with significance for the socialization of the child's emotions. If the parent allowed for a full discussion of the punishment episode, which would allow the child to voice any feelings, including those of unfairness or resentment, such a practice would fit within Braithwaite's model of reintegrative shaming. After punishment is over, the parent takes care to repair the bond.

But in the Smith family, the practice of having the child show affection toward the parent who has just spanked her smacks of repression, rather than reintegration. The child is not allowed to voice its actual feelings, but required to embrace and kiss the parent. In behavioral perspectives, such a practice might be thought of as "extinguishing" negative feelings. But in a more realistic view of emotion dynamics, the child is surely being taught to repress its feelings, especially anger and resentment.

Gender and crime

As already suggested, a detailed theory of the social bond-emotions might also explain the differential crime rates between men and women. Given that the crime and violence rates among men are enormously higher than among women in all industrial societies (Braithwaite 1989), the criticisms of Straus's theory by Kurz (1991) and Loseke (1991) that it ignores gender differences are well taken. In this section I will try to provide a preliminary theoretical explanation for these differences.

Alienation in the family of origin drives men and women in different directions. The socialization of men in such families directs them toward an isolated style of relationships, and toward bypassed shame. That is, they are taught to swallow their shame, to deny it completely to the point that it is no longer available to consciousness. This type of shame is correlated with the practice of masking shame with anger, giving rise to a pervasive sense of resentment toward others, including the world outside of the family. This emotional pattern could drive the vendetta pattern that governs male violence and criminality, both in first offenses and in repeated ones.

On the other hand, alienation in the family of origin would drive women into a different pattern. The normal pattern of socialization of girls moves them, in alienated families, toward the engulfed style of relating to others, which is correlated with overt, undifferentiated form of shame. In the bypassed format, shame is so disguised that the bearer is likely to be completely unaware of it. But in the overt form, the sensation of unpleasant affect is exaggerated. For example, the blush is associated with overt shame; blushers become aware of their own blushing, in a feedback loop of increasing arousal.

For these reasons, overt shame is associated with shame–shame sequences: women's socialization in overt shame and engulfment leads them, in the world outside the family, toward passivity and withdrawal rather than hostile aggression. This hypothesis would explain the frequent instances of wives who remain loyal to violent and abusive husbands. In the engulfed style, one gives up important parts of one's self, even the right to fairness and justice.

Although Adler (1956) did not use shame terminology, his analysis of the consequences of insecure bonds in childhood (lack of parental love, in his terminology) parallels mine. He argued that children who lack parental love at critical junctures in their development go in two different directions: what he called the "inferiority complex," on the one hand, and the "drive for power," on the other. The inferiority complex corresponds to what I have called the engulfed, overt shame dynamic, and the drive for power, the isolated, bypassed shame dynamic. My scheme makes explicit the details of moment-by-moment causal sequences and observable indicators in a way that Adler's does not.

The condition of having no secure bond, not a single one, is so painful that it is usually banished from consciousness: the counter-dependent behavior it generates is compulsive. In the emotional dynamics of insecure bonds, the feeling of complete alienation from others or self generates feelings of rejection (shame) so overwhelming that they are bypassed, surfacing only as aggressively active and/or hostile behavior.

If this theory is correct, it would explain why the Smith parents responded so negatively to the good advice about alternatives to corporal punishment that was offered them in the 20/20 broadcast. They were antagonized by the advice offered them, acting as if it were an attack. According to the theory, they have developed a self-right-eous rationale for their practices, but their behavior is actually compulsive; they are usually out of control in spanking their children. Their actions are not rational choices, but involuntary results of denial of their isolation and shame.

To reach parents like the Smiths would require an indirect route, one that would give them time to develop some trust in the instructor, which would probably involve support for their low levels of self-esteem. Given a bond with the instructor, he or she might find a way to allow the parents to acknowledge some of their hidden feelings and their sense of alienation. Such a program might require many sessions rather than a single one, to the extent that the parents are trapped in their patterns of isolation and denial of feeling. To teach parents how to deal with their children without spanking might require changes in the family system as a whole.

Future research directions would be to systematically analyze the Smith family's interactions, and those of other families, using part/ whole analysis of discourse. This method of analysis allows for the systematic interpretation of verbatim discourse, in its biographical and ethnographic context. It can be used to confirm the results of the informal analysis reported here, and to elaborate a theory of social bonds. Such a study might then be used to develop reliable measures of alienation in the family. With such measures, perhaps one might show that spanking of children is associated with later crime, as Straus's findings suggest, but only because it is highly correlated with alienation. Having considered the bonds in a single family, the next chapter will examine social bonds among the members of children's groups, moving from single case toward comparative morphology.

Appendix I   Smith breakfast
Dad: 1. Your nutu-rous, your nutritious in the morning.
        (Dad being sarcastic towards mother.)

Mom: 2. Vit-a-mins, vitamins . . .
          (Mom's response is also sarcastic.)
          (Child 1 is whining to Mom.)
Ashley: 3. This is hot!
          (Mom slaps Ashley on the leg and yells.)
Mom: 4. This isn't a circus, don't play with your food.
          (Ashley coughs.)
Dad: 5. That's what you get.
          (Referring to Ashley, while he removes a glass from Jordan's hand.)
Mom: 6. You have a problem!
          (Raising her voice to Ashley.)
Dad: 7. You haven't touched nothing yet.
          (Dad talking to Jordan.)
Mom: 8. Eat something Jordan! . . . Eat!
          (Mom raising her voice with a stern expression.)
Dad: 9. (inaudible)
          (Mom begins to fumble with food in her plate.)
Mom: 10. Yeah right, I forgot what happened . . .
          (Dad continues to eat, while mumbling.)
Dad: 11. (inaudible)
          (Mom looking down at her plate playing with her food, while talking
          to Dad.)
Mom: 12. Suppose to get cold again though . . . S'ppose to go down to 58
          some time this week.
          I'm gonna miss "All My Children" if I have to take her to the
          doctor's.
          (Mom appears frustrated.)
Mom: 13. Damn. (Whisper.)
Dad: 14. To the doctors?
Mom: 15. I should've had an appointment for the morning.
Dad: 16. (Inaudible)
Mom: 17. 'Cause, Sandra told me. Paula has to go too.
          (Looking down at the table, with her finger in her mouth. She
          suddenly screams while getting up to run over to infant in ' high
          chair, while Dad continues his breakfast.)
Mom: 18. Oh she's got her arm caught under her again . . . Your gonna
          break your arm one of these days . . .
          (Returns to table being humorous.)
Mom: 19. You silly goose.
          (Children chattering/singing, gesticulating at the table. Mom in high
          patronizing voice, referring to infant, is talking to Dad.)
Mom: 20. There you go . . . One of these days she's gonna break that arm.
          (While resuming her position at the breakfast table Mom smacks
          Cindy, and then yells.)
Mom: 21. Do you want to sit there right and eat?
          I just smacked you for that.
Cindy: 22. Mama.
Dad: 33. (To Cindy) Uhhg . . . What are you doing?
          (Ashley and Jordan chattering and singing.
Mom: appears disturbed and disgusted by Cindy, who is picking her nose.)
Mom: 34. I can't tell you what she was doing.

(Mom looks at all of the children, appears annoyed and yells.)

Mom: 35. Eat! . . . Eat!

Mom: 36. (In normal tone.) We don't have to leave right after umm, we take them to school.

(Dad makes eye contact.)

Dad: 37. I know . . .

Mom: 38. You want lunch first?

39. (Dad nods his head.)

Mom: 40. Appointments not 'til 1.30.

(Cindy chattering.)

Cindy: 41. Hey . . .

(Mom mimics Cindy.)

Mom: 42. Hey. (To Dad) We'll be there at one o'clock.

(Ashley points to her chest.)

Ashley: 43. Mommy right here hurts . . .

Mom: 44. Down there's gonna hurt if you don't eat that . . . (Mom points to Ashley's rear, then begins to impatiently tap her fingers on the table. Mom looks around nervously, touching her empty plate.)

Mom: 45. It's hot in here . . .

(Dad grunts while eating, not focusing on her.)

Dad: 46. Hmmmm?

(Mom seems annoyed.)

Mom: 47. It's hot in here.

Dad: 48. Something else? . . . Mo, more bacon?

(Mom shakes her head no in silence, looking across at Dad.)

Mom: 49. Did you cut the heat back?

Dad: 50. (Mumbles,looking down at his plate) No . . . inaudible).

Mom: 51. Would never nobody never accuse you of being intelligent!

(Mom continues drinking orange juice.
Dad is looking down, shuffling his fork in his plate.
Cindy: yells in baby talk.)

Dad: 52. Ummm.

(Cindy continues talking and starts to sing.)

Cindy: 53. Yum . . . Yum . . . Yummy . . .

(Mom looking in direction of hall door, not focusing on Cindy. Talking in harsh tone of voice.)

Mom: 54. Yummy . . . Eat.

(Looking at Jordan and Cindy, speaking in an irritated tone to Ashley.)

Dad: 55. Ashely don't play with your food . . . if you're not going eat go put your plate in the trash. Please . . .

(Mom slaps Ashley on the leg, yelling angrily.)

Mom: 56. What do you think you're doing? . . .

(Mother grabs Ashley's fork from her hand.)
(Father looks at Ashley.)

Dad: 57. Just get down , go put your plate in the trash.

Mom: 58. But I've told her that already, about playing with it.

Ashley: 59. But I can't eat more food.

(Dad looks at Ashley, speaking in a low tone.)

Dad: 60. Put it down . . .

(Mom, sneering, says)

Mom: 61. Solves . . . the blanket again.
       (Infant in high chair mumbles baby-talk. Ashley and Jordan turn away from table to look.)
Dad: 62. (Speaking to Ashley and Jordan.) Never mind . . . concentrate on eating.
Mom: 63. (Looking at infant, talks to Dad.)
       She's got the keys in her mouth, and she's going like this . . .
       (Shaking her head from side to side in a comical manner, then points to infant.)
Dad: 64. (inaudible).
       (Mom screams in a laughing manner for Dad's attention in reference to infant.)
Mom: 65. Look at her . . . ! She's mugging on them, Oh I bet ya her teeth hurt.
       (Mom looks at her finger, picks at it.)
Mom: 66. Got some Orajel upstairs.
       (Mom looks at Dad. Dad looks at infant and becomes animated.)
Dad: 67. Oh, she's struggling . . . all by herself.
Mom: 68. (Laughing, referring to infant.) Look at her! . . . Look at her. . . . Look at her . . . How did I do that, Oh goooh.
       (The Mom seems to be speaking for the infant, who's teething. Suddenly she smacks Ashley, who's looking at the infant.)
Mom: 69. (Yelling) Eat! . . . Well I'm tired of telling you. You too, Jordan!
Ashley: 70. (Crying) I don't want more pancakes.
Mom: 71. We have Sebastian (?) working.
       (Mom is fumbling with her wedding ring.)

Appendix II   20/20 report
Smith family spankings

I. Ashley did not clean her room
Mom: Didn't I tell you (pulls her towards her by the arm, rhetorical calm, expressionless)
A: (shrugs away from her and nods her head)
M: (spanks her behind)

II. Jordon runs towards the street
Dad: Get up there (spanks her, Jordon puts her hand behind her to protect her bottom. Dad's voice is assertive and angry)

III. Ashley did not pay attention
M: (turns and faces Ashley) Pay attention to me when I am talking to you (smacks her hand). (Ashley looks up at Mom, face has a look of deference, appears to have nervous, childlike insecurity, voice is soft, the smack appears to be almost habitual, because she does not seem angry)

IV. Cindy is picking her nose
M: (approaches Cindy) Do not put your fingers in your nose and then put it in your mouth. That's nasty (strikes her hand five to six times. Cindy cringes during the spanking, face tightens up, begins to cry after Mom has left, words are punctuated with each smack, appears to be less instruction than a disgust with the action, angry)

V. Ashley plays with her food
M: (smacks A.) Eat (emphatic frustration, voice is whiney, eyes raise to make pleading gesture, helpless anger)

VI. Jordon hits Ashley
M: You like to hit You like to hit Come here. (hits Jordon on the bottom) Jordon immediately backs away when she realizes she is about to be hit, puts hands over her eyes, moves out of range of the first attempt, when she is told to "come here" she follows directions and moves towards her Mom hesitantly and cowering. (Tries striking Jordon twice, when she misses the first time she throws her head back in rage and yells "come here", voice is calm until she is unable to make physical contact and then voice elevates, throws hand down emphatically, tantrum like, spank is forceful but appears not to reflect the intensity of the previous outburst as if the "tantrum" was a result of the humiliation felt when Jordon refused to be punished.)

VII. Ashley pulls Jordan's hair
M: (pulls Ashley's hair) Ashley thinks Mom is coming at her to smack her, puts hand up instinctively and shies away, Mom turns Ashley around, head is thrown back from the force of the pull, Ashley begins to cry and walks away slowly) You like to pull hair (calm, routine-like, after she gets hold of Ashley's hair seems satisfied, appears to act as if she is teaching a lesson, seems pleased with herself)

VIII. Dad spanks Cindy for wetting pants
D: (touches Cindy's pants and spanks her; Cindy lets out a faint moan) You know better than that (again, spanking appears to be habitual, calm, tone does not seem angry, picks Cindy up immediately, lovingly)

IX. Child spanked for ignoring Dad
D: (spanks child several times; child looks terrified, standing back afraid to get any closer, bending up and down at the knee in a panic-like state, crying extremely hard) Don't ignore me (calm until gets hold of the child, anger is very apparent seems to "lose it" for a minute, face clenches up, force of spanking intensifies, starts to say something but then becomes so engrossed in spanking he stops and continues his sentence only after spanking is finished, booms out instruction at the end but appears to have regained some control over his anger)
D: (child has hand on her bottom) Move your hand, you want more (child moves hand and is spanked several times; child has waited dutifully for her turn to be spanked, face is frozen in a pained expression, appears very fearful when she is called over, crying uncontrollably before, during and after spanking. Most of Dad's anger seems to have dissipated, face seems more relaxed, even during the battle over moving her hand, perfunctory, voice stays calm)

20/20 broadcast
Reporter: It seems to me that someone is being spanked all the time
M: Not all the time (tone is indifferent and cool, dismissive as a defense)
D: Well there are certain things they haven't learned yet (defensive)
M: Ya I have thought about that but no better be hit now than electrocuted in the electric chair later (believes in what she is saying, looks detached, indifferent defensive, direct denial with the words "but no," appears fearful

about what could happen, almost fanatical, has a warning in her voice, hard direct glaring at end, rhythm irregular)

D: Until they get spanked they won't realize (reserved, mixed smile, appears very confident), but is interrupted by Mom:

M: NO means NO (loud, assertive, challenging , eyes averted, rapid condensed speech possibly because she feels uncomfortable with having interrupted Dad, playing with hands)

D: Most of these kids growing up who don't get spanked are uncontrollable (patiently explains, has air of superiority, mixed smile)

Reporter: There is a fine line between spanking and abusing your children, there's a very fine line and it's easy when you're angry to cross that line

M: *We never cross that line* we're very careful (seems to have taken on Dad's calm and confident mannerism, is direct, monotone, looks to believe that what she is saying is the truth and is the proper way to handle disciplining children, playing the role)

D: Let's try the time out chair and the privileges taken away you know . . . oh please give me a break (laughs) it did not work . . . it seems to have gone from bad to worse (tone and expression change three times with each segment, first part eyes are darting nervously, tone is monotonous, sarcastic, stops mid sentence, changes tone, accusatorial, eyes close to emphasize frustration with the situation, third change occurs with the laughed words, authoritative tone, makes eye contact with reporter, looks to be justifying previous "outburst," rhythm irregular, fragmented speech throughout)

Reporter: Why do the experts say this? (puts hands in the air)

M: It might work for some people but it does not work for us (voice gets higher, assertive, heavy stress on word "does not and "work")

Reporter: Can't she forget she is only two years old?

D: Yes she can forget but there's certain signs with her that I know she knows what she is doing (mixed smile, condescending tone, words, tone, and facial expression all take on the "I am the parent, I know best, don't try to challenge me" demeanor, seems a bit defensive)

Reporter: You think she does this just to bother you?

D: No, not particularly to bother me . . . but just to be bad (mixed smile, stammer, rapid speech in conclusion frustrated, the reporter is challenging his authority, again condescending)

Reporter: But that's why they are called training pants

D: RRRight, right, but she does know (mixed smile, looks threatened and a bit flustered, stammers, heavy emphasis on words "does know", reporter seems to have been successful putting him on the defensive)

Reporter: Sometimes in your house you see fear

D: Fear restrains them from doing bad things . . . you know bad things

Reporter: The child care experts say that if children behave out of fear that they will never learn how to behave for the right reasons, just because it's right

D: No, I think that is bull too . . . AAA UMMM (fixed smile, cocky, cool, laughter in speech, indignant, rudeness to the reporter may be sign he's losing his temper)

M: I don't care if they learn it for the right reasons or not as long as they learn it (sarcastic tone, laughter in speech, almost belligerent, again seems to have taken on Smith's attitude towards the reporter, gaze averted, appears to be

overcome with frustration regarding both the reporter and his line of questioning, cynical of the "child care experts", heavy stress on last words)
Reporter: It is almost as if you're abusive . . . you're you're cruel
M: It might look cruel but it be more cruel not to let them grow and be evil little brats I mean I see kids now that are . . . I mean downright evil and cruel to each other. My kids are not (calm until emphasis on the word "evil", rhythm becomes irregular, rapid speech, eyes light up, voice becomes urgent, face looks frightened, fanatical voice carries with it a warning, speech slows down again, direct gaze at the end)

Conversation with sociologists Favarro and Straus
Favarro: I have worked with parents who have unintentionally injured their children while spanking and they feel terrible about it
M: *Neither of us spank when we're angry We have time out first and we talk about it* (calm, controlled, direct eye contact, appears to be playing a role, lies)
D: No we don't AAAA (first time he appears nervous, stammers, over-soft tone, hesitation, self- interruption, withdrawn, face is blank, embarrassed that Rebecca has lied and/or appears ashamed about his action on the tape)
M: I'd love something else to work because it makes me feel worse than it makes them feel to do it (tired expression, breathiness, false exasperation, eyes averted, often dart)
Favarro: I believe that
M: But nothing else seems to work (voice fades out, almost incoherent, eyes averted, helpless and tired expression, resigned)
Straus: (comments on spanking not working)
D: Oh it works most of the time (face lights up when faced with this challenge, cocks his head to the side, assertive, interrupted by Strauss, changes phrasing)
Straus: Most of the time it has not worked
M and D: Most of the time it has (unified and defensive, both sound threatened, Rebecca has jumped in to help Smith)

CHAPTER 4

Boy's talk, girl's talk: a theory of social integration

Here I re-analyze some of the results of a study of children's discourse by Goodwin (1990). I show how the implications of her data might reach far into our understanding of child development and social organization. Here is a preliminary example, which will be examined in more detail later in the chapter. One boy (Chopper) is ridiculing another (Tony) for his supposed cowardice. This episode goes on for a long time, about two pages of text, with the other boys siding with Chopper, laughing at his imitations of Tony's behavior, and by implication, at Tony.

> Chopper: We was coming home from practice, and three boys came up there and asked us for money and Tony did like this (Chopper raises his hands up, miming Tony's alleged submissiveness) "I AIN'T got no money." (ll. 19–25, p. 295).

My purpose is to show that this excerpt from Goodwin's study, and others like it, might have strong implications for our understanding of the child's world, if it can be positioned within a theoretical framework, one that would connect emotions, social bonds, and social structure. During the entire episode, Tony makes no verbal indication that he has been humiliated, or that the bond between him and his tormentors has been damaged. Like the excerpts involving the other boys in the study when they are being taunted or insulted, Tony maintains his "cool," keeping up the appearance of toughness. But a close examination of the least parts of this and other excerpts show tell-tale signs of embarrassment, shame, and damage to the bond. I argue that a theory of social integration, backed up with morphological study of the least parts and greatest wholes in the excerpts, could be used to elaborate and expand the significance of this study.

The main purpose of abstract theory is to generate empirical research, and the purpose of empirical research is to test a theory, the more abstract the better. The more abstract the theory that is tested, the more it connects with largest possible frameworks, the more

An earlier draft of this chapter benefited from advice by Mitchell Duneier.

reverberations of the study that tests it. Descriptive studies, no matter how well carried out, can have little influence on advancing science until they are framed in terms of general theory. There is probably near unanimity on this idea in the human sciences. But we pay it only lip service in our actual research. The reality is that abstract theory and empirical research have become two separate realms, with little or no contact between them. The divorce between theory and research is a long-standing one. Is there any possibility of reconciliation?

Although there are many reasons for the disparity between our professed beliefs and our practice, I will single out what I think might be the most important one, specialization. Social scientists, like other scholars and scientists, are under pressure to specialize, concerning themselves with only a narrow portion of the spectrum of possible issues. Each discipline is already a specialization, but this specialization is no longer sufficiently narrow; one must have a field, special method, or belong to a "school of thought". Among the many forces to bear, one important one is a moral or ideological imperative: specialization is good in itself. Although few would agree with this proposition in the bald form in which I have stated it, I think that the overwhelming majority subscribe to the underlying *feeling*. Perhaps because everyone has become increasingly specialized, there is bias that highly specialized work is not only more worthwhile, but morally superior to studies which are broad and general.

This bias occurs equally among theorists and researchers. Theorists seem to feel that it is mandatory for them to avoid branching out into issues of method and actual findings. For them it seems more commendable to restrict themselves to textual analysis and emendation, and the study of the origins and influences of theories. Increasingly, the field of theory is defined as dealing *only* with concepts, that is, with abstractions.

Similarly, empirical researchers restrict themselves, for the most part to atheoretical, descriptive studies. Some studies refer to abstract theories, but make only the vaguest connection between their actual design and findings and the theory, which serves as little more than window dressing. Studies which actually use theory almost always deal with low-level abstractions, rather than a general theory. Increasingly, the specialty of empirical research in the human sciences is defined by the absence of sustained attention to theory.

The scientific value of a study is mainly a matter of how closely connected its findings are to a general theory. In the long run, this connection is much more important than even reliability and validity, which are often used as excuses for triviality. Data which directly support, modify, contradict, or even help build a general theory reverberate throughout all of science. Current practices of journals and granting agencies, which outrageously over-emphasize reliability and are hardly aware of validity, let alone theoretical relevance, are draining science out of the human sciences.

The spectre of psychologism

One of the principal causes of the divorce between theory and research is the strong bias that social scientists have against psychological concepts and data. It is more than a mere bias; it amounts to a taboo. Most social scientists seem to find "psychologism" revolting; they hold it in contempt. The attempt to avoid psychology seems to be a strong element in our identity. We are not sure what we are, there are too many diverse strands. But we are sure of who we are *not*; we are not psychologists. (For a thoughtful and thorough critique of social scientists' attitudes toward psychology, see Moscovici 1993.)

The repugnance that sociologists feel toward incorporating psychological concepts and data into their work is ostensibly based on Durkheim. After all, he announced in one of his early works (1895): "every time a social phenomenon is explained directly by a psychological phenomenon, we may rest assured that the explanation is false." What was only a preliminary tactic in Durkheim has become for modern sociologists a call to arms and a badge of identity. In his later work, particularly, in *The Elementary Forms* (1912) and in *Education and Sociology* (1903–1911), he reversed himself; his mature work explicitly concerns the reciprocal interaction of psychological and social process.

Furthermore, even in his early work, Durkheim's rejection of psychology was much more qualified than the current bias. In the quote about social facts, the word "directly" suggests that he was not rejecting all uses of psychology in social science, but those which attempt to explain a social phenomenon only or entirely in psychological terms.

Unlike even the early Durkheim, modern social scientists dismiss psychological elements in their entirety, and without qualification. The manner in which this dismissal occurs implies that this dismissal is not only intellectual, but also moral and emotional. Here are some sample statements (only a few of those that are cited in Moscovici 1993, ch. 1):

Ferraroti (1984): "The . . . 'psychologizing' of hard social facts . . . has the effect of destroying any serious critical stance *vis-à-vis* existing institutions . . ."

Baudrillard (1976): "The jurisdiction exercised by psychological mode of discourse . . . is more dangerous than the economist's mode of discourse . . ."

Bloor (1983), in his book on Wittgenstein: "There is, said Wittgenstein, a kind of general disease of thinking [which both Bloor and Wittgenstein call "psychologism"] which always looks for (and finds) what would be called a mental state from which all our acts spring 'as from a reservoir'."

Habermas (1988), reproaching theories which mix psychological and social elements, saying they can be consistent only if "the theory of society shrinks down to *social psychology*."

Boudon (1979), claiming that a book on history by Simmel, which contains many obvious psychological elements, "does not run the mortal risk of psychologism."

Sperber (1985), an anthropologist: "Tyler, often considered the founder of cultural anthropology, was guilty, in the eyes of his successors, of the sin of psychologism."

It takes no deep interpretation of these and similar statements to note the strong moral and emotional repugnance for all things psychological, which are referred to as a mortal risk, dangerous and destroying, as illness, disease, and sin.

Oddly, the same aversion for "psychologizing" is found within the discipline of psychology itself. One would think that members of this discipline, at least, would be licensed to use psychological reasoning. But academic psychologists hold it in the same contempt as their social science colleagues, but for different reasons. Academic psychology, since it is strongly dominated by quantitative and experimental approaches, contemptuously rejects any kind of analysis not directly related to quantitative measurement. The steel corset that restricts innovating thinking in psychology is based not on theoretical grounds, as in the social sciences, but on methodological ones. The human sciences as a body have developed a powerful *taboo* against psychological reasoning. I use this word because of intense emotional aura which surrounds these attitudes: its advocates not only reject the forbidden fruit on intellectual grounds, but also show fear of contamination, a taboo.

This moral-emotional taboo is interfering with the advance of the human sciences. Morin (1984) has suggested that the detachment of social science from psychology and other relevant disciplines "prevents the exercising of thought." If we are to bring our theories, macro-concepts and research designs to life, we need to relate them to the micro-world on which they are based, a central theme in Weber's discussion of methods (1947): "In general, for sociology, such concepts as 'state,' 'association,' 'feudalism' and the like, designate certain categories of human interaction. Hence it is the task of sociology to reduce these concepts to 'understandable' action, that is without exception, to the actions of participating individual men [*sic*]." The task that Weber charged us with has not been carried out, not even by Weber himself. We have been content, using excuses like "the ecological fallacy," to use abstract macro-concepts that have no connection with human reality and experience. Weber called this usage "reification," mistaking abstractions for concrete reality. Social science theory as it stands today, separated from the micro world and from empirical studies, is a giant reification.

At the other pole, in empirical research, the result of specialization has been to create a literature which is divided between descriptive studies, on the one hand, and studies oriented toward low-level generalizations. Qualitative studies are increasingly descriptive, and quantitative studies dedicated to simple atheoretic propositions (such as: achievement is determined by one's class of origin). What is primarily needed for advance is the quest for general theories of human behavior, theories which can be tested and modified in the light of empirical studies. Such a quest would require a breakdown of specialization, since all relevant theories, concepts, method and data would be needed. In trying to solve an important problem, one must catch as catch can, utilizing any and all approaches and data that might be relevant.

If the human sciences are to advance, we must begin to integrate disciplines, theories, methods and data into some semblance of cooperation and mutual influence and stimulation. In this chapter I undertake Weber's task, by relating a complex and abstract macro theory to data of human interaction. To this end, I relate a general theory of social integration to the findings of a study of children's discourse. The first section outlines a theory of integration, drawn from existing sociological and other theories.

Alienation and solidarity as poles of social integration[1]

The concept of social integration, of the balance between solidarity and alienation, is basic to social science theory. It is particularly prominent in Marx's theory, where it is an explicit core for his analysis of alienation in capitalist societies. Marx suggested that alienation is a structural feature of capitalism, and that solidarity would be a

---

[1] This section is based in part on pp. 15–18 of Scheff (1994).

structural feature of socialism. As with most other uses, Marx never defines the terms alienation and solidarity, allowing his theory to float free of concrete reality. Without even conceptual, let alone operational definitions, Marxian analysis builds castles in the air.

To the present day, there is still no definition of alienation which relates conceptual and empirical indicators. Seeman (1975), a leader in the empirical study of alienation, did not establish formal definitions, but instead used pragmatically derived scales. The link between these scales and the concept of alienation remains unclear, just as the link between theory and data is unclear in Marx and other conceptual approaches.

The polar dimensions of social integration are also central to Durkheim's basic study *Suicide* (1897), and prominent in virtually all of his work. Although he does not use the term alienation, it is clearly implied in his study of suicide. Durkheim sought to explain the constancy of suicide rates in religious and other groups in terms of the types of social relationships in each group. He showed, for example, that rates of suicide in predominantly Catholic regions in Europe were consistently and uniformly lower than rates in predominantly Protestant regions. He also considered variations in rates between nations and between occupations. These observations led him to formulate a cultural theory of suicide: differences in culture lead to variations in suicide rates, because culture influences the types of social relationships that prevail in a group.

At the core of Durkheim's theory is the distinction he made between two kinds of cultures. On the one hand, there are cultures which are suicidogenic because they give too much prominence to individuals (as against the group), characteristic of modern industrial societies. In his formulation, such cultures lead to egoistic or anomic suicide. On the other hand, there are cultures which give too much prominence to the group, such as the cultures of small traditional societies, which leads to what he called altruistic or fatalistic suicide.

Durkheim sought to explain high suicide rates in traditional groups (too little emphasis on individuals), leading to culturally prescribed forms of suicide (as in *hara kiri* in Japan), and in groups promoting change and innovations (too much emphasis on the individual), like the most ascetic forms of Protestantism. Although Durkheim did not use the term, his analysis is clearly focused on what would today be called social integration, of being either too loosely or too tightly bound to the group.

In his analysis, Durkheim took two important steps: he formulated an abstract theory of suicide, and he gathered data which supported his theory. In combining these two steps into a single study, he invented modern sociology. But a sociology composed of only these two steps is not the last word. Durkheim's explanations of the link between his abstract concepts and his data are phrased in terms that are quite vague. Durkheim continually speculated about such linkages, but in a way that was undisciplined by theory or method. For the formulation of a complete theory, explicit, detailed description of the *steps in the process that links abstract concepts to empirical data* is necessary.

Explicit models that link concepts (names for precisely defined abstract classes) to data at many levels are characteristic of successful sciences. The periodic table, which classifies the chemical elements, is an example: its form is finished because it grows organically out of a micromodel of the atom. On the other hand, Linnaen classification in biology is a continuing embarrassment, because it is still an arbitrary taxonomy: there is no underlying micromodel of the processes that lead to speciation to give it form.

Durkheim's classification of the types of suicide is Linnaen, since he did not specify a precise model of the process through which types of social relationships at the microlevel lead to suicide rates at the macrolevel. His theory gives a bird's-eye view of society, but suicide rates are discrete events. How can the two levels be connected?

In this chapter I link actions and social institutions (micro and macro-levels) by specifying precise models of causation at the level of individual actions, providing theoretical and empirical links in chains of actions, moment by moment. In this way, I give a systematic basis for what Giddens (1984) has called "instantiation," and Geertz (1983), "thick description" of a single case. I am not arguing, however, that macro theories like Durkheim's are unnecessary. Theory construction at each level is *equally* necessary. By moving back and forth from the top down and from the bottom up, it may be possible to advance understanding much more quickly than isolated efforts in each direction. I describe a bottom-up strategy as one step toward building a theory of degree of social integration.

I show how language can be an indicator of the state of the social bond between two people. I focus on the use of pronouns, particularly *I, you, we*, and *it*. The disposition of these pronouns within a sentence, and the relative weight accorded them, can be used as cues to three different states of the bond: solidarity and the two opposite forms of alienation, isolation and engulfment. As discussed below, this analysis can be backed up with a study of emotion cues, showing how pride cues signal solidarity, and shame cues signal alienation.

My approach draws upon and overlaps with Buber's (1958) discussion of I–thou, and many other formulations. What I call solidarity language (I–I) corresponds exactly to his I–thou. What I call the language of isolation (I–you) corresponds exactly to his I–it. I use different terms because Buber, like most philosophers and social scientists, did not consider the other form of alienation, what Bowen (1978) called engulfment (me–I). The idea of engulfment is centrally important in family systems theory (sometimes called enmeshment or fusion) but is rare elsewhere in the human sciences. Social scientists usually confound engulfment with solidarity. In engulfed relationships, one or both parties subordinate their own thoughts and feelings to those of the other(s). In solidarity, each party recognizes the sovereignty of the other, but balances respect for the other's position with respect for one's own.

My use of I and me is quite different than Mead's (1934). His social psychology seems to assume perfect solidarity, without any considering the possibility of alienation. In Mead's scheme, the me is made up of the internalized representation of the roles of others. For example, the citizen utilizing a criminal court is prepared by already knowing the role of the judge, the jury, the policeman, jailer, etc.

Mead did not consider the accuracy with which each member of a society knows the roles of the other members. By ignoring this issue, he evades the issue of imperfect relationships, of alienation. Consider the doctor–patient relationship. Obviously the patient has only a superficial knowledge of the doctor's role, and superficiality of her knowledge can cause impediments to cooperation. For instance, since the patient understands very little of what the doctor knows of the relationship between the patient's illness and the medication that the doctor has prescribed for treatment, the patient might fail to follow the doctor's orders. The relationship is asymmetric in this way.

The relationship is also asymmetric the other way round. Although the patient has never learned the role of the doctor, the doctor should certainly know the role of the patient, since she has been a patient before becoming a doctor, and will continue to be a patient as a doctor. We would expect, therefore, that the doctor would understand patients. But as it turns out, there are impediments to such understanding. As part of their training, and as part of their management of their roles, many doctors seem to "forget" the patient's experience; they do not understand their patients, not because of lack of knowledge, but because of emotional barriers which doctors erect against them.

This process of forgetting also occurs in the teacher's role. Most teachers call very little upon their own role as students to guide their teaching; rather their teaching seems to conform to the way other teachers teach. Once we have learned a body of knowledge, we seem to repress the difficulties we had in learning it, which erects a wall between us and our students. In the language I will use here, in our role as teachers, we are engulfed with other teachers, and isolated from our students. Bi-modal alienation seems to be the most common form of social relationship in the modern world (Scheff and Retzinger 1991; Scheff 1994). In this format, individuals or groups are engulfed within, isolated without, as in sects, cults and academic schools of thought. In the social sciences it has been customary to refer to this system of relationships in terms of ethnocentrism, but this concept is imprecise and static.

As already indicated, the theoretical approach to social integration most similar to the one advocated here is found in Elias's (Introduction 1987) discussion of the "I-self" (isolation) and the "we–self" (engulfment). Elias discusses the "I–we balance" (solidarity) in a way that is quite similar to my usage, but he does not apply it to actual instances. Elias proposed a three-part typology of what he called social figurations: independence (lack of cooperativeness because of too much social distance), interdependence (a balance between self and other that allows for effective cooperation), and dependence (lack of cooperativeness because of too little social distance). Although this typology grows out of Elias's long-standing commitment to the concept of interdependence, his attention was usually limited to this concept, rather than to the other two components of the typology. In this chapter, I give equal theoretical and empirical weight to all three types.

The concept of the I–we balance is oriented largely to the verbal components of interaction, ignoring the non-verbal. My approach is oriented to both verbal and nonverbal elements. The emotions of pride and shame are directly related to the state of social relationships, and can serve as indicators of the nature of that relation from moment to moment. Pride is the emotional cognate of a secure, unalienated bond, and shame signals threat to the bond.

It would appear that careful analysis of the state of social relationships might require using both the I–we and the pride–shame approaches. The first is simpler, the second more subtle and complex, requiring use of the technique developed by Retzinger (see Appendix) to identify cues to shame. The limitation to determining the I–we balance is that human beings often use language in a less than straightforward way, disguising their own motives and goals. Word choice is largely voluntary and intentional; we can easily hide our motives and goals in our verbal expressions. Since shame signals are, for the most part, stereotyped and out of awareness, the analysis of nonverbal cues can detect strains in relationships even when they are covert and hidden. The two approaches can be used to complement each other in determining the state of the bond.

Elias's scheme comes closest to what seems to be needed, if we are to connect the micro and macro-worlds. Many other theories are closely related to this scheme, but contain only two of the three types. Durkheim, Doi (1971) and Seeman (1975) considered only the two forms of alienation that I am calling isolation and engulfment, but did not relate them to the third, solidarity. Buber's typology contains isolation and solidarity, but not engulfment, as do Marx and Braithwaite (1989).

Braithwaite's theory of reintegrative shaming in crime control (1989), which he has applied to the practice of community "conferences" in Australia, excludes one of the types of alienation, engulfment. Since he invited Retzinger and me to observe such conferences, I can report on one of them, a case involving driving under the influence, which illustrates engulfment, rather than reintegrative shaming (solidarity) or stigmatization (isolation). The offender was an adult male with three previous arrests on this charge. With the help of most of the other participants (except for the arresting officer), he successfully denied his responsibility. Even the policeman who ran the meeting colluded with his defense, that because of the extenuating circumstances in this instance, drinking a six-pack, apparently a norm among working-class men, and driving was not morally wrong. Rather than being overshamed, often the case with juvenile offenders, this offender was undershamed, because of engulfment between him and other participants. This outcome was unusual, in that the outcome of most of the conferences is closer to reintegrative shaming than to either engulfment or isolation (stigmatization).

All three types of relationships are implied in the work of Satir (1971), who contrasts defensive postures that I would call isolated (blaming, computing) or engulfed (placating, distracting) with what she calls *leveling*. By leveling she seems to have meant communication which is direct but respectful. Being direct without being respectful involves isolation, just as being respectful but not direct implies engulfment, as I have used these terms here. Leveling involves balancing the claims of the individual with those of the relationship, an I–we balance.

The classifications described here, as already indicated, are closely related to those developed by Ainsworth et al. (1978). What I am calling isolated corresponds exactly to her *avoidant* type. What I have called engulfed seems closely related to her *anxious–ambivalent type*. Finally her secure type is exactly equivalent to what I call solidarity or a secure bond. The great advantage of linking my classification with Ainsworth's is that there is a sizable body of empirical research which utilizes her scheme (Shaver and Clark 1994). The advantage of my

Social integration			
Too little		**Too much**	
Anomie	solidarity	Altruistic	*Durkheim*
Alienation	communism	?	*Marx*
Stigmatization	Reinteg. shaming	?	*Braithwaite*
Independence	Interdependence	Dependence	*Elias*
United States	?	Japan	*T. Doi*
Isolation	secure bond	Engulfment–fusion	*M. Bowen*
blame-compute	Leveling	placate–distract	*V. Satir*
I–it	I–thou	it–thou?	*M. Buber*

Empirical indicators			
Alienation	?	self-estranged	*M. Seeman*
I–we	I–WE	i–WE	*N. Elias*
Bypassed shame	Pride	Overt shame	*Scheff-Retzinger*
Avoidant	Secure	Anxious ambivalent	*Ainsworth*

Figure 4.1 Theories of social integration

scheme for the Ainsworth studies is it can be used to link them both to the microworld of thoughts and feelings, and to the larger institutional and societal structures within which they are embedded.

Figure 4.1 shows the relationship of the present approach to the various theories. It would seem that most earlier discussions of social alienation and solidarity and related concepts are misleading, since they ignore one of the three types of relationships described above, or confound one with another. Most classic Western studies which compare Asian and Western societies seem to have valorized Western isolation and individualism by confounding it with solidarity based on rational outcomes (Durkheim's description of organic solidarity), as Markus and Kitayama (1991) have charged. But it seems likely that Markus and Kitayama have made an equal and opposite error, valorizing Asian (unity-based) societies by confounding engulfment with interdependence. A similar confusion seems to exist in classical studies of autonomy, which feminist scholarship has shown to be male oriented, or in Elias's terminology, oriented toward independence rather than interdependence. But again, most feminist scholarship may be making the equal and opposite error, confounding engulfment with interdependence or solidarity (as discussed below).

In this chapter the theory of social integration outlined above is applied to the concrete data of social interaction. To show how this can be done, I draw upon the findings of a thorough, hands-on study of discourse by Goodwin (1990).

A study of children's discourse

Goodwin recorded the speech of forty-nine working-class black children in a small neighborhood in Philadelphia for a year and a half in 1970–71. She apparently spent many, many hours on the street with these children. What emerges is a comprehensive and rigorous description of behavior and discourse over a considerable period of time. I know of no record remotely like it in the literature on discourse.

By observing the children over such a long period of time, Goodwin may have at least partially overcome some of the difficulties usually associated with the analysis of verbatim discourse. In the typical study, some passage or passages are analyzed intensively, but in the absence of background knowledge. Often the researcher has none whatever; the text itself is the only data. Even in the most powerful studies, this insularity imposes limitations.

Cicourel , in a large number of theoretical and empirical studies (for an example, see 1985), has been the foremost critic of the analysis of texts isolated from their physical and social context. He has long advocated the use of extensive ethnographic study to supplement each and every text that is analyzed. Although Goodwin shows ethnographic knowledge (e.g. she visited the homes of the children and talked to their parents), it is of a general kind, not one that is meant to supplement each episode of discourse, in the manner proposed by Cicourel. For this reason, there would seem to be, at first glance, an imbalance in the text–context ratio. Goodwin's approach is heavily weighted toward text, as against context.

Field ethnographies are usually weighted towards context, with little or no verbatim text. (Cicourel's empirical work is an exception.) Sociolinguistic and psycholinguistic studies are usually weighted the other way, with little or no biographical, historical, or ethnographic context. Lewis's (1971) study of psychotherapy sessions again provides an example. She found that shame or embarrassment was the emotion by far the most frequently evoked in the patient, but neither the patient nor the therapist seemed to take any notice of it. This finding gives rise to her classification of a type of shame that is bypassed, one that is not acknowledged. But since she had access only to the transcripts, she was unable to determine whether bypassed shame was actually out of awareness, or merely being hidden from others. Had she interviewed even a small sample of the patients and therapists afterwards, this ambiguity might have been overcome.

Goodwin's resolution of the problem of context does not involve interviews. She questioned the children occasionally, with the question and answer duly transcribed and reported in the same manner as the children's naturally occurring discourse. But the year and a half of observing the same children in a wide variety of settings yields contextual data of an entirely different sort. Each episode of discourse provides context for every other episode. I am presuming that Goodwin, over the course of 18 months of observation, obtained what might be called global knowledge of each child's behavior and discourse.

Goodwin does not often make her global knowledge explicit, or use the temporal order of her observations for the prospective-retrospective understanding for the meaning of her data. In order to do this, she would have had to time-mark the discourse, which is not done in the book. But the reader of the book is often impressed by her asides, which strongly suggest Goodwin's encyclopedic knowledge of each child. I will return to the strengths and limitations of her use of this resource below.

Although some of the children were aged 4–8, most (38) were 9–14, and most of the discourse Goodwin recorded was from the older group. The children spent much of their non-school time playing in the streets near their homes, usually involved in games. The boys told stories, made and used slingshots, and played yo-yos, go-carts, and dead blocks (a sidewalk game using chalked boundaries and tokens). The girls also told stories and played house and jump-rope.

Goodwin found substantial differences between the speech and activities of the older boys (23 children aged 9–14) and the older girls (15 children aged 10–13). Much of her analysis is focused on these gender differences. She uses studies in related fields, such as anthropology, developmental psychology, sociology and linguistics to compare her findings with those of earlier studies. But her analysis is basically descriptive and atheoretic: she does not attempt to relate her data to social institutions, much less any theoretical explanations of the children's behavior. Because her findings with regard to gender differences are relevant to the theory of social integration outlined above, I will re-analyze them in theoretical terms.

The I–we Balance

Goodwin notes many large differences in the format of girls' and boys' discourse. One major difference is in the use of first-person plural pronouns. The girls, she says, seldom give commands ("bald imperatives"). Instead they make suggestions, a form which always involved a plural pronoun : "Let's play house." (That is, Let us play house.) The boys, on the other hand almost never (Goodwin recorded only two instances) make suggestions using plural pronouns. Rather, they give direct commands: "Get out of here, Tony." (That is, you get out of here, Tony). Goodwin shows a striking difference between the boys and girls in what I (1994) have called the language of division (boys) and the language of unity (girls).

Another difference is in the use of honorific and pejorative labels. The boys virtually never used honorifics, but instead frequently used pejoratives: Stupid, dummy, ain't no good, sucker, big lips. They also used terms critical of the recipient's dress or other possessions: "you and your dingy little sneakers." Less frequently, neutral terms were used: you, man, boy, or the recipient's actual name.

The boys frequently engaged in a practice of what appears to be ritual combat, each participant hurling insults and innuendoes at the other. There are many instances where each boy appears to stand his ground, giving as good as he gets. There is an atmosphere about these disputes that is difficult to convey, in that they often seem to be both serious and playful at the same time. Goodwin's comments suggest that the play side usually predominates; she notes that these verbal fights are often brief, with the boys resuming play as if nothing had happened.

In some of the incidents, however, it is possible that the serious side may have predominated. One example, already quoted above, is the encounter between Chopper and Tony, with other boys present, all supporting Chopper rather than Tony. This encounter is one of three for which Goodwin supplies the full text; in this case, 164 lines. The central issue is Chopper's insinuation that Tony is a coward. Although Tony defends himself, Chopper seems to browbeat and overwhelm him.

> Chopper: We was coming home from practice, and three boys came up there and asked us for money and Tony did like this (Chopper raises his hands up, miming Tony's alleged submissiveness) "I AIN'T got no money." (ll. 19–25, p. 295).

Chopper acts out this allegation repeatedly, ridiculing not only Tony's words but also his manner, milking the line for laughs. Tony attempts to counter each repetition, but to no avail. The other boys, including Malcolm, Tony's brother, confirm Chopper's allegations, and laugh at his miming, rather than at Tony's rebuttals.

Even though Goodwin reported no negative consequences, the content and duration of this dispute suggest that it might have been extremely painful for Tony. We know that Chopper (12) is younger than Tony (14), and that Tony is bigger and stronger, and that Chopper and Malcolm, Tony's brother, are best friends. According to Goodwin (1995), Tony did not seem hurt by the episode. His attitude seemed, rather, to be one of indifference. I will raise a question about this issue in the discussion below.

There is much less overt aggression among the girls. They seldom used pejorative labels, at least they did not use them in the face-to face encounters like the boys did. They used many more honorifics, such as dear heart and hon (honey). They also used neutral terms, such as you, girl, or the recipient's name.

These differences, so far, are consistent with differences in the I–we balance. The girls talk much more the language of we (the language of unity), the boys the language of I and you (the language of division). Both in Elias's scheme and in mine, each group lacks balance: too much *I* and *you* in the boys' group, too much *we* and *us* in the girls'. In my terminology, both groups show signs of alienation; the boys in the isolated mode, the girls in the engulfed mode.

Goodwin's interpretation of these differences is different than mine. She sees the boys' relationships as determined by hierarchy, with the girls more equalitarian. She admits that like the boys, the girls rank each other according to proficiency in their games. But for the girls, she argues, these rankings are specific to the moment, and much less consequential than for the boys. Although Goodwin is not explicit on the point, her interpretations of the gender differences lends itself to the proposition that the relationships between the girls are more solidary, cooperative, and perhaps humane than that of the boys. Since this proposition has some standing in literatures of child development and of feminism, it may be important to examine some other data from Goodwin's study that seem to contradict it.

Covert conflict among the girls

Goodwin's interpretation that the girls are more egalitarian and cooperative with each other than the boys is based entirely on the girls' face-to-face behavior. She also goes to great pains, however, to establish that there is conflict among the girls, but it is covert. The title of the book (*He-Said-She-Said*) refers to the practice of generating dispute with an absent girl, behind her back. Goodwin devotes two whole chapters to it (8 and 11). In this example, Bea is talking to Annette (p. 195):

> Kerry said you said that I wasn't going to go around Poplar no more

This utterance is what the girls themselves call an "instigation," in that it generates conflict between Annette and Kerry, with Kerry absent. Such an instigation leads to a complex situation, entangling not only the absent person, but also the two that are present. The recipient of the instigation, in this case, Annette, needs to make a number of choices before responding. Shall she accept the report as true, or should she test or challenge its veracity? This kind of decision and others related to it each have an immediate effect on the alignments in the relationships between the three parties. Goodwin deftly analyzes this minefield in some detail.

Instigations of this kind are an instance of what Bowen, in his analysis of family systems, calls "triangling," the practice of referring to an absent person in order to avoid dealing directly with the relationship between the two persons who are face-to-face. Bea apparently wants to test the extent of Annette's alignment or conflict with herself. Instead of approaching this issue directly, she masks her desire by informing on Kerry. This utterance is also an attack on Kerry, implying that Bea is not aligned with her.

Goodwin points out that Kerry, who is often the target of instigations, is by far the best student of all the girls, having skipped a grade because her proficiency. Among the girls, one basic reason for criticizing another girl is that she "thinks she is better than us." The girls may sometimes criticize Kerry to her face on this ground, but it appears they attack her deviously more frequently behind her back.

The data and analysis that Goodwin provides about covert conflict among the girls raises a question about Goodwin's contention that the girls have a higher state of egalitarianism and cooperation than the boys. The data on covert conflict implies that this higher state is only a matter of surface behavior. The girls give the appearance of unity in each other's presence, but actually they seem to be as divided as the boys. Their mode of conflict is much more surreptitious than the boys' mode, and therefore at least as intractable. The boys insult each other face-to-face, the girls behind each others' backs.

There is one suggestion that the consequences of the girls' conflicts are more serious than those of the boys. One of the girls, Annette, appears to have been ostracized by the other girls for a month and a half. She stayed at home after school during this period, and her Mother talked about the possibility of moving to another neighborhood. There is nothing remotely as consequential as this mentioned with respect to the boys.

It would seem that the girls are as alienated in their relationships as the boys, but in a different mode. The boys' alienation is in the isolated mode, they speak to each other in the language of division. But the girls, speaking in the language of unity, are alienated in the engulfed mode. The practice of speaking courteously in someone's presence but critically behind their backs means that the girls are withholding their hostile feelings in one situation (face to face), but voicing them in another (target girl absent).

The practice of withholding thoughts and feelings is a primary indicator of the state of engulfment. Out of loyalty or prudence one suppresses parts of the self. This practice can be as disruptive as outright hostility, in that it makes trouble both for relationships and the self. In engulfed relationships, the participants find it difficult to know where they stand with each other, because one or both is withholding their thoughts and feelings about the other. Withholding also makes trouble for the self, in that given sufficient voluntary, conscious withholding, one may forget where one actually stands, to the point that withholding becomes automatic. Engulfment may deform the contours of the self as it does relationships (Bowen 1978; Bowen and Kerr 1988).

Discussion

In describing the Goodwin study, I have already alluded to some of its strengths, particularly the massiveness and precision of its coverage of the children's behavior. In this section, I describe two limitations, one quite specific, concerning gestures and emotions, the other very general, the relationships of parts and wholes.

Already mentioned above is the difficulty in ascertaining from Goodwin's report the seriousness of the conflicts that she observed. This issue has strong implications for my analysis of the degree of integration of the children. If the conflicts reported are mostly rituals, one might argue that far from undermining social bonds and coopera-tion, they actually contribute to it. This is certainly the case in the juvenile conflicts reports by animal ethnographers. In these sparring matches, the animals virtually never cause actual injury. On the contrary, as individuals learn their rank in the group through combat, they are building, rather than disrupting social solidarity.

In Goodwin's report, we know of only one social injury, when Annette found herself in Coventry for six weeks. Although the disputes of the boys might have led at times to physical battles, none are reported. The boys threaten each other frequently with blows, but none are resorted to. What about emotional pain and injury to social standing? Chopper's effective attack on Tony's courage has already been mentioned. Also reported is an instance where two teams were forming that led to a rejection of one boy (Dave, p. 77) by both teams.

The effect on the rejected boy is not mentioned by Goodwin, but I surmise that it and similar rejections and exclusions can be quite painful. Even when all present are included on one of the teams, being in the role of the ones who are always chosen last can leave its mark.

I assume that the practice of instigation and exclusion would cause frequent feelings of rejection among the girls. Surprisingly, Goodwin reports no incidents of crying. It is possible, of course, that crying occurred, but not in public. Perhaps the girls cried only in the privacy of their homes, when telling their travails to parents or other relatives. As indicated, the intensity and duration of injury is a crucial question for assessment of the nature of the social integration between the children.

Of course the researcher could have privately questioned the children and their parents about these matters. Another approach, perhaps complementing the interview method, would have been to report and analyze nonverbal gestures in the children's discourse. By analyzing his facial expressions and intonations during and after his encounter with Chopper, we might have been able to determine the extent and intensity of Tony's emotional reaction. Since he was being publicly humiliated, we might expect him to feel ashamed, and that this feeling might have persisted long after the incident. As already indicated above, Goodwin (1995) has stated that Tony was indifferent to the episode, rather than hurt by it. But cool indifference can be a mask for pain; it is very commonly so among male adolescents. Without additional interview and/or gestural evidence, we can not be sure which way to interpret this and similar incidents.

This analysis points to an issue that has gone unnoticed in the literature on child and adult development: at what degree of frequency and intensity does rejection cause permanent damage? Or alternately, at what level does affirmation and respect lead to an inviolate sense of self and high levels of self-esteem? If systematically followed up in later years, data such as Goodwin's might provide an answer to this vital question.

The type and extent of the children's emotional reactions implies a very general problem in the conduct of research, the extent to which the relation between parts and wholes can be assessed. Given a text, how can we relate it to the larger whole of which it is only a part? In this regard, I have already mentioned the balance between parts (text) and wholes (context). Goodwin's study, although supplying far more context than most analyses of discourse, still attends much more to text than context. Like most micro studies, although far less so, it emphasizes text at the expense of context. I have already suggested, in the dispute between Chopper and Tony, that too little background information is provided. To understand this incident, we need to know more about Chopper and Tony, and more about the history of their relationship, before and after the incident. Individual and joint biographical information of this kind would allow us to judge the duration and intensity of their conflict.

This kind of biographical information can be thought of as providing larger wholes, the character of individuals and of relationships, within which we can judge the meaning of parts, in this case an incident of conflict. Other, larger wholes that might be relevant to the meaning of the data could involve issues of race and class. Although the children do not invoke social class directly, many of their insults involve class and economic standing indirectly: the superiority and inferiority of clothing worn by children is a frequent cause of comment among them. One dispute involved the allegation of vermin in the house of one of the children, which may indirectly related to the economic standing of the family.

There are no direct allusions to race in the children's discourse, but several indirect ones. One boy referred to another as "thick lips," another commented on the bushiness of another's hair. The children probably rank each other not only in terms of economic and class standing, but also in terms of degree of blackness. This latter issue would pose a delicate problem for the researcher, since it would be intrusive to ask direct questions. But it would probably help us better understand the relationships between the children; like social and economic standing, at least some of their alignments and disputes are generated by these larger patterns. Race and class are social institutions, but they probably have strong influences in the daily lives of these children.

Emotions in discourse

I have critiqued Goodwin's study in terms of the need to look at larger wholes, biographical, ethnographic, and historical, in the manner of Cicourel. But in discussing the matter of gesture and emotion, I also invoked a level of data smaller than the words and sentences that Goodwin analyzed. To understand the intensity and duration of the emotions generated in the disputes between children, and therefore the nature of their relationships, we would need to study not only small parts of their discourse, the words and sentences, but also their gestures: facial expressions and intonation contours. To what extent were these children being emotionally wounded in their daily interaction? To answer this question, we need to look at not only the larger patterns in which they were involved, but the smaller: sequences of emotions.

Were these children hurt by the insults and rejections that were frequently their lot? To ascertain the answer to this question, we could interview them and their parents, but we could also examine the smallest parts of their discourse, the patterns of visual and audial cues which indicated painful emotions like anger, embarrassment, shame, fear and grief. Because Goodwin did not interview children and parents about feelings, or report most of the gestural accompaniment to discourse, we are unable to make many inferences about emotional responses from her data. (However, her precise method of transcription is a help, because it indicates some of the nonverbal components of discourse: stress patterns, pauses, laughter, etc.) But Goodwin's transcriptions omit some key nonverbal components, such as direction of gaze, intonations, and other nonverbal signs, that are needed to support inferences about emotion. Without substantiated inferences about emotion, we cannot be sure about the degree of integration between the children.

Given the nature of research in the human sciences today, it is not being critical to suggest that Goodwin did not examine the least parts and the greatest wholes that we would need to determine the degree of integration between the children. I think she did better than most current studies, even the best ones. Because most research is so specialized, it is a rare study that shows the breadth necessary to relate micro and macro, small parts and large wholes. Part/whole analysis enables the researcher and the reader to position data and analysis within the steps of the part/whole ladder: how any particular set of words and gestures is related to the dialogue in which it is embedded; how that dialogue is embedded in the whole past and future relationship of the participants, and how that relationship is embedded within all the children's relationships in their community, all relationships in their community, including the adults, and finally, making a large leap, within all relationships in our civilization.

If we were more certain about the balance between solidarity and alienation in the children's relationships, Goodwin's study might make a contribution to the study of the social institution of gender. One implication of my analysis concerns the institutional aspect of gender relationships. Most feminist theory urges that causality in gender relationships is highly asymmetric; oppression of women is caused more by men than by women. In the physical world, this suggestion may be true: men's greater size and strength, and their greater control of property and the means of violence gives them power over women.

But in world of culture and relationships, Goodwin's data suggest that the present institution of gender differences might be jointly determined by males and females. The practices of discourse between the girls could be creating alienated relationships, a false solidarity among them, just as the practice of discourse among the boys might be creating alienation through open, contentious disputes. In this view, tension between the sexes is created equally by males and females, because each group creates cultural versions of maleness and femaleness which lead to alienated relationships not only within the sexes, but between them. To understand the strains in gender relationships, and what to do about them, we may need to know more about the parts and wholes of social relationships.

Summary

This chapter shows that connecting abstract theory with concrete data can provide illumination for both theory and data. A general theory of alienation was used to interpret instances of children's discourse. The results suggest several new directions. One is the outline of a general theory of integration, one which could be applied to assessing the state of the bond in actual human relationships. Another direction is the need for augmenting studies of discourse with systematic follow-up studies. Such studies might provide answers to hard questions, such as the long term effects of repetitive patterns of social relationships, which studies with conventional research designs have not yielded. A final direction concerns modifying theory, method and interpretation of data through the use of part/whole analysis. Although theory and empirical research are now divorced, reconciliation might bring rapid advance for the human sciences.

CHAPTER 5

Origins of the First World War: integrating small parts and great wholes

We are all just prisoners here of our own device.

Don Henley (The Eagles)

This chapter marks a departure from the others in this book. Here the emphasis shifts from the close examination of small parts to integration of microanalysis with macro analysis of the causation of the First World War. The immediate causes of this and other wars lie in the alienated relationships that are endemic in our civilization. These causes are equally present in the smallest unit of sociation, the family system, as much as they are in the relations between nations. The patterns of secrecy, deception, and self-deception which prevail in the relationships of family members can also be found, in parallel forms, in the relationships among nations. Drawing upon family systems theory and the sociology of emotions, I outline a theory which describes how alienation and unacknowledged shame produce wars. To illustrate this theory, I apply it to a hotly contested problem, the origins of World War I. To illustrate part/whole morphology, I analyze the texts of several crucial telegrams exchanged between heads of states in the context of the historical and political situation in which they occurred.

In claiming an isomorphism between interpersonal and international relations, I realize that I challenge an article of faith of modern social science, that structure and process at the societal level is fundamentally different than that at the level of persons; society, as Durkheim claimed, is a reality *sui generis*. Although I agree that societal relationships are in some ways different than interpersonal ones, they are also in other ways the same. I will show parallels between the communication tactics and emotion that occur in families and in relations between nations.

In classical political theory, as in Machiavelli, the parallel between personal and political relations was taken as a truism. With the rise of

This chapter is a revised version of chapter 4 of my earlier book (Scheff 1994).

nationalism and the nation state, however, an opposing presumption appeared, that reasons of state were utterly different from those of individuals and mere social groups, and sacrosanct. This presumption still bedevils political theory, since it privileges one social formation at the expense of all others. Kissinger's study of the maneuvers of Metternich can be taken as a representative example of the fallacies which result from this presumption. (I am indebted to Edward Muir for the ideas in this paragraph.)

For a discipline to retain its cutting edge, it is necessary to maintain a balance between accepting the established consensus and challenging it. A scholar need not challenge every tenet in a discipline, starting from scratch with every problem, nor should she or he accept every tenet on faith. Maintaining a judicious balance between skepticism and faith is a demanding task, but a necessary one, if one's work is to be more than a mere exercise.

T. S. Eliot observed that one "cannot inherit a tradition; it must be acquired by hard labor." In modern social science there is a tendency to evade that hard labor by conforming to the established tenets on faith, creating an imbalance. As my contribution toward decreasing the imbalance, in this chapter I challenge not just one article of faith, but two. The first has already been mentioned, the conjecture that societal process is fundamentally different than that between persons, a tenet of theory.

I will also challenge a second, substantive tenet, Germany's war guilt. The problem of the origins of World War I is recognized in the disciplines of history and political science to be of considerable scope and complexity, one of the principal conundrums, like the fall of Rome. George Kennan puts the matter very well (1980):

> Were we not in the face of some monstrous miscalculation – some pervasive failure to read correctly the outward indicators on one's own situation . . . ? Must not the generation of 1914 have been the victim of certain massive misunderstandings, invisible, of course, to themselves but susceptible of identification today . . . ? Was there not a possibility that if we could see how they went wrong, if we could identify the tendencies of mass psychology that led them thus astray, we might see where the dangers lay for ourselves in our attempt to come to terms with some of the great problems of public policy of our own day?

It is also acknowledged that in spite of a very large number of attempts, no one has come even close to solving this problem. Consensus reigns on both these points. Yet at the same time, the great majority of researchers seem to tacitly agree that the solution is to be found in the analysis of aims and actions of one of the nations who fought the war, Germany.

To be sure, there are minority positions, one being taken by those researchers who propose that France played a vital role in instigating the war. Nevertheless, it is stated or assumed in a sizeable majority of studies that the basic causes of the war are to be found in German militarism and imperialism.

In this chapter, I challenge the assumption that Germany was the sole culprit; I claim that all five of the major powers were *equally* responsible for the onset of the war: Germany and Austria-Hungary (The Central Powers), and France, Russia, and England (The Allies).

This argument is a familiar one in family systems analysis; in *interminable* family conflict, it is argued, all members contribute more or less equally to never-ending discord. The onset of World War I was mutually and jointly caused by the five major combatants. To argue that one or the other of the nations was most culpable is to mistake the part for the whole.These nations had created a system of alienated relationships between persons and between groups. Both as individuals and groups, they denied their own responsibility, creating, through this maneuver, their own entrapment.

Most studies of war fall into one of two camps; either they evade or ignore the problem of causation, or alternately, assume that causes are to be found in some discrete event, person, or nation. My argument contradicts this assumption. Our civilization is a *system*, one that produces the character of the actors and the organization of communication. This system is not directly visible to its members; if allowed to function uninterrupted, it will produce intermittent wars in the same way that it produces shoddy consumer goods, prisons and ecological disaster. By becoming aware of the system, perhaps we can escape its imperatives.

The alienation between France and Germany which led to two world wars can be represented dynamically in terms of unacknowledged shame. Alienation, threat to a bond, causes and is caused by shame. Humiliated fury by the French toward Germany after their defeat in 1871 was the prime mover in the part that France played in starting the First World War. Humiliated fury by the Germans toward the French and their allies after their defeat in 1918 created Hitler's appeal to the Germans, which led to the Second World War. Shame and anger are both cause and result of alienation. Since the cues to these emotions are clear in discourse, they allow us to assess the state of the bond in every message exchanged between disputants.

Conflicts of interest and outlook between the major powers do not seem compelling as a cause of World War I. Unlike the situation prior to the Second World War, where there were intractable differences between the worldviews of the Allies and the Axis powers, in 1914 the differences of outlook were relatively minor. Although there were many, they seem in retrospect all capable of being sorted out by negotiation.

Bertrand Russell, who was jailed because of his opposition to the war, provided a clue to the social-emotional causes: he called it a "vanity war." Goffman's (1967) idea of "character contests" strikes a similar chord. In an alienated state, individuals and groups can be quickly humiliated to the point that irrational emotions determine behavior. The dynamics of the headlong rush to war can be understood in terms of unacknowledged shame.

It is possible that other emotions are involved in irrational destruction. It seems to me that the nations of Europe had good reason to fear each other: fear as well as shame might generate rage, as Gaylin (1984) has suggested. Anxiety is another emotion that is frequently evoked to explain irrational behavior. In this chapter I limit my analysis to alieantion and the emotions of shame and anger.

Figure 5.1 shows the major nations involved in World War I. I have placed England at the equipoise because of its last-minute entry into the war.

In order to understand the origins of this war, it is first necessary to consider the relationship between France and Germany, and between these two countries and the other three, in the years prior to the war. Germany and England were by far the most powerful and stable of the group, with France next, followed by Russia and Austria-Hungary. These last two countries were particularly weak and unstable; Russia because it was vast, underdeveloped, led by an incompetent elite, and riven by political and ethnic animosities; Austria-Hungary was smaller and more developed, but its situation was otherwise similar to Russia's. The onset of World War I can be seen as the way in which the weaker members of the family manipulated the strongest.

I argue that this manipulation could only occur in a system of dysfunctional communication tactics and repressed emotions. Unacknowledged shame was transformed into self-righteous anger. Deception, self-deception, and secrecy allowed these emotions to generate an irrational and unnecessary bloodbath.

My analysis suggests that prior to the onset of World War I the relationships *between* the five principal nations were dysfunctional. In the case of England, we now know that *within* that nation, secrecy obtained between the foreign minister and the rest of the nation; vital information was withheld even from the members of the Cabinet.

To show the power of a systems analysis of the origins of war, I reassess a standard work, the chapter on World War I in the Stoessinger (1990) study of the causes of modern wars. This study is a

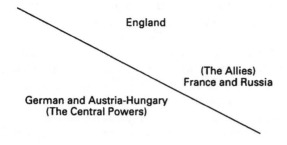

Figure 5.1 The major nations involved in the origins of World War I

useful one for my purposes for several reasons. First, it represents the majority position on World War I; Stoessinger makes a careful analysis which seems to incriminate Germany. His study is stronger than most of the others in two ways, however.

Stoessinger bases his core argument on an analysis of some of the *discourse* that took place between the major powers: Germany, Russia, and England, immediately prior to the onset of the war. Such an approach makes possible a part/whole analysis of social systems, since it offers data at both the level of individuals and of groups. Social structure and emotion ride upon manner and implicature; they are deeply embedded in the *context* and in the *details of specific events*. Secondly, Stoessinger's approach is comparative and analytic: his chapter on the onset of World War I is the first in several similar analyses of the causes of other modern wars.

Stoessinger's study stands out because it combines an interest in the details of the particular case with a comparison with other cases. Most attempts to understand the causes of war are either particularizing and descriptive, or abstract and generalizing, but not both. Either type of specialized study precludes part/whole analysis. Stoessinger's approach allows one to see further than he did by standing on his shoulders, and those of others who have attempted to deal with this problem.

Of the many efforts, the one most frequently praised is that of Joll (1984). Although it is balanced and temperate, it is also abstract and descriptive. A review of the various earlier studies, on which most current scholarship is based, can be found in Remak (1967). Although they come to no definite conclusions, I admire the dispassionate tone of most the authors in the volume edited by Evans and von Strandmann (1988), which stands in stark contrast to the narrowness or partisanship, both open and covert, of most of the standard studies.

However, it is only fair to say that the chapter by one of the editors, von Strandman, is highly partisan in arguing the majority position, that Germany was most guilty of instigating the war.

Like all of the other analyses of the origins of World War I published since 1977, von Strandmann does not cite the study by Goodspeed (1977) which will play a large part in my analysis. Of the studies published since 1984, von Strandmann is the only one to cite Kennan's (1984) study, which is quoted at some length at the end of this chapter. Von Strandmann cites Kennan's study three times, but very briefly. He criticizes several specific points that Kennan made, especially his conclusion that the alliance between France and Russia made World War I inevitable. But his criticisms are weakly documented, and ignore Kennan's overall thesis. His response to Kennan's powerful study is superficial, almost a formality.

Of course, there is no way of knowing why the two most powerful recent studies of the origins of World War I have been all but ignored. One possibility is that they both go so much against the grain of the established position among experts that they have found it expedient to act as if they do not exist. If such were the case, it would not be the first time such a reaction has occurred in the history of scholarship.

A useful comparative study of the causes of war can be found in a book of great scope by Blainey (1988), a survey of the virtually innumerable wars fought between nations since 1700. Although it is also descriptive and abstract, like Joll and most of the other better studies, the author deftly points out the utter uselessness of conventional wisdom about the causes of wars. Although he does not make the point explicit, Blainey's analysis strongly suggests that we do not understand human behavior, neither in the small or in the large. Like the causes of most human actions, the causes of war remain a mystery and an enigma.

Given the large number of prior studies on the origins of the war, and the diversity of their approaches to the problem, some comments on how the problem has been defined to this point are in order. Some of the earlier studies are purely descriptive, or attempt to be. They ignore the problem of causation, or at least do not deal with it explicitly. The way in which authors title their studies is usually revealing of their overall approach. Descriptive studies use the phrase "the coming of World War I" (Schmitt 1930; Laqueur and Moss 1966; Evans and von Strandmann 1966) or some similarly passive construction, such as "the approach of the First World War" (Bosworth 1983; Berghahn 1973) or "the outbreak of World War I" (Lee 1963). Kennan's (1984) study is an exception. Although he used a passive construction in his subtitle (*The Coming of the First World War*), his study moves from description to generalization, as will be discussed below. Several studies have titles which are completely descriptive, since they involve only a date, such as *July 1914*.

Another common approach is to explicitly discuss causation, but only briefly and in passing. For example, in what is otherwise a useful and balanced discussion, Sontag's (1933) approach to causation is to reject an analysis made by other authors. He acknowledges that Germany should share some of the blame for beginning the war, but rejects the contention that Germany alone was responsible. However, he does not offer his own counter-hypothesis. This kind of maneuver is found in many of the studies.

The most common approach is to make a strong and explicit statement about causality, but only about one country, usually Germany. The most notorious example is the work of Fritz Fischer (1967; 1969; 1974). One of the chief criticisms of his work is that he fails to compare the causal sequences he attributes to Germany with similar sequences in the other major participants (Kock 1972; Moses 1975). The contributions in this vein may not be completely erroneous, but they are certainly narrow and incomplete, neglecting the big picture in favor of the small.

Studies in this genre usually use a word or phrase in their titles that is stronger than the "outbreak" or "coming" of World War I. Some of the title words in these studies are "causes," "roots," "genesis," and two words which imply causation, "culpability" and "guilt," as in Barnes (1928). The most commonly used word is "origins," as in Fay (1930), Albertini (1952–57), Lafore (1965), Fleming (1968), Turner (1970), Steiner (1977), Kieger (1983), Lieven (1983), Joll (1984), Hentig (1989), and Remak (1968). I will single out Remak's study for criticism not because of its weakness but because of its strength. It comes closest to the kind of analysis I believe to be needed: an assessment of causation that is comparative, rather than limited to a single country, person, or event.

Remak (1968, 133–143) ranks the major participants in terms of the part they played in instigating the war, in this order: Austria, Serbia, Russia, Germany, England, and France. The eleven pages in which he explains his rankings, from the most culpable (Austria), to the least, France, form a coherent narrative. But his explanation seems arbitrary, if not chaotic. His reason for ranking Austria, Serbia, and Russia so high is that they all made overt moves toward war before the other three powers, either mobilization or a declaration of war, or both. He ranks Germany, England and France lower because they went to war only after the first three had done so.

Remak's explanation of the ranking of Germany, England and

France relative to each other shifts from the proximate issue of overt war moves to more distal issues. Germany is ranked fourth largely because it had planned, for many years, a highly detailed aggressive move against France, through Belgium, the Schlieffen plan. England is ranked next because of its imperialism and control of the seas for 100 years prior to the war. France was least culpable, in Remak's view, because it was attacked, rather than being an attacker, and did not have aggressive war plans, as did Germany, nor large number of colonies and control of the seas, as England did.

Although Remak's analysis is thoughtful, its piecemeal nature raises a host of questions. With respect to the high ranking given to Germany, it has been pointed out by many of Fischer's critics that there is a vast difference between having war plans and instigating war. Remak chooses to ignore the more proximate question of comparing each of the countries' response to the crisis, moment by moment. The same criticism applies to his explanation of England's rank; Remak neglects to tell us the causal links whereby imperialism and control of the seas led to war.

Finally, perhaps the most glaring difficulty in Remak's analysis, is his ranking of France as the least responsible for the onset of the war. His explanation, that France was attacked by Germany, refers only to the highly visible surface of conflict, without taking into account the underlying realities. He acknowledges that France conspired with Russia against Germany and Austria, but does not seem to give this fact the same weight as the overt attack by Germany. Remak, like all the other researchers who have sought to understand the origins of the war, faces the difficult problem of selecting and comparing motives and actions of a large number of individuals and groups in an extremely complex situation.

Remak's ranking of Austria, Serbia, and Russia high in culpability implies a neglect of the covert springs of behavior in favor of the overt. In particular, it ignores or discounts the possibility of *conspiracy* as a key factor in causation of collective events. As I will demonstrate below, French diplomacy may have played a considerable role in the genesis of the war; in particular, the evidence suggests that French diplomacy led to a conspiracy with Russia and Serbia. This conspiracy seems to have led to the assassination of the Archduke and in the preemptive mobilization by Russia, two key events in the chain that led to war. In the absence of a theory, it is tempting to point only to the most obvious element in a situation, simplifying it by using only common sense concepts.

It seems to me that the arbitrariness and confusion to be found in the explanations of this particular problem grow out of a more general problem in the human studies, the lack of explicit models of causation of any kind of behavior. In the absence of a commonly accepted model, each author is left with the unenviable task of creating his or her own model. I believe that this is the main reason that so little progress has been made in understanding the origins of World War I and other wars. I will return to this issue at the end of this essay.

In this context, my reassessment of Stoessinger's study is both appreciative and critical. I accept his analysis of the parts played by Austria-Hungary and by Germany in the immediate triggering of the war. This part of his analysis is masterful. But I extend it by adding the roles played by France, Russia, and England. His portrayal of them as victims of the aggression by the Central Powers seems to me erroneous. On the contrary, I argue, all played more or less equal roles in causing the war. To persist in locating causation in one or the other nation may signal that the scholar has become almost as emotionally enmeshed in the conflict as the participants. Whatever the tone of voice or content, it is difficult to avoid blaming, or alternatively, whitewashing, if one nation is singled out for analysis.

For his assessment of the causes of World War I, Stoessinger analyzed three exchanges that occurred immediately prior to the outbreak of hostilities. The first is between the Kaiser and Franz Joseph, the Emperor of Austria-Hungary, Germany's ally (pp 3–5). The second set is the "Willy–Nicky" telegrams (pp. 11–14). Willy is the Kaiser Wilhelm of Germany, and Nicky is the Czar Nicholas of Russia. (Willy and Nicky were first cousins). The third set is two notes from Lord Grey to the Kaiser, and the Kaiser's private responses to them (pp 13–14).

Stoessinger's analysis focuses on the Kaiser's reactions, since he is the recipient of all three sets of communications. He says nothing about the communications given and received by France, thus entirely omitting one of the principal parties. I will argue that Stoessinger's method of selection of texts leads him to erroneous conclusions. His analysis is doomed from the outset, since it begins by excluding one of the parts of the system, France, rather than considering all of them.

Stoessinger is not alone among analysts of World War I in excluding France from consideration, although few of them do so completely. A more representative method is to downgrade France's role by making it subsidiary to that of some other nation. An example is provided by one analysis (Williamson 1988) which discusses France only insofar as it is an ally to Russia. Williamson's discussion begins on a tendentious note (p. 225): "World War I began in eastern Europe. The war started when Serbia, Austria-Hungary, Russia and Germany decided that war or the risk of war was an acceptable policy option."

The implication of these two sentences, which exclude France from consideration, is that wars can only be started by nations whose boundaries are contiguous to the location of the earliest declaration of war, i.e. Austria-Hungary and Serbia, surely a flagrant *non sequitur*. By this kind of reasoning, since Chile is in South America, then the US could have had nothing to do with the destabilization of the Allende government. Nevertheless, the subsequent discussion brings in French activities as if they were subservient to those of Russia. Like Stoessinger's, Williamson's conclusions seem to be determined by his initial assumptions. I will argue, however, that in order to resolve this problem, it will be necessary to consider all of the nations, the parts, and the system in which they were involved, the whole.

Family systems theory (Bowen 1978) suggests that in cases of *interminable* conflict, all parties are more or less equally involved in causing the conflict. The same theory also suggests that it is impossible to point to a single event as causal; in interminable conflict, each event is part of a long causal chain. My analysis of the onset of WW1 will illustrate and amplify these basic ideas.

On June 28 1914, the Archduke of Austria and his wife were assassinated during a visit to Sarajevo. On July 5, the Kaiser pledged Germany's "faithful support" to Austria for punitive action against Serbia. As Stoessinger points out, Wilhelm used a special term in his declaration of support, promising to be "Nibelungentreue." The Nibelung is a blood bond from Teutonic legend which is sacred and irrevocable. The Kaiser was deeply attached to Archduke Ferdinand and his wife. When he heard of their assassination, he reacted emotionally, pledging himself to support Austria whatever the consequences. This was an utterly reckless act, since it amounted to giving Austria a blank check. This act represents Germany's hand on the final trigger.

Austria-Hungary had been hesitating about responding to the assassination, because Berchtold, the Foreign Minister, was unsure of German support. But when the Kaiser sent Berchtold a blank check, he issued an ultimatum to Serbia that contained a series of conditions arrogant and insulting enough to insure non-compliance. The phrasing of this ultimatum, calculated to insult, was Austria's contribution to the actual starting of the war. When Serbia failed to comply to the letter, Austria declared war on Serbia.

When the Kaiser learned of the Austrian declaration of war against Serbia, he sent a conciliatory note to his cousin, the Czar of Russia, offering to act as a mediator, and to hold back Austria from fighting until a peaceful settlement could be reached.

It is with the gravest concern that I hear of the impression which the action of Austria against Serbia is creating in your country . . . With regard to the hearty and tender friendship which binds us both from long ago with firm ties, I am exerting my utmost influence to induce the Austrians to deal straightly to arrive at a satisfactory understanding with you. I confidently hope you will help me in my efforts to smooth over difficulties that may still arise.

Your very sincere and devoted friend and cousin.

At virtually the same moment, Nicholas had also sent a note to the Kaiser:

Am glad you are back. In this most serious moment, I appeal to you to help me. An ignoble war has been declared on a weak country. The indignation in Russia shared fully by me is enormous. I foresee that very soon I shall be overwhelmed by the pressure brought upon me and be forced to take extreme measures which will lead to war. To try and avoid such a calamity as a European war, I beg you in the name of our old friendship to do what you can to stop your allies from going too far.

The telegrams appear to suggest that both monarchs wanted to avoid war.

Wilhelm responded to the Czar's telegram by wiring his cousin not to take military measures that Austria would interpret to be threatening, i.e. mobilization. The Czar answered on July 30:

Thank you heartily for your quick answer. The military measures which have now come into force were decided five days ago for reasons of defense on account of Austria's preparations. I hope from all my heart that these measures won't in any way interfere with your part as mediator which I greatly value. We need your strong pressure on Austria to come to an understanding with us.

The tone of the Kaiser's response abruptly changed when he received this note. His comments on the margin of the telegram have been preserved:

The net has been suddenly thrown over our head, and England sneeringly reaps the most brilliant success of her persistently prosecuted, purely anti-German world policy, against which we have proved ourselves helpless, while she twists the noose of our political and economic destruction out of our fidelity to Austria, as we squirm isolated in the net.

Instead of responding to the Czar's continuing support for conciliation in the last two sentences, the Kaiser reacted to a detail in the second sentence that he apparently had not known before, that Russia had made the decision for mobilization five days earlier.

The second exchange also involves the Kaiser's reaction to a telegram, this time from Lord Grey, who warned, on July 30: " . . . if war breaks out, it [would] be the greatest catastrophe that the world has ever seen." The Kaiser's reaction is again highly emotional, as his note on the telegram indicates: "This means they will attack us; Aha! The common cheat."

On one of Grey's later notes, the Kaiser wrote:

> According to this the Czar has simply been tricking us with this appeal for assistance and has deceived us . . . Then I must mobilize too. . . . The hope that I would not let his mobilization measures disturb me in my role of mediator is childish, and solely intended to lure us into the mire . . . I regard my mediation action as brought to an end.

Stoessinger gives a name to the emotional quality of the Kaiser's reactions to Grey's notes; he calls it "paranoia" (p. 13), an interpretation which I challenge. Stoessinger also interprets the notes from Grey and from the Czar to be entirely in good faith, which I also will challenge. After receiving the notes from the Kaiser and from Grey, the Kaiser issued an ultimatum to the Russians to immediately demobilize. When they refused, he ordered full mobilization for Germany. Since Russia had already begun full mobilization, the two movements together meant war. These telegrams and notes, and the Kaiser's reactions to them constitute the basic data for this chapter. The rest of what follows is my interpretation of the context and the meaning of these texts.

One purpose of my analysis is to challenge and modify Stoessinger's interpretation of these communications. Before beginning, I will describe the larger study of which his comments on the onset of World War I are a part. Stoessinger compares the beginnings of six other sets of wars in addition to World War I: Hitler's attack on Russia, the US wars in Korea and Vietnam, the wars between India and Pakistan, those between Israel and the Arabs, and finally, the Iran–Iraq war. By comparing the onset of these wars, he comes to several conclusions about the causes of war.

His first conclusion concerns the role of leaders of nations, as compared to impersonal forces (p. 209, emphasis added):

> Conventional wisdom has blamed the alliance system for the spread of the war. Specifically,the argument runs, Kaiser Wilhelm's alliance with Austria dragged Germany into the war against the Allied Powers. This analysis, however, totally ignores the role of the Kaiser's personality during the gathering crisis. Suppose Wilhelm had had the fortitude to continue his role as mediator and restrain Austria instead of engaging in paranoid delusions and accusing England of conspiring against Germany. The disaster might have been averted; the conventional wisdom would then have praised the alliance system for saving the peace instead of blaming it for causing the war. In truth the emotional balance or lack of balance of the German Kaiser turned out to be absolutely crucial.

It seems to me that this conclusion is vague and misleading. My interpretation is that *the personalities of leaders had less to do with causing the war than the system of relationships and communication tactics in which the leaders were involved.* The leaders were but parts of a more complex whole, the civilization in which they and their nations functioned.

Stoessinger's second conclusion concerns the role of the leaders' misperceptions. He argues that wars are caused by leaders' mistaken perceptions about themselves, their allies, and their adversaries (210). They have what Stoessinger calls delusions about their own strength and virtue, and that of their allies, and the enemy's weakness and deceit. They also believed that a war was inevitable, in itself a powerful cause of war (211).

Both the Kaiser and his ally, Franz Joseph, the monarch of Austria-Hungary, had nothing but contempt for the fighting prowess of the Russians, which turned out to be a grave error. Stoessinger provides many examples of such misperceptions and delusions on both sides in each of his seven cases. My analysis supports, extends and conceptually organizes Stoessinger's interpretation. Misperception of self and others is a facet of bimodal alienation in a social system: alienation within (engulfment) and between (isolation) disputing groups.

My critique of his study focuses on three interrelated issues. First, Stoessinger's approach is *atheoretical*. His interpretations and findings are couched in the commonsense terms of ordinary language, rather than using concepts and propositions generated by a theory. The second and third problems follow from his lack of theory. Secondly, although he is dealing with a social system, his concepts and findings are *individualistic*; they concern leaders and their personalities, rather than the relationships between the leaders and their communication tactics. Thirdly finally, his data are *incomplete*, as already indicated. He leaves out one of the principal participants, France, from his analysis. If exchanges between France and Russia, and between France and England are included, a different picture emerges with respect to what Stoessinger calls the Kaiser's "paranoia."

As already indicated, my analysis will draw upon family systems theory, as stated by Bowen (1978). This theory concerns communication tactics between and within parties to a conflict. To understand the role of intentional secrecy and deception, Bowen's conception of triangling is crucially important. He noted that in what he called dysfunctional families, two parties to a dispute seldom negotiate directly with each other with regard to the dispute (*leveling*, Satir 1978). Rather one party, A, conspires with another party C, against B, in secret, i.e. excluding B, instead of negotiating with B directly.

Triangling was a predominant pattern of French diplomacy in the years preceding World War I, with France extremely active in con-spiring with Russia and with England against the Central Powers. The same pattern can also be seen within and between nations, with French leaders communicating secretly with English leaders, but excluding their own countries.

One of the corollaries of family systems theory is that in dysfunc-tional families, it is usually a mistake to isolate a single member as the culprit. In interminable conflicts, not only is there no single event that is a cause, there is also no single member to blame. All are caught up in a dysfunctional *system* of conflict. Blaming one party to an interminable conflict serves two functions: if we blame one single event or party, we are apt to ignore the systemic nature of the conflict, a way of denying the social nature of the human condition. Secondly, blaming serves to perpetuate the conflict; one becomes as emotionally enmeshed as the parties themselves, which destroys objectivity and impartiality.

Although the majority of historians still single out Germany as the prime instigator of World War I, a countercurrent points to France as equally culpable. The clearest and most detailed statement of this point of view is by the Canadian historian D. J. Goodspeed (1977). Since his argument bears directly on the context of the discourse I will be interpreting, I will give a brief summary of his position.

Goodspeed argues that of all the major powers, France was the most powerfully motivated to start a war (1977, viii, 6, 20, 91, and *passim* in chapters 1-5, book I). He proposes that France experienced its defeat in the Franco-Prussian War (1871) as a humiliation, one that continued to rankle because of the loss of its provinces of Alsace and Lorraine. He argues that the French government's policies during the years from 1871–1914 were strongly influenced by the motive of *revanche* (revenge). This motive was seldom publicly avowed, as suggested by Gambetta's advice to the French about the defeat of 1871: "Speak of it never; think of it always," a counsel of obsession, denial, and bypassing of shame.

Goodspeed argues that the French of this period were obsessed with recovering their lost provinces. This obsession seemed to in-crease rather than decrease with the passage of time; the French feared that the population of Alsace-Lorraine were becoming Germa-nized as the young people learned that language rather than French in their schooling.

In order to remove what the French considered a stain on their honor, after the Franco-Prussian war, France created a secret alliance with Russia, the Dual Entente, for mutual aid against Germany. Even though France was a republic and Russia an absolutist monarchy, France sought to help develop Russia into mighty military power, as an ally in its defeat of Germany. In particular, France provided the loans that would enable Russia to build a railroad network, so that its troops would have the mobility needed to help defeat the Central Powers.

Although French diplomatic policy toward Germany became aggressive immediately following defeat in the Franco-Prussian War, matters came to a head in 1912, with the rise to power of Poincaré as the French Premier. His appointment was precipitated by the Agdir crisis, a quarrel between France and Germany over the French plan to acquire Morocco as a colony. France's wish to "annex" Morocco was foiled by Germany's resistance to the plan. The French public thought the premier, Caillaux, had been too submissive to the Germans.

Poincaré, a native of Lorraine, would be another matter entirely. He had said publicly that his generation "had no reason for existence other than the hope of recovering the lost provinces." When he came to power, French secret activity against Germany became much more intense and aggressive.

Two thrusts of this activity will concern us here: the events leading to the assassination of Archduke Ferdinand, the immediate trigger of the war, and the attempts of the French to gain England as an ally in a possible war with Germany. Goodspeed argues that these two trains of events were intimately connected.

It is clear that England, unlike the other four major powers, attempted to remain neutral in the event of the war, at least at the level of public actions. France and Russia were pledged allies, as were Germany and Austria-Hungary. Both sets of allies sought repeatedly in the years leading up to war to assure themselves of England's position: the Entente wanted assurance that England would enter the war, the Central Powers, that it would not. Until the very day of mobilization, England never gave a clear answer to either question. The leadership actually equivocated: although allowing Germany to expect that it would remain neutral, it planned for military participation with the French.

Goodspeed argues that England's refusal to make a clear pledge to either side was one of the proximate causes of the war (p. 131). If the Central Powers knew that England would fight on the side of the Entente, the Kaiser might have been less careless about pledging his support for whatever action Austria-Hungary decided to take toward Serbia. The Kaiser was certain that the Central Powers could defeat the Entente if it was not aided by England, but he had doubts about defeating the three powers together. Similarly, France's leaders were convinced that the Entente would win with the aid of England, but anxious about winning without it.

Because of these two conjectures by French leadership, capturing England as an ally became the principal thrust of French diplomacy. Although not able to secure a formal treaty, the French gained a secret alliance, because the English leadership was a house divided. Although a majority of the Cabinet and of the public would never pledge involvement in a war on the Continent, a minority of the leadership, Grey, Asquith, Churchill and others, did. They were able to do so because Grey was the Foreign Minister, and because he was willing to act in secret.

Beginning in 1905, Grey arranged for secret meetings between the French and English General Staffs, to plan for cooperation in the event of a war. He kept these meetings secret not only from the Central Powers, but also from his own Cabinet. By the time Poincaré came to power, England's involvement in a war was virtually a *fait accompli*. Grey and Poincaré triangled not only against Germany, but against England.

Less than a year after he took office, Poincaré took care to secure an opinion from the French General Staff as to the probable outcome of a war, should it occur during his premiership. He was told that the advantage would be on the side of France, assuming that Russia and England were its allies. It would appear that from the moment he secured this favorable opinion, all of his considerable energy and skill were devoted to triggering a war.

Poincaré's problem was to instigate war in a way that assured the entry of Russia and England on the side of France. He probably assumed that if the French began a war by marching on Alsace and Lorraine, neither Russia nor England would involve themselves. He may have decided that the ideal trigger would have its location in the Balkans, and its ostensible cause, an action by one of the Central Powers. That is, the location in the Balkans would insure Russian entry into the war, and the aggressive action by a Central Power, English entry.

Goodspeed traces the incredibly intricate plotting by the French which led to the assassination of the Archduke. It is so byzantine that I will only give the briefest summary here. Poincaré conspired with the pro-war group in the Russian government to encourage nationalism in the Balkans against the domination of Austria-Hungary, particularly Serbian nationalism. Russia's motive was to reassert its dominance in that area against both Austria and Turkey.

In particular, Poincaré guaranteed that France would support Russia and the Balkan nations against Austria-Hungary, even if it meant war with the Central Powers. French guarantees were essential in this matter, since without them neither Russia nor Serbia would have acted. That is, Russia would not take on Austria-Hungary alone, because of the likelihood that Germany would also be involved. For any of the Balkan nations, action without Russian guarantees would simply have meant annexation by Austria-Hungary.

Under these conditions, Russian diplomats constructed a plot with the most violent and irresponsible of the Balkan governments, Serbia, to assassinate the Archduke. The actual assassins were members of a secret terrorist group, but as Goodspeed shows, this group was led by the highest officials of the Serbian government, and coached by Russian military advisors. However, these details became known only in 1925 (Goodspeed 1977, 114–118).

We can use the concept of *interlocking triangles* to describe the web of deception which led to the assassination. Instead of negotiating directly with Germany about their dispute, France triangled with Russia, who triangled with Serbia, who triangled with the terrorist group, three interlocking triangles which excluded the three parties whose interests were connected with the outcome: Germany, Austria-Hungary, and England. It is possible that not even Lord Grey, who conspired with the French about military cooperation against the Germans, had knowledge of the assassination plot, much less the English anti-war majority. England was as much a target of the conspiracy as the Central Powers.

Given knowledge of the interlocking triangles described above, the Kaiser's emotional reaction to the Czar's and Grey's notes takes on a new meaning. I will consider his reactions to Grey's notes first, since the backdrop of Germany's attempts to get assurances of England's neutrality casts the matter in a new light. England had refused to pledge its neutrality, but also would not promise to enter the war on the side of France and Russia. In this context, Grey's warning about a war being "the greatest catastrophe the world has ever seen" can be read as the first indication of England's commitment to fight. To clarify this point, it will be necessary to consider some details in German strategic thinking.

According to Germany's war plans, France and Russia alone could be readily defeated, even though waging a war on two fronts against a much larger combined army would seem disadvantageous to Germany. The Russian Army, even though much larger than Germany's, was also more ponderous due to the lack of railway and other transportation. The German plan was to attack France first, safely ignoring the slow-to-mobilize Russian armies. After quickly defeating the French by a massive thrust through Belgium, the entire German army could be brought to bear on defeating Russia.

The Kaiser guessed, however, that the likelihood of a quick victory depended on England not entering the war. If an English army landed in France to help defend Paris, a quick victory became problematic. The actual events in the first month of the war confirmed the accuracy of this idea. Russia was slow to mobilize, as expected. Had it not been for the presence of a British Army, and the stiff resistance of the Belgians, Paris would probably have fallen with the German attack, and with it the whole nation.

The implication of Grey's telegram was that England would enter the war on the side of France, since a war of the Central Powers against France and Russia would be unlikely to last long, and there-fore would not be the catastrophe that Grey predicts. It is important to realize as Poincaré had that Lord Grey would have made exactly the same calculations. In his memoirs he reports that the reason that he and his clique decided for war was that they did not want France to fall under German domination, which they thought would happen if France and Russia fought against the Central Powers alone.

For these reasons, Grey's telegram implies the very encirclement that the Kaiser complains about in his private response. Even if the Kaiser had been unaware of the joint war planning by the French and English General Staffs, the chain of reasoning discussed above implies it. The Kaiser's emotional reaction was not paranoid, as Stoessinger argues, but closer to being a sudden awakening to the realities around him.

The Kaiser's reaction to the Czar's admission that mobilization had been decided five days earlier (July 25) can also be interpreted in a new light. It would suggest to the Kaiser that Russian mobilization had been planned *prior* to the declaration of war of Austria on Serbia on July 28. That is to say, although the Austrian mobilization was only partial, aimed at Serbia, full mobilization by the Russians could only be aimed at the Central Powers, implying collusion between France and Russia at the very least, and perhaps England as well.

Since the Russians had by far the largest army, its mobilization had to be the signal for mobilization by all of the other powers, so that it was virtually a declaration of war. Had Russian mobilization been partial and subsequent to Austria's, it would have signaled only defense. But since it was complete and prior to Austria's move, it was a clear signal of offensive purpose and pre-planning.

Taken out of this complex and extended context, the Kaiser's highly emotional reaction to the two sets of notes can easily be seen as violent over-reactions (as in Stoessinger's view that the second note from the Czar "completely destroyed [the Kaiser's] sense of balance" (Stoessinger 1990, 13). However, in context, his responses seem to me the normal response of one who justifiably felt betrayed.

A closer comparison of the contents of the Czar's telegrams, as against the Kaiser's, provides further support for Goodspeed's interpretation. In this comparison, I draw upon the description of dysfunctional communication tactics found in family system theory (Bowen 1978). I show how microscopic analysis of texts support an argument at the macrolevel.

In the Czar's first note, there are several indications of *indirection, denial of responsibility* and *threat*. There is a slight indirection in the fourth sentence: "The indignation in Russia fully shared by me is enormous." A more direct acknowledgment of responsibility would have been a sentence like *"I am indignant, as are my subjects." (As already indicated, the asterisk * is used as the symbol for a "counterfactual", an imagined statement.)

The choice of the word *indignation* particularly suggests a certain kind of anger, self-righteous anger, and therefore, perhaps, rather than anger alone, shame-anger, with the shame component unacknowledged. This sentence is also used to prepare for the intense denial of responsibility and threat in the next sentence: "I foresee that very soon I will be overwhelmed by the pressure brought on me and be forced to take extreme measures which will lead to war."

Although phrased in polite language, the Czar is actually threatening war, and at the same time denying his own responsibility for it, and even the responsibility of his countrymen; it is not his fault or theirs, but Austria's. The Czar seems to see the coming war as exterior and constraining, with himself and his countrymen playing no part in its causation.

By comparison with the Czar's note, the Kaiser's is a monument to directness, acknowledgement of responsibility, and absence of threat. He simply offers his services as mediator, who will restrain the Austrians.

The Czar's second note continues in the same vein as his first. The second sentence contains a denial of his responsibility for his own actions, as did the first: "The military measures which have now come into force were decided five days ago for reasons of defense on account of Austria's preparations." It is Austria that is to blame for his actions, not the Czar himself.

Note also the awkward syntax in the two occurrences of the passive voice in this sentence; he does not say: *"I have decided to mobilize the army," which would have been direct and forceful. The indirection, vagueness and denial of personal responsibility in this sentence strongly suggest either deception, self-deception, or both. Was the Czar feeling a guilty conscience, or trying to deceive his cousin, or both?

In any case, both of the Czar's telegrams strongly suggest bimodal alienation. The threat implied in both telegrams, and the blaming of Austria, both imply isolation from without, against both Germany and Austria. The vagueness, passive tenses and indirection all suggest that the Czar is fooling himself by denying his own feelings and responsibility for the threats he is making. In engulfed relations, one gives up parts of oneself to be loyal to one's group. The giving up of parts of self corresponds to what Seeman (1975) calls "self-estrangement" in his analysis of alienation.

To further support my argument about the Czar, however, it would be necessary to find addition biographical evidence from his earlier letters. Does he have a record of passivity and denial that is characteristic engulfment not only in this crisis, but in all of his dealings? My impression is that he does not. On the contrary, he was usually headstrong and defiant. But an examination of his letters would be needed to clinch this point. The issue here is of filling in the rungs of the part/whole ladder. What is needed is more biographical evidence concerning the relationships attested by earlier letters, to see if they differentiate them from his behavior at this crucial moment.

I now return to the historical record for collateral evidence that is relevant to my interpretation of these texts. The issue of the early mobilization of the Russian army brings us to the most bizarre episode that Goodspeed and others unearthed in the events leading to the war, the meeting of Poincaré and his entourage with the Czar in St. Petersburg on July 15–18. This meeting occurred immediately following the assassination of the Archduke, and before the Czar's decision to mobilize.

The trip of the French premier to meet the head of a foreign state would be unusual enough whatever the circumstances. But in this case, since it took place when the peace of Europe was at stake (because of the assassination), the eyes of the world were upon it. What transpired during the three-day meeting? The answer is, no one knows. There was no announcement of the outcome at the time by participants from either side, or afterwards. What is extraordinary is that the mystery has never been removed, since none of the participants clarified the matter, not even in their memoirs. Comments in the memoirs are brief, bland and vague. Whatever occurred has been obliterated from history.

In the face of such an absence of information, Goodspeed has examined the circumstantial evidence that would link the meeting to the onset of the war. He argues that since convictions in courts of law can be made upon the basis of circumstantial evidence alone, scholars should not hesitate to make similar judgments, since the stakes in a case like this are so much higher.

Goodspeed proposes that the evidence all points to collusion between the French and the Russians to instigate the war. In effect, Poincaré and the Czar could have decided that the Russians would mobilize before the Austrians. From the French point of view, such a premature action would have a triple advantage: it would insure a war, it would insure Russian entry into the war, and provide a military advantage to the French. That is, the quicker Russian mobilization, the sooner German troops would be needed on the Russian front, removing them from an attack on France.

It may be significant that the official French diplomatic history of the war goes to the extraordinary length of stating that the Austrian general mobilization occurred first, and uses forged documents to support the claim. It is also significant that all of the participants sought to put their own actions in the best light, but only the French and the Russians used forged documents in their official histories (Goodspeed 1977, 137). Secrecy and deceit appear to have been instrumental not only in the causation of the war, but in continuing the interminable conflict from which it grew.

Conclusion

In the light of this discussion, Simmel's support for the social functions of secrecy (and, more recently, Komarovsky 1967) seems ill-founded. This position, for which there is actually little evidence, is on the verge of becoming another article of faith in modern social science. For further evidence which seems to contradict Simmel, see Cottle (1980), which suggests that children's shameful secrets have disastrous effects, and Retzinger (1991) who shows how deception and secrecy produce alienation in marriages.

The broadest critique of secrecy is by Bok (1983). Although her analysis is comprehensive and precisely balanced, her conclusions are overwhelmingly opposed to secrecy in public matters, except under highly delimited circumstances. My analysis supports and extends hers by adding the component of self-deception: secrecy, deception, and self-deception support and feed into each other, generating and reflecting alienation between and within persons and nations. Far from being functional, as Simmel claimed, secrecy and deception seem to be generated by, and supported by the status quo, the social arrangements which distribute power, wealth and esteem.

Following the lead of family systems theory, it may be useful to see the major wars of the last 100 years as an interminable conflict in the family of nations. My analysis of the origins of the First World War points in this direction. All five of the large nations which began it can be seen as equally involved. In the long-term, the militarism of Germany and France, and the secret diplomacy of France were certainly factors. In the period immediately preceding hostilities, the Kaiser's blank check to Austria, the active instigation of war against Serbia by Austria-Hungary, and by France and Russia against Germany was equally important.

A systems analysis suggests that the listing of factors, however detailed and accurate, is not a parsimonious explanation. In family systems, conflicts of long duration and limitless destructiveness are caused not by individual parties or specific events, but by the elemental structure-process of the social system in which they occur. Since 1870, nations in the world system have been and still are trapped in bi-modal alienation: engulfment within nations, isolation between them.

War fever, the lust for conflict, whatever the cost, can occur because *members of the public within each nation maintain a false solidarity (engulfment) with their fellow nationals, and fail to identify with the enemy as persons like themselves (isolation).*

My emphasis on the importance of deception and self-deception in understanding social systems is also found in O'Connor (1987, 182–183):

> Theory is no more or less than the critique of the self-deceptions which we use to legitimate to ourselves the deceptions of others. This means simply that we cannot know why we are deceived or why we deceive others until we first know why others deceive themselves and why we deceive ourselves. No trust, hence no morality, is possible without knowledge of our own and others' self-deceptions.

It might be argued that by concentrating entirely on alienation, my analysis has concerned only subjective causes, neglecting the "objective" causes of wars, such as scarcity of resources, and cultural and linguistic differences, for example. However, I counter by proposing that objective differences can always be negotiated, where there is free communication and an absence of unacknowledged emotions. That is, however great the conflict of interests, there will always be some most rewarding or perhaps least punishing compromise.

In some ways the arguments which favor objective causes are another form of denial and projection: it is not we humans who make war, but objective conditions. If not tempered by part/whole understanding, structural explanations of human actions inadvertently become part of the causal chain which leads to war.

The "realist" interpretations of conflict insist that material conditions, money, territory, and technology play a part in causing war, which of course they do. But these same interpretations also insist, *sub voce*, that *only* material conditions are causal, surely a non sequitur. Such an argument seems blind to the force of human motives, perceptions, and emotions responding to material conditions. It represents an *a priori* assumption that of the two parts of human action, stimulus and response, only the stimulus is causal.

Family system theorists have pointed out how unending conflict is generated in families when members focus only on *topics*, such as money, sex, children, etc., ignoring relationships and feelings. If members are disrespectful in their *manner*, they insult each other continuously. In this way, *any* topic can become the cause of conflict. The obverse is that if members are respectful in their manner, any conflict can be resolved or at least reduced to manageable levels.

The realists' arguments about material conditions are parallel to the focus on topics in family systems. To paraphrase Shakespeare's character Hotspur (*Henry IV*), anything can become a cause for fighting when honor is at stake.

To this point, my analysis has concentrated on the actions of leaders of nations, with little attention to the masses of people within these nations. A true systems theory, however, implies that the peoples of these nations are just as much a part of the chain of causation as their leaders. This postulate gains support from the work of Eksteins (1989), who has described the crowds in Berlin, St. Petersburg, Vienna, Paris, and London (pp. 56–64).

In Berlin and the other major cities in Germany, large crowds began to form on Saturday, July 25, awaiting Serbia's answer to the Austrian ultimatum. Beginning on Thursday, July 30, excited crowds fill the streets of Berlin, remaining "an almost permanent feature of the German capital for the next seven crucial days" (p. 58). Both in arriving and leaving their sessions in the capital, the Kaiser and his advisors have difficulty getting through the throng on the Unter den Linden on the next day: "All the major decision makers are confronted directly by the massive outpouring of enthusiasm from the Berlin public. None of them has ever witnessed such demonstrations before. None of them can ignore the popular mood" (pp. 59–60). By August 1, the crowd has grown to a huge size, estimated at 100–300,000 people (p. 60). The order for German mobilization has "been made against the back drop of mass enthusiasm. No political leader could have resisted the popular pressures for decisive action" (p. 61): "Elsewhere in Germany, whether in Frankfurt, Munich, Breslau or Karlsruhe, the scenes are similar. . . . Emotionally Germany has declared war by July 31 . . . certainly on Russia and France. Given the intensity of public feelings, it is inconceivable that the Kaiser can, at this point, turn back" (p. 62). Although Eksteins does not make the point explicitly, he implies that similar mob scenes were occurring in all of the other capitals. In the illustrations (following p. 174) he shows photographs of vast crowds in Berlin, Paris, St. Petersburg and London. The crowd, he says, is as potent a force in causing the war as the leaders. A *war fever* swept through the participating nations, involving virtually everyone, as suggested by a systems theory approach.

Even the leading intellectuals were caught up. Freud and Weber, to mention only two, were both of the opinion that a war would be a cleansing experience. Of the few who had a clearer vision of the consequences of a war, the poet Yeats and the woman he loved, Maud Gonne, stand out. Gonne's critique of the war, in a letter written by her on August 26 1914, is particularly prescient: "This war is an inconceivable madness which has taken hold of Europe – It is unlike any other war that has ever been. It has no great idea behind it. Even the leaders hardly know why they have entered into it, and certainly the people do not . . . The victors will be nearly as enfeebled as the vanquished." Unlike the leading politicians, intellectuals, and social scientists, Gonne was crystal clear on the two most important features of the war, that it would be the most destructive event in the history of the world, and that there was no good reason for it. Her comment that the leaders and people do not know why they are going to war parallels my argument that the emotional and relational roots of the war were deeply repressed.

I do not believe that Gonne had the gift of second sight, as she herself would have liked to believe. I think rather that her worldview as artist, Irish nationalist, feminist, and occultist distanced her from the collective illusion which held most of Europe in thrall.

Contemporary biography provides further hints at the causes of war fever. A representative instance occurs in the life of the philosopher Ludwig Wittgenstein, a citizen of Austria at the beginning of the war. Wittgenstein's life was closely tied to that of Bertrand Russell, his teacher, who was a close observer of the First World War. One of his biographers (Monk 1990, pp. 111–112) explains Wittgenstein's motives in the social context of the times:

> Although a patriot, Wittgenstein's motives for enlisting in the army were more complicated that a desire to defend his country. His sister Hermine thought it had to do with: "an intense desire to take something difficulty upon himself and to do something other than purely intellectual work". It was linked to the desire he had felt so intensely since January, to "turn into a different person".
> The metaphor he had then used to describe his emotional state serves equally to describe the feeling that pervaded Europe during the summer of 1914 – the sense of perpetual seething, and the hope

that "things will come to an eruption once and for all". Hence the scenes of joy and celebration that greeted the declaration of war in each of the belligerent nations. The whole world, it seems, shared Wittgenstein's madness of 1914. In his autobiography, Russell describes how, walking through the cheering crowds in Trafalgar Square, he was amazed to discover that "average men and women were delighted at the prospect of war". Even some of his best friends, such as George Trevelyan and Alfred North Whitehead, were caught up in the enthusiasm and become "savagely warlike".

We should not imagine Wittgenstein greeting the news of war against Russia with unfettered delight, or succumbing to the hysterical xenophobia that gripped the European nations at this time. None the less, that he in some sense *welcomed* the war seems indisputable, even though this was primarily for personal rather than nationalistic reasons. Like many of his generations (including, for example, some of his contemporaries at Cambridge, such as Rupert Brooke, Frank Bliss and Ferenc Békássy), Wittgenstein felt that the experience of facing death would, in some way or other, *improve* him. He went to war, one could say, not for the sake of his country, but for the sake of himself. In the diaries Wittgenstein kept during the war (the personal parts of which are written in a very simple code) there are signs that he wished for precisely this kind of consecration. "Now I have the chance to be a decent human being", he wrote on the occasion of his first glimpse of the enemy, "for I'm standing eye to eye with death." It was two years into the war before he was actually brought into the firing line, and his immediate thought was the spiritual value it would bring. "Perhaps", he wrote, "the nearness of death will bring light into life. God enlighten me." What Wittgenstein wanted from the war, then, was a transformation of his whole personality, a "variety of religious experience" that would change his life irrevocably. In this sense, the war came for him just at the right time, at the moment when his desire to "turn into a different person" was stronger even than his desire to stay alive.

There are a number of points in this passage relevant here. First, Russell's comments support those of Ecksteins's, concerning the support of crowds for the war, in this case, the crowds in London. Elsewhere, Russell classified this war as one whose base source was vanity and prestige rather than conflicts of interest. This analysis, which was the reason he chose to be a conscientious objector, closely parallels my own, since prestige is a code word for honor and the avoidance of shame.

Note also that this passage concerns four young men from three different countries, indicating that all of them had the same basic motive for going to war, the hope that it would improve them (Brook and Bliss were English, Wittgenstein an Austrian, and Békássy a Hungarian). Although these men were on opposing sides (Austria-Hungary was an ally of Germany) they seem to have had the same motives, which were personal rather than political.

In terms of the approach of this book, these men may have wanted war because they were alienated from their respective societies. Because of their age and their education, they had yet to be integrated into positions of respect in their societies. Instead of investigating their feelings of alienation, they acted them out by going to war.

War and social science

It is understandable that nations and their leaders are lost in the nightmare of their history, that they view the wars that they themselves create as exterior and constraining. Their own characters and social institutions were created by a dysfunctional civilization founded on secrecy, deceit, self-deception, and repressed emotion, the accompaniments of massive alienation.

Although alienation and shame are almost universally repressed at the level of governments in our civilization, repression may occur to different degrees. Shame appears to have been most deeply repressed in the stronger countries, England and Germany, and therefore less obvious in their actions. That is, it can be seen most clearly at the level of character, rather than at the level of institutions. Shame was close to the surface in the actions and rationalizations of the weaker governments like France, Russia, and Austria-Hungary. I have already indicated how notions of honor, insult, and revenge played a major role in French politics during the period 1871–1914. Stoessinger (1990, 6–7) points out comparable motives in the actions of the leaders of Austria-Hungary, with their denial of the weakness of their nation, and their emphasis on maintaining their "prestige" among other nations in the face of their fading power.

To see the role of shame in English and German politics, it becomes necessary to focus on the level of character. An approach to this problem can be found in the work of Hughes (1983), who compared the character of English and German leaders in the years prior to 1914. Her analysis of the German leadership, particularly, seems to support the approach I have taken here. Although she does not use the concept of shame, her data and interpretations suggest it.

Hughes stated that the style of the German leaders was characterized by what she calls "the fatalistic temper," the denial of one's own responsibility by projecting it on to the outer world. The best known example of this maneuver is the reaction of the German leadership to the initial stages of mobilization: "Events take control." Rather than acknowledge that they themselves were contributing to events, and that they had the power to interfere with them, they projected this power onto "events."

The way in which the repression of shame leads to the fatalistic temper is implied by Hughes' analysis of the character of the two male protagonists of a popular nineteenth century German novel *Effie Briest* (Hughes 1983, 215–218). One of the male characters in the novel receives what he experiences to be an insult from the actions of another man toward his wife, who is completely innocent. Even though he realizes the futility of dueling, he feels compelled to it because he has, in a moment of "weakness" revealed his experience of insult to the other protagonist, his closest friend. Although Hughes does not name the shame component, it is clear from her description that the man who felt insulted is compelled to remove the stain from his honor because he anticipates seeing himself in a negative way in the eyes of the other man, the generic shame context. He acts out the code of honor to bypass shame.

Hughes's analysis of the character of the English leadership does not touch as clearly on the repression of shame as a motive. Perhaps unacknowledged shame was less of an issue, or it was more deeply repressed. What may be needed is a knowledge of the particular shame–honor vocabulary in use at the time.

The repression of shame at the level of character probably did not influence English and German group behavior directly, the way it appears to have done in the cases of France and Austria-Hungary. Nevertheless, it still could play a vital role, since the English and German leaders missed the opportunity of interfering with the chain of events, even when they could clearly see their futility, somewhat like the protagonists in *Effie Briest*.

Perhaps the dysfunctional system between nations is invisible to national leaders and their publics because the same system occurs within their nations, and indeed, within their own families, even their own characters. The triangling, threats and counter-threats, idealization of self and allies, vilification of enemies and other tactics that led to World War I go on apace in all nations and most families, wartime or peacetime, no matter. The war is everywhere. We have been down so long it looks like up. Unless this system is changed, it will continue to perpetuate itself to the end of time.

It may be that our job as social scientists is to at least awaken ourselves from this nightmare. How can one escape from the limitations of one's own character and social institutions? Although by no means an easy task, three directions might make a start. Firstly, in studying a complex problem such as the one discussed here, one needs an explicit theory and method, to help maintain one's objectivity in the face of the ocean of facts and the conflicting approaches. In this essay I have called upon a theory generated from family systems approaches and the sociology of emotions. I have applied a method based on the analysis of discourse. This theory and method has served as a guide through what otherwise might have been an overwhelming mass of studies and viewpoints.

Another theory and method which might bring some order to the study of the origins of wars is legal theory and practice. In courts of law there is already an existing framework for determining causation, a theory of human behavior and methods for presenting evidence as to actions and motives. In criminal law, for example, the prosecution must prove not only that the defendant committed a crime, but also that he or she *intended* to do so. Conviction for a crime requires the presentation of physical and of subjective evidence showing *mens rea*, criminal intent.

It is possible that the legal approach to proving *conspiracy*, particularly, might solve some of the many problems of showing causation of collective actions, and avoid some of the arbitrariness we have seen in explanations such as those by Remak (1968) and Williamson (1988). However, I am not saying that researchers need adopt all the features of the legal model; it seems particularly important that we ignore the issue of intent. In family and world systems, wars seem caused less by human intentions than by alienation and by the repression of emotions.

A second direction suggested here is the need for a new approach to self and society relationships, part/whole understanding. In this type of endeavor, one studies not only the part or the whole, but both together, and the relationship between the two. In such an analysis, the analyst escapes from entrapment in the situation being studied by making explicit one's theory and method directly. In particular, one avoids singling out only one part or the other of the larger system for blame, the capitalists, the leaders, the men, the Germans. In Stoessinger's study of the origins of World War I, he included some detailed parts and some wholes, but he excluded others, notably the actions of France.

A good example of part/whole thinking can be found in the work of Elias (1978 1982) on the civilizing process. He develops a theory of development of modernity, of our contemporary status quo, by considering verbatim texts, mostly advice manuals, literary works, and diplomatic notes, within the context of larger historical movements. In this way he is able to include the building of character, interpersonal relations, and the formation of national cultures and states within the same framework. His analysis is specialized, but it is also general, attempting to include many levels of analysis and disciplinary viewpoints. His work as a whole, like Goethe's before him, exemplifies what I have called the specialist-generalist (Scheff 1990; see also Mills' [1959] description of the sociological imagination).

To be sure, specialization of function is unavoidable in modern societies. Not everyone can be an opera singer. But we are under no compulsion to *think* in a specialized way. Hyperspecialization of both function and thinking may be no more than one of the myriad forms that alienation from others and from self takes in our civilization.

Of all the earlier approaches to the causes of the First World War, the one that is closest to my own is that of Kennan (1984), in his study of what he calls "the fateful alliance," the secret military treaty completed between France and Russia in 1894. There are many parallels between my theory, method, and findings with those of Kennan. The first involves methods. Like my study, Kennan uses part/whole reasoning. The bulk of Kennan's book concerns his very close reading of verbatim letters and documents showing the origins of the treaty and the way in which it came to be written, sequentially, step by step.

Yet in his conclusion, Kennan proposes several extremely abstract generalizations about the causes of the war. (I will review these assertions below, in my discussion of theory.) Like my study, Kennan's falls in neither of the two camps; he does not evade the issue of causation, as those in the descriptive camp do, nor does he limit his conclusions to a single event, person, or nation, the approach in the other camp. Kennan uses general concepts, but he is careful to ground them in concrete events, the essence of the part/whole approach.

Like my study, Kennan demurs from the majority position that Germany bore a heavier responsibility for starting the war than the other powers. By giving so much prominence to the French-Russian alliance in the origins of the war, he implies that these two countries played as much a role as Germany or any other country in instigating the war.

Finally, Kennan's conclusions support a theory of alienation like the one proposed in this book. By comparing earlier wars with limited goals to World War I, in which total destruction of the enemy is the only goal, Kennan outlines a change from a mixture of solidarity and alienation between nations in the eighteenth and nineteenth centuries to one of virtually total alienation in the twentieth (p.254):

> As late as the eighteenth century, wars, being conducted in the name of dynastic rulers rather than entire nations, were generally fought for specific limited purposes. The amount of force was made, if possible, commensurate to the purpose at hand – no more, no less. When the immediate objective had been obtained, or had proven unobtainable, one, desisted. One did not try to carry hostilities to the

point of the total destruction of the adversary's armed power and his complete humiliation and political emasculation.

Kennan goes on to link the specialization of the professional establishment, especially the military establishment, nationalism, and alienation to the causes of war (p. 255):

> Precisely because of the higher degree of specialization and profes-
> sional concentration to which he was subject, the senior military
> figure of the new era tended to have his eyes riveted more exclu-
> sively on the technical-military aspects of his dedication than were
> those of his counterparts of earlier ages, and to be less familiar and
> less involved with the wider political interests military forces were
> supposed to serve.

In his discussion of nationalism, Kennan focuses on its emotional power in a way that parallels my analysis (pp. 257–257):

> The nation, as distinct from the dynastic ruler of earlier times, is –
> even in theory – a secular force. Ready as it is to invoke the blessing
> of the Almighty on its military ventures, it cannot claim the divine
> right of kings or recognize the moral limitations that right once
> implied. And it is outstandingly self-righteous – sometimes to the
> point of self-adoration and self-idealization – in its attitudes towards
> any country that appears to oppose its purposes or threaten its
> security. The kings and princes of earlier times were usually cynical,
> indeed; but their cynicism often related, in a disillusioned way, to
> themselves as well as to their rivals. The nation-state is cynical, too,
> sometimes pathologically so, but only in relation to opposing mili-
> tary-political force. In the view it takes of itself it is admiring to the
> point of narcissism. *Its* symbols always require the highest reverence;
> *its* cause deserves the highest sacrifice; *its* interests are sacrosanct.
> The symbols, causes, and interests of its international rivals are, by
> contrast, unworthy, disreputable, expendable. Once involved in a
> war, regardless of the specific circumstances that gave rise to the
> involvement in the first place, the nation-state fights for vague,
> emotional, essentially punitive purposes. *They*, the opponents, must
> be punished, made to regret their recalcitrance, made to be sorry. *We*,
> on the other hand, must be vindicated by victory.

Kennan's last comment links alienation, specialization, and nation-
alism in a way that closely parallels my proposal that bimodal alienation – isolation between nations and engulfment within them – is the systemic cause of modern wars (p. 257):

> These, as will readily be seen, are anything else but limited aims.
> And it is not difficult to see how beautifully they dovetail with the
> hopes and anxieties of military men charged with the planning or
> pursuing of sweeping military victories over hypothetical opponents
> in essentially purposeless wars. The nationalistic euphoria provides
> the moral-political justification for those visions of all-out military
> effort and of total military victory that unavoidably command the
> imagination, and shape the efforts, of the military planner. And

between the two of them they tend to obliterate, in minds of both statesman and popular masses, all consciousness of that essential community of fate that links, in reality, all great nations of the modern world and renders the destruction of any one of them the ultimate destruction, too, of the country that destroyed it.

Although Kennan does not make it explicit, it is clear enough in context that his analysis of these generic causes applies equally to all of the major participants in the war, not just to France and Russia. As in my conclusions, Kennan seems to argue for equal responsibility among the participants. My statements are explicit and somewhat flatfooted, Kennan's are more implicit and graceful, but we seem to reach a very similar conclusion, linking war to alienation and emotion.

The third direction might lead to more self-understanding by social scientists. Our own understanding of social relationships is conditioned by those in our families, both our family of origin and our nuclear family. To some extent we have all learned to see the relationships in these two families as external and constraining, even though by the time we became teenagers, we were as active in sustaining them as anyone else. If social scientists are not to be as entrapped in social systems as everyone else, we must try to understand the relationships in our own families. With such understanding, and using part/whole thinking, we then might help to bring peace, and not just between nations, and not just during wartime.

The next chapter will continue my analysis of destructive conflict, but will return to microdynamics, with an analysis of the relationships between the principal characters in a play by Shakespeare.

Generating theory: emotions and conflict

The next three chapters apply the theory and method developed here to a central problem for the human sciences and for humanity as a whole, the origins of protracted and destructive conflict. This problem is especially puzzling when there is very little difference between the combatants, as was the case with the First World War, in contrast with the Second World War, in which the vast difference in outlook between the Allies and the German, Japanese and Italian dictatorships made war inevitable. It is also puzzling when continued conflict brings suffering and ruin to both parties equally, to the point of self-destruction, which was also the case with the First World War.

The part/whole method and the theory of shame/anger spirals offers an explanation of destructive conflict at both interpersonal and intergroup levels. The next three chapters focus on generating an explicit theory that is only touched on in the earlier chapters. Hints as to the affinity between anger and shame in the empirical work of Helen Lewis (1971) were developed and elaborated by Retzinger and myself. We proposed that a necessary condition for destructive conflict is unacknowledged shame, feelings of rejection and/or inadequacy that are so disguised and transmuted as to be almost invisible to the combatants. My analysis of emotions in this book is based on the coding system developed by Retzinger (see Appendix) that enables one to identify shame and anger even when they are elaborately disguised.

The theory proposes that destructive conflict is generated by threatened social bonds and unacknowledged shame. The core idea is that shame that is acknowledged is painful, but does not lead to disruption of social bonds and destructive behavior. Unacknowledged shame, on the other hand, always generates threats to bonds and to self-control. To those completely trapped in spirals of unacknowledged shame, shame and anger, or guilt (I treat guilt as a shame-anger spiral directed at self), the endpoint may be madness, suicide, or murder.

This idea is so abstract that I will briefly illustrate it with an incident

147

in Shakespeare's *Macbeth*. The title character, Macbeth, with his wife's full collusion and even prodding, has murdered his king, Duncan, in order to take the crown for himself. After the event, however, Macbeth is virtually overwhelmed with a crushing sense of guilt. Since Macbeth and his wife are co-conspirators, the differences in their reactions to guilt and their subsequent behavior provides a dramatic illustration of our theory.

In scene II, act II, immediately after he has murdered the sleeping king, Macbeth returns to his wife's room with his hands steeped in blood. His reaction to the blood on his hands is intensely expressive of the feeling of guilt:

> Will all great Neptune's ocean wash this blood
> Clean from my hand? No; this my hand will rather
> The multitudinous seas incarnadine
> Making the green one red.

Macbeth expresses his feeling of unbearable guilt by the metaphor that his hands are so bloody that they would turn all the oceans red. In real life, such an emotional verbal expression of guilt would usually reflect acknowledgment, rather than denial of guilt.

Lady Macbeth is contemptuous of Macbeth's intense feelings. Since she has gone to the king's room to place the murder weapon in the hands of a guard, and smear all the guards with the king's blood, her hands are also bloody. But she says to Macbeth:

> My hands are of your color, but I shame
> To wear a heart so white . . .
> Retire we to our chamber.
> *A little water* clears us of this deed.
> How easy it is then! (emphasis added)

In real life, such a belittling of her husband's feelings, and discounting of her own guilt, would be a sign of denial, rather than acknowledgment of feelings. As the drama plays out, full acknowledgment of guilt feelings by Macbeth is followed by intrepidness in his behavior: he is not paralyzed by guilt, but fights on the end. Lady Macbeth's denial of guilt is followed by madness and suicide, an exact illustration of an important aspect of the shame theory of destructive conflict.

Chapter 6 gives another example of the nature of relationships that can be inferred from fictional discourse, but in much greater detail than the example from Macbeth. In this case, two romantic relationships are compared in a classic drama, Shakespeare's *Much Ado about Nothing*. My analysis suggests that although the Beatrice–Benedick relationship is unconventional, compared with the Hero–Claudio relationship, the same underlying patterns of conflictual communication can be uncovered in their discourse. This play illustrates dramatically how the small parts of discourse, the phrasing which make up manner, reveal a microworld that plays a crucial part in conflict and cooperation.

Chapter 7 examines the minute details of the development of a relationship between therapist and patient in an actual psychiatric examination. By carefully examining the smallest parts, the words and gestures as they occur in utterances, the analyst can make systematic inferences about the thoughts and feelings of the participants, and the kind of relationship that develops between them. This study suggests that any segment of human discourse, no matter how brief, is a microcosm which contains many elements of the entire relationship between the participants, their relations with others, and indeed all human relationships. In this case, although quite unintended by either of the participants, the relationship is threatened by feelings of rejection and inadequacy (that is, by shame).

Chapter 8 continues the idea that protracted conflict is generated by unacknowledged shame. In this case, however, we move from single cases, the most elementary morphology, to comparisons between cases of the same type, parent–child quarrels. This study shows, in several cases, that in a quarrel between one parent and a child, the other parent is also involved, but in a way that is mostly hidden, even from the participants. By examining the actual discourse of quarrels, the observer can uncover patterns of communication that are relentlessly repeated by the members of a particular family, their family system. These patterns have immediate implications for the family members' understanding of themselves and each other, and for the researcher's understanding of social systems, and they illustrate the theory of unacknowledged shame.

Chapter 9 summarizes the main points of the preceding chapters, and draw out their implications for integrating the human sciences, and for increasing communication between the human sciences and the humanities. This chapter proposes first that the current human sciences are deeply mired in conventionality, both disciplinary and societal conventions. Secondly, it suggests that part/whole morphology may provide a path for freeing up the disciplines from their own conventions and those of the society in which they are located.

Since the last chapter will take up this issue in detail, here I give only one example of a convention which is inhibiting the growth of the human sciences. All of them assume in most instances a model of human nature in which the individual is in full control of their thoughts, feelings and behavior. "Rational choice" theory makes this assumption explicit, but it pervades all the human science disciplines and subdisciplines. As a result of this assumption, the human sciences deal almost entirely with surface of behavior, rather than investigating its depths. Experiments and surveys assume that their subjects are aware of their own motives and feelings, and that they say what they mean and mean what they say. The academic disciplines deride psychoanalytic writing, the one discipline which does not make the full control assumption, because psychoanalytic methodology is shoddy.

But even though the hypothesis of unconscious control of thoughts, feelings and behavior has not been adequately investigated, it is quite likely that it is true anyway. There is a small empirical literature in psychology which confirms the importance of the unconscious in determining behavior. Certainly the work that Retzinger and I have done with verbatim transcripts of quarrels demonstrates that our subjects do not have the faintest idea of their own motives and feelings, that they often do not mean what they say, and virtually never say what they mean. The meaning of most discourse, as I indicated in the first chapter, is a technical problem that requires concerted investigation of the three-way relationship beween expressions, context, and meaning. Our findings, like psychoanalytic reports, suggest that most people, most of the time, seem to be out of control: their motives are unconsciously determined in a way that is a mystery to themselves, their associates, and to most human scientists.

The human science convention of assuming humans to be in full control except in unusual circumstances is generated by (and to a lesser degree generates) the same assumption in our society. In modern civilization we assume that we are rational individuals who are acutely aware of our most important thoughts and feelings. The idea suggested above in the example from Macbeth, that Lady Macbeth had repressed her feelings of guilt in order to carry through her part of the murder of Duncan, would be unacceptable to almost all laypersons, just as it is to most academics. But if we are to understand ourselves and our societies, we need to investigate this assumption and indeed that whole tissue of conventions which shape our disciplines and our civilization. The method of part/whole morphology, described and illustrated in this book, offers a path in this direction.

CHAPTER 6

Gender wars: love and conflict in *Much Ado About Nothing*

> I hate and love. If you ask me to explain
> The contradiction,
> I can't, but I can feel it, and the pain
> Is crucifixion
>
> Catullus 85 (trans. James Michie)

In this chapter I apply part/whole morphology to a fictional text. In order to explore the relation between love and war, I apply the theory of shame and the social bond to show the affinity between romance, shame and anger. Unlike the love relationships in the second half of chapter 2, which were somewhat idealized, in this chaper they are closer to what passes as normal love relationships. On close inspection Shakespeare's plays present a grim portrait of the relationship between men and women. Even his lighthearted treatment of this theme in *Much Ado about Nothing* suggests that love between a man and a woman involves unending tension and conflict, much like the distrust, deception, and outright warfare between nations. A close reading of the text of *Much Ado* shows shame/anger sequences both in conventional courtship (Hero and Claudio) and in the unconventional relation of Beatrice and Benedick. Both relationships involve infatuation. My analysis shows that acknowledging shame and anger between men and women may be an important first step toward resolving their conflict.

Attachment, shame, and images of human nature

Until recently, it has been customary to view human nature in one of two ways, as either inherently destructive, or as a blank slate upon which culture writes human character. The first view is associated with Hobbes and in a later form, Freud; the second view with cultural relativity, as implied in learning theory and in postmodern trends.

In the last twenty years, however, studies of infant–caretaker relations raise the possibility that a new perspective is needed which will be in better accord with infant studies and with clinical findings

---

This chapter is based on Scheff 1993.

151

on adult emotions. This new viewpoint begins with the postulate that social attachment is the fundamental human motive. Although it has been formulated by many authors, I will follow, in outline, the position developed by Helen B. Lewis (1976; 1981; 1983).

The recent infant studies strongly suggest that human infants have, at birth, a strong, genetically programed capacity for social interaction and for attachment. Early in the first year, infants are able to engage in the game of taking turns at looking and looking away, and in smiling at the caretaker. This game forms the basis for mutual delight between parent and child, and falling in love. Love between child and parent, a secure bond, is not certain however. If the parent or child fails to play the game, love may not develop.

In conjunction with her clinical studies, Lewis (1977) subsumed these findings in a theory which relates attachment, shame, and anger. In this theory, love involves neither independence nor dependence, but interdependence. Bowlby (1969) characterizes such a relationship as a secure social bond. Shame and anger are instinctive and therefore universal emotional responses to, and signals of, threatened bonds. If this is the case, shame and anger would figure prominently in all love relationships.

Lewis's work, like Freud's, suggests that ambivalence is inevitable in intimate relationships. Unlike Freud, however, especially in his later work, Lewis argues that hatred and destructive relationships are not a fixed part of the human condition, but are produced by alienated social relationships. In this chapter, I argue that romance may mask unconscious shame and anger.

Shame and anger seem to play a key role in relationships that involve extensive idealization or hostility. In this chapter, I consider the role of these two processes in romantic relationships, at both the interpersonal and cultural levels.

The tradition of courtly love and romance provides a cultural script for idealization in Western civilization. Although there is more emphasis on idealization of the woman, especially in the origins of the tradition, considerable encouragement for mutual idealization is provided. "Falling in love," especially at first sight, is considered to be an extraordinary state, far different than the mundane aspects of everyday life. Ideas of a fated or destined relationship with a unique person are also prominent.

Separate from cultural tradition, yet strongly interacting with it, is the psychological process of infatuation. Individuals may merely act out the cultural script of idealized romance without feeling it. But often, the script is deeply felt; one falls "head over heels" in love with the "perfect" partner. Idealization in this case is not merely conforming to a culturally sanctioned role, but is also a compelling emotional experience. Both the cultural and psychological elements in idealized romance can be understood in terms of the dynamics of shame and anger.

Suppose, as suggested in the discussion of attachment, that shame and anger are both biologically programed to signal threats to important relationships. Further, these emotions would be roused frequently in intimate relationships: one is so dependent on the other that they frustrate us, leading to anger, and we feel criticized or rejected, leading to shame. Frequent episodes of shame and/or anger may be an inevitable part of all intimate relationships.

If these emotions are immediately acknowledged, as is sometimes the case, they may be quickly dispelled (Scheff 1979; Scheff and Bushnell 1984). Perhaps in early infancy, before strong social sanctions are applied by self or other, these emotions are frequently aroused but immediately expressed. For adults, however, the case may be quite different. Especially in Western societies, these emotions are severely controlled. They may be acknowledged only under extremely restricted conditions, if at all. They are often seen as evidence of self-indulgence, weakness, or lack of self-control; they are taboo (Scheff 1984).

Under these conditions, the affects of shame and anger lead a shadow life, expressed only indirectly. One channel, I will argue, involves idealization. One may deny one's own shame by linking self with an idealized person or class of persons. Excessive patriotism may be seen as one route that idealization may take, snobbery attached to one's lineage or social class is another. Idealization may also take a more personalized route, romantic infatuation with another person, or hero-worship.

The process of infatuation, whether with a class of persons or a particular person, can be understood in terms of a combination of idealization and shaming. It begins with the denial of one's own shame: feelings of inadequacy and rejection. One links oneself with an idealized other, who manifests the desirable qualities that are missing in one's self, and has none of one's own undesirable qualities, especially weakness and commoness. The other is seen as "special," possessing glamour, charisma, or magic. Perhaps this route is a distorted version of the process referred to by Durkheim (1915) as the differentiation between the sacred and the profane.

Idealization, which begins with the denial of shame, also increases shame. Having created a perfect other, one may come to view one's self from the point of view of that hypothetically perfect other. The process is self-perpetuating to the extent that one underplays the imperfections of the other, and overplays one's own. Viewing one's self from the point of view of a scornful other is the prototypic context for generating shame. The more idealization, the more shame, and the more shame, the more idealization; an aspect of what Lewis (1971) called a feeling trap. In order to illustrate some of its features, this model and the theory of shame dynamics on which it is based will be applied to *Much Ado*.

Shame/anger sequences in a Shakespearean Comedy

Although *Much Ado about Nothing* is certainly a comedy, it displays the usual Shakespearean dark underside with considerable prominence: physical and emotional violence between men, and between men and women. I will first describe this element in the play, then interpret it in terms of a theory of emotion. Hopefully, this treatment will further understanding of the ambivalent love that occurs between men and women.

Much Ado concerns two parallel male–female relationships: the conventional courtship between Hero and Claudio, and the unconventional one between Beatrice and Benedick. These courtships take place within a framework of physical violence, and themselves involve both physical and emotional violence. Since the violence is skillfully woven into a plausible narrative, it often goes unremarked. I will begin by describing the violent elements in the story.

The play opens with a reference to warfare. A messenger is reporting to Leonato (Hero's father), Hero, and Beatrice that Don Pedro is arriving, after a victory in battle. In answer to Leonato's query, they learn that the victory was won with the loss of only a small number of men: "But few of any sort, and none of name." That is to say, a few men died, but they were common soldiers, not gentlemen. The reminder is faint, but occurs in a strategic place. The first topic of the play is a war in which men died.

The second topic is weeping. The messenger reports the tears shed by Claudio's uncle when he learned that his nephew had distinguished himself in battle. Presumably the tears also reflect the uncle's relief that Claudio is unhurt. We have learned in the first few seconds of the first scene, that in war, some men die, others survive, and that the survivor's kin weep for joy. Violent death, survival, and weeping mark a somber beginning for a comedy.

The topic of violent death is taken up by Beatrice, when she enters the dialogue, in her jests about Benedick's adequacy as a soldier. Her first line is: "I pray you, is Signior Mountanto returned from the wars or no?" She refers to him as Mr. Swordthrust, a reference which Hero is able to translate for the others as Beatrice's playful name for Benedick. As we shall see below, the use of impromptu labels rather than proper names occurs frequently in references Beatrice and Benedick make to each other.

In this case the sobriquet refers to a potentially lethal act. Beatrice goes on to deny, in her next comment, that Benedick is deadly, however. Her next reference is to a shooting contest with blunt arrows, between Benedick and Cupid. Finally, in this same comment, she ridicules Benedick as a soldier, as a killer, by promising to eat all "of his killing." In her initial comments, Beatrice refers to swords, bow and arrows, and finally to killing, all aspects of warfare.

After Beatrice makes several more jests at Benedick's expense, her uncle, Leonato, explains to the messenger the background of Beatrice's jesting, that there is a "merry war" between B and B. He goes on to use another military term: each of their conversations, he says, is a "skirmish of wit." Beatrice, continuing the metaphor of warfare, refers to her last meeting with Benedick as a conflict in which he was vanquished, to the point that he lost "four of his five wits." The initial dialogue moves, without transition, from the warfare between men to the warfare between men and women. The beginning of the play seems to suggest a parallel between warfare and romance.

The next dialogue in the first scene involves one of the skirmishes between B and B that Leonato referred to. This is one of the six dialogues between B and B in the play. Each involves a disagreement or a quarrel. As I will explain below, each also involves a considerable amount of hostile innuendo by both parties toward the other. Since both of the contenders are present, and they both seem capable of defending themselves, the skirmishes can be considered to be fair fights between equals. This is not true of the opening dialogue, however, in which Beatrice ridicules Benedick in his absence, moving Leonato to defend him and mildly reprove Beatrice. Since she berated Benedick when he was unable to defend himself, one is left with the impression that Beatrice's animosity toward him is not completely in good humor.

At the center of the plot are two scenes involving emotional and physical violence. The first is the denunciation and humiliation of Hero in the church; in the second, Beatrice asks Benedick to kill Claudio, his best friend.

In the first scene, Claudio carefully orchestrates the situation so as to disgrace Hero. The night before the wedding was to take place, Don John, the villian, has caused Claudio to believe that Hero had been unfaithful to him. Rather than canceling the wedding, Claudio arrives at the church with his seconds, Don Pedro and Don John, and allows the ceremony to begin. He halts it dramatically at the point where the minister asks if any impediment to the union is known. At this point he declares that she has been unfaithful, seconded by Pedro and John. The men denounce Hero as a "rotten orange" and as a "common stale," a prostitute. She is publically disgraced.

The most intense violence in the scene comes not from Claudio's party, however, but from Hero's. Her father's first reaction to the denunciation is to wish death for himself. After Hero faints, his next response is to wish for her death, to hide her shame. At the height of his fury, he hopes that she will die so that he will not have to kill her himself. After Hero has been questioned, Leonato acknowledges the possibility that she has been wronged. Even so, he vows revenge, either against her, if she is guilty, or against her accusers, if she is innocent. The public shaming of his daughter rouses Leonato to extremes of shame and anger.

The second scene occurs immediately after the denunciation, when B and B remain in the church after the others have left. Benedick declares himself in love with Beatrice. In the course of his declaration, he asks her if there is anything he can do to prove his love. Her reply is succinct: "Kill Claudio." Beatrice wants her cousin's honor avenged. After an intense quarrel in which Beatrice expresses strong anger and outrage, Benedick agrees to challenge his friend Claudio to a duel.

In the first scene, a denunciation by one man has aroused humiliated fury in another, to the point of desiring first his own death, then that of his daughter. In the second, a promise of physical violence between two men was instigated by a woman. This comedy begins within a framework of war to the death between men; the plot hinges upon the potential for deadly revenge when honor is impugned in the relations between men and women.

Both of the romantic relationships in this play involve violence, but the violence is disposed differently in each case. In the courtship of Hero by Claudio, there is no violence on the surface, it is hidden beneath a façade of romantic love. (Some of these issues are touched on by Hays 1980). It comes to the surface only through outer circumstance, a conspiracy against Hero's sexual honor. Until the moment when Claudio was informed of Hero's supposed faithlessness, he had idealized her, referring to her as a "jewel beyond price," as the "sweetest lady" he had ever seen (I.i. 175,182). Such idealization of the beloved is conventional in Western societies. Parallel to, and interacting with, the cultural process of idealization is a psychological one, the phenomenon of infatuation. In the discussion of shame dynamics below, I will return to idealization and its relation to shame and anger.

On the surface, at least, the element of idealization seems to be absent in the relation between Beatrice and Benedick. If anything, they seem to engage in the opposite process, profaning each other at every opportunity. Once again, their relationship can also be interpreted in both cultural and psychological terms. Benedick's role conforms to that of the misogynist, the woman-hater, lady-killer; Beatrice occupies the complementary female role,the shrew, who is "curst" with ill-temper and hatred of men. (In II.i. both Leonato and his brother Antonio make this point.)

The psychology of their relationship is more ambiguous than its cultural components, however. One possibility is that their warfare is an open expression of the hostility that is a part of all intimate relationships. One of Freud's most important insights was that all love is ambivalent, a mixture of love and hate. In intimate relationships, each person is so dependent on the other that frustration, which leads to anger, and loss of face, which leads to shame, is inevitable. In this view, humiliated fury toward the beloved is a natural part of any intimate relationship. The only question is whether it will be hidden by idealization and infatuation, or acknowledged openly.

My reading of the dialogues between B and B, to be discussed below, indicates that they are involved in an interminable quarrel, a quarrel based not on the open acknowledgment of shame and anger, but on the suppression of these emotions, so that they are expressed only indirectly, in sarcasm and other forms of hostile innuendo.

Skirmishes

Although the characters in Shakespeare's plays are fictional creations, I will treat them as if they were actual persons. It may be argued that writers are much more revealing of themselves and their world in fictional work than in ostensibly factual work such as autobiography. This seems to have been the case with Goethe. His autobiography dealt, in large part, with lofty intellectual and philosophical themes. His novels, on the other hand, apparently were almost entirely based on his own experiences and to a lesser extent, on those of persons who were well known to him. Since so little is known of Shakespeare's life, there is no way of evaluating the extent to which his characters are based upon actual observations of real behavior.

Whatever the case, however, his dramatic scenes have the character of lived experience: they evoke our emotional responses as if they were real. For this reason they may serve the purpose of illustrating some ideas about emotions, and their relationship to thought and behavior.

In this discussion I will describe how both of the love relationships in *Much Ado* seem to be driven by shame–anger. In the case of Hero and Claudio, the spiral is made up largely of emotions which are bypassed and therefore invisible except under gross provocation. The bypassing operation is not only a psychological process (infatuation) but a cultural one, as well. The cultural script provides a disguise for hostility: the process of idealization which is part of the Western tradition of romantic love. When cultural and psychological processes act in conjunction, the repression of shame and anger is virtually complete under ordinary circumstances.

As will be seen below, the dialogue between B and B also suggests the presence of bypassed shame–anger, but in addition, considerable amounts of overt, undifferentiated versions of the same emotions. I will refer to relations like that between Hero and Claudio, where shame–anger is usually bypassed, as *silent impasses*, and relations like that of B and B, where some of the shame–anger is overt and undifferentiated, as *interminable quarrels*.

Since B and B's first exchange foretells much of their relationship, I will discuss it at length. Beatrice's first line to Benedick is: "I wonder that you will still [always] be talking, Signior Benedick; nobody marks you." Benedick replies in kind: "What, my dear Lady Disdain! Are you yet living?" (ll. 113–116)

Beatrice's first word to Benedick is not a greeting, as would be expected in any conventional social relationship, but a hostile jest. The fact that she did not welcome him but berated him instead is important for several reasons. Firstly, it implies that instead of an ordinary social relationship in which peace at least outwardly prevails, they are involved in an ongoing quarrel. Furthermore, this skirmish, like the larger quarrel in which it is an incident, is unmotivated. We are never given a cause for the hostilities.

For most of Shakespeare's lovers, the path of love is blocked by palpable impediments. In the history plays and the tragedies, *Realpolitik*, either of nations or families, militates against the lovers. Even in the romances, there is usually some real obstacle. For example, in *Twelfth Night* Viola is in love with a man who loves another woman. But in *Much Ado*, there is no obstacle in the outer world. The only obstacles are within. In this respect, the relationship between B and B resembles that between Leontes and Hermione (*The Winter's Tale*): their peace is shattered by Leontes' jealousy, which is utterly without foundation.

Finally, there is one more reason that Beatrice's unmotivated hostility in this line is of importance. According to Lewis (1981), the most intense shame is generated in a context in which one is expecting affection, but gets instead rejection. It seems plausible that a man in Benedick's position, returning from a war, might hope his personal war with Beatrice might also be over. I will return to this conjecture below. First I will consider one more layer of innuendo in Beatrice's comment.

If she had said *"I wonder that you keep talking; nobody is listening to you," the remark would still be disparaging, since it suggests not only that no one is listening, but that he is unaware that no one is listening, i.e. that he is a fool. (Remember that the asterisk (*) indicates counterfactual phrases that might have been said but were not.) But as stated, the remark is even more disparaging than that, because the word "still," which Shakespeare uses to mean "always," implies that Benedick is foolish not only in this particular situation, but that he is always a fool. Her remark about nobody listening is also obviously exaggerated, since she at least is listening, in order to surmise that no one else is. I will now turn to Benedick's response.

His comment escalates the level of hostility begun by Beatrice. Since the layers of innuendo in this sentence are complex, I will divide it into three parts, as follows: (a) "What (b) my dear Lady Disdain! (c) Are you yet living?" The first word "what" implies the affect of surprise, which is to be a part of the main insult, delivered in part (c). That is, Benedick affects surprise that Beatrice is still alive. If (b) had been "my dear Lady *Beatrice!," then his retort would have been similar in form to Beatrice's initial disparagement, an address followed by an insult. If anything, this form of address would have been somewhat more familiar and/or affectionate than hers, since it adds to her name and form of address, "Lady *Beatrice," the phrase "my dear."

Since Benedick does not call her by her name, as she did him, but instead substitutes the disparaging label "Disdain," the effect of the phrase "my dear" is not added familiarity or affection but rather sarcasm, an effect missing from Beatrice's address to him. The substitution of a disparaging label and the sarcasm in its use is one way in which Benedick's comment escalates the level of hostility. A second way involves his main insult, affecting surprise that she is still alive.

It appears that Benedick's main insult was much more hostile than Beatrice's, just as his form of address was more hostile. Raising the issue of the possible death of another person is insulting in itself unless the topic is handled with considerable deference. The casual way in which Benedick introduces it is an insult. Furthurmore, affecting surprise alone is also insulting, as if the life or death of the other is of no intense concern to him. The socially correct affect would be pleased, or even joyful surprise, that the other were still alive, if death were possible. Even though in the present case, the comment is obviously intended as a jest, it is still a hostile jest, for the reasons mentioned.

Since it is not mentioned in the comment, the putative reason for Benedick's supposed surprise is ambiguous. In the absence of mention, Benedick's label "Lady Disdain" can be seen as particularly insulting since his retort does not eliminate the inference that she is so disdainful that this trait might have somehow led to her death. The two-pronged nature of Benedick's assault, involving labeling and sarcasm, on the one hand, and jesting about Beatrice's death, on the other, makes her initial insult seem moderation itself.

There is one way in which Beatrice's initial comment is immoderate, however, in that it dispenses with the greeting and expression of concern which conventional etiquette requires. It is this aspect of her quip which may have occasioned Benedick's extreme response. If, as already indicated, he had been hoping for a truce, if not yearning for an affectionate welcome from the wars, then Beatrice's initial jab would have struck him like a slap in the face. In this context, the surprise he affects at seeing her alive might have been an inadvertant defensive maneuver: if you are still warring against me, then I deny having thought of you at all, much less of having had fond thoughts. In terms of the theory used here, his reaction to what he perceives to be her rejecting initial comment is to feel first intense shame, then extreme anger directed toward her.

The model of the shame/anger spiral hypothesizes that it occurs not only within, but between the participants in an interminable quarrel. There are three feeling traps involved, not just one. In the present case, the shame is completely bypassed for both participants. None of the anger is expressed completely, but its presence is felt as hostility and sarcasm. As long as these affects are neither acknowledged nor dispelled, the quarrel will not be resolved.

The quarrel under discussion seems to fit, in outline, the requirements of the model. Beatrice's initial hostility toward Benedick, in his absence, suggests resentment on her part, an interior spiral of bypassed shame and anger. This state occasions her attack on him, which touches off his resentment, leading to his even more hostile rebuttal. Following this first round of barbs, they trade several more insults. Although they stop quarreling without outside interference, there is no resolution:

> Benedick: [. . .] But keep your way, a God's name! I have done.
> Beatrice: You always end with a jade's trick. I know you of of old.
>   (ll. 139–142)

Beatrice gets not only the first word, but also the last. She complains that his tactics are like those of a "jade," a vicious horse. The editor of the Signet edition suggests that Beatrice refers to the trick of the sudden stop, by which the horse tries to throw the rider. In an interminable quarrel, all of the other's moves, even those that are not hostile, are suspect.

Benedick's ambivalence towards Beatrice is implied by his only reference to her after she leaves the scene. Immediately following the quarrel, Claudio reveals his suit for Hero to Benedick, at one point describing her, as already indicated above, as "the sweetest lady that ever I looked on." Benedick compares Hero unfavorably to Beatrice: "There's her cousin, and she were not possessed with a fury, exceeds her as much in beauty as the first of May doth the last of December." In Benedick's eye, it is Beatrice, not Hero, that is the beauty. However, as is characteristic of chronic resentment, he sees only the anger in her, not his own, or that for which they are mutually responsible.

The feeling trap model predicts that if left to their own devices, participants in an interminable quarrel are quite unlikely to escape the trap unless one or both undergo substantial changes in their personalities: the quarrel is compulsive and involuntary. In the present case, however, the participants are not left alone. Their friends concoct a plot, a conspiracy, actually, to bring B and B to the altar. Benedick's friends, led by Don Pedro, and Beatrice's friends, led by Hero, surmise that B and B love each other, but are unable to acknowledge this fact, even to themselves.

The plot is as follows: Don Pedro instructs the friends of B and B to follow two parallel devices. The male friends, Don Pedro, Claudio, and Leonato, will arrange so that Benedick will hear them talking about Beatrice's secret love for him. The female friends, Hero and two "gentlewomen" (Margaret and Ursula) arrange so that Beatrice will overhear them discussing Benedick's secret love for her. This plot is carried through without hitch. Both B and B swallow the bait. Each is unsuspecting until the last scene, as the marriage is about to take place. Each is also greatly gratified by the supposed love of the other, transformed immediately from a cynic to a passionate lover, but only in private soliloquy. In actual contact, the two lovers continue their hostility, which is only slightly abated by the turn of events.

The next dialogue between B and B occurs before Don Pedro's plot is carried out; the lovers are still completely at odds. The scene is a masked dance. Benedick is pretending to Beatrice to be someone else, repeating a disparaging comment about Beatrice. She appears to suspect that he is in fact Benedick, because she launches into a diatribe, calling him a "dull fool" among other things. Characteristically, however, she also commends him: she ends her tirade on a sexual note: "I am sure he [Benedick] is in the fleet; I would he had boarded me!"

It is of interest to note that the last dialogue in the play also involves masks; Beatrice and Hero come to their weddings veiled. Benedick's first line in this scene is: "Which is Beatrice?" Masks or other disguises are a common ingredient in Shakespeare's male–female relationships. One very common device is for the heroine to disguise herself as a man, as in the case of Portia, Rosalind, and Viola. In many instances, the disguises are used to advance the courtship, which serves the interests of both parties. In other cases, however, the disguise may be a form of trickery, as in the case of Helena and Marianne, who both disguise themselves not as men, but as other women. In some of the cases, however, disguise is used merely as a means of assault, as in the case of Iachimo's attack upon Imogen's sexual honor, in *Cymbeline*. Although each of these deceptions serves to advance the plot, Shakespeare may also be commenting, *sub rosa*, on the large role that deception plays in the relation between men and women.

The third dialogue between B and B is very brief; it involves only three exchanges. It occurs after Benedick has overheard the plotters describe Beatrice's secret love for him, but before Beatrice has been similarly duped. Although the scene is brief, it is precisely constructed. Beatrice, not yet practiced upon by her friends, is still cranky: "Against my will I am sent to bid you come in to dinner."

Benedick, whose attitude toward Beatrice is transformed, is gallant: "Fair Beatrice, I thank you for your pains." But Beatrice seems oblivious to the change, she persists in her hostilities. Benedick, in his way, also is oblivious; before he saw hostility in Beatrice's comments even where there was none. In this scene, he insists on finding fair meaning in her hostility: "Ha! 'Against my will I am sent to bid you come in to dinner,' there's a double meaning in that . . ."

Although Benedick's attitude is changed, it is also unchanged. It is still based upon error, but now a different error. First it was excessively rejecting, now it is excessively accepting. Benedick has merely moved from one mode of distortion to another, from profaning Beatrice to idealizing her. Perhaps this scene serves as a wry comment on the difficulty of changing a romantic relationship. Unless both parties change simultaneously, the impasse will continue.

The fourth dialogue occurs after the play's central crisis, Hero's public humiliation. This dialogue occurs when B and B remain in the church after the others have left. Like all the other dialogues between these two, it also involves a quarrel. Beatrice has been practiced upon by her friends by this point in the play; she now thinks that Benedick is in love with her. For the first time, he declares his love. But he is appalled when she demands that he kill his best friend, Claudio. When he hesitates, she attacks him, with only slight indirection, by complaining about the fashion of men who only talk, rather than act: "men are only turned into tongue."

This disparagement, though indirect, is reminiscent of her direct criticism in her first comment, on Benedick's manliness: "I promised to eat all his killing." She is in a high fury, most of which, but not all, directed at Hero's detractors. Some of it however, is directed toward all men, and therefore, in part, at Benedick, when he hesitates to do her bidding.

In this case the quarrel is both emotional and physical. In her fury, Beatrice continually interrupts Benedick, at first allowing him a few words ("Hear me, Beatrice, – "), but finally, only part of one word, her name.("Beat – ") At one point the contest becomes physical. Beatrice vows to leave the scene because he will not meet her demand for action. Apparently he tries to restrain her physically; she says "nay, I pray you, let me go." This scene is a realistic description of a violent quarrel between lovers.

The fifth (and next to last) dialogue is relatively brief, only ten exchanges. It is the least quarrelsome of the dialogues. Benedick is now the complete gallant: "I will live in thy heart, die in thy lap, and be buried in thy eyes . . ." Beatrice, however, though not quarrelsome, is by no means amorous. She is, rather, businesslike. She is still concerned about her cousin's honor. Her business with Benedick is to find out if he has indeed challenged Claudio as he had promised to do. When she finds out that he has, she relents somewhat, but not completely. When Benedick asks her what it was about himself which first made her fall in love with him, she answers in her usual tart manner, which combines praise and blame in the same breath in more or less equal measure. She goes on to asks him the analogous question, but changing the phrasing from "fall in love" to "for which of my good parts did you first suffer love for me?," implying that love is less a reward than a punishment. Perhaps because of the continuing uncertainty of her cousin's position, Beatrice is much less in a hurry to idealize Benedick than he is to idealize her.

The sixth and last dialogue occurs in the last scene of the play, the wedding of B and B and of Hero and Claudio. Once again, the dialogue is short but dense with meaning. It begins with a quarrel.

> Benedick: Which is Beatrice?
> Beatrice: I answer to that name.What is your will?
> Benedick: Do not you love me?
> Beatrice: Troth, no; no more than reason.

> Benedick: Why, then, your uncle and the Prince and Claudio have been deceived – they swore you did.
> Beatrice: Do not you love me?
> Benedick: Troth, no; no more than reason.
> Beatrice: Why, then my cousin, Margaret, and Ursula are much deceived: for they did swear you did.
> Benedick: They swore you were almost sick for me.
> Beatrice: They swore that you were well-nigh dead for me.
> Benedick: 'Tis no such matter. Then you do not love me?
> Beatrice: No, truly, but in friendly recompense. (ll. 72–83)

At the last minute before the wedding, the friendly conspiracy has come unstuck. Benedick has balked, apparently because of Beatrice's initial tentativeness. (When she identifies herself to him in the first exchange, she merely asks for his will, rather than affirming hers: *"I am Beatrice, come to marry my loving Benedick." When he asks if she loves him (instead of affirming that he loves her) she responds, as she usually does, by both affirming and denying: "Why, no; no more than reason." They are back in impasse: if they are left to themselves, the marriage might not occur.

Once again, they are not left to themselves. Their friends intervene, producing letters by both lovers, attesting their love. The marriage goes forward, but under protest:

> Benedick: Come, I will have thee; but, by this light, I take thee for pity.
> Beatrice: I would not deny you; but by this good day, I yield upon great persuasion, and partly to save thy life, for I was told you were in a consumption. (ll. 93–96)

Perhaps it will be necessary for the friends to attend the honeymoon as well as the wedding. The quarrel has been disrupted by outside intervention. Since the combatants have not changed, it is likely to continue.

Discussion

In this chapter, I have focused on the quarrelsome romance between Beatrice and Benedick, suggesting that their love and attraction toward each other, though genuine, is also ambivalent. In essence my analysis unpacks the meaning of the abstract concept of ambivalence. This analysis is intended to develop a new approach to an old problem, the roots of interminable conflict.

In the case of Beatrice and Benedick, ambivalent love means that the attitudes of the lovers toward each other involve three layers of emotions. As the play demonstrates, the first layer, surface hostility, masks love and attraction. My analysis, however, argues that beneath this second layer there is yet a third, unknown to the characters, unacknowledged shame and anger. My analysis of the discourse appears to support this conjecture about the sources of quarrels: interminable conflict is driven by unacknowledged emotions.

My discussion of infatuation and idealization also points toward what might seem to be an utterly different problem, the place of obsessive love in relation to large scale political issues like charisma. By comparing the unconventional romance of Beatrice and Benedick with the conventional one of Hero and Claudio, it may be possible to advance our understanding of these larger issues.

Since the play involves virtually no discourse between the second pair of lovers, Hero and Claudio, I have had very little to say about their relationship, which is much more conventional and therefore prevalent in the real world, than that of Beatrice and Benedick.

How could the Hero–Claudio romance be central to the plot of the play, yet show little dialogue between them? Discourse between the two is unnecessary, because the marriage that finally occurs was arranged by others in its entirety. Claudio approached Hero through three intermediaries: Benedick, Don Pedro, and Leonato, her father.

When Claudio tells Benedick his intention to marry Hero, he had not yet met her. He had seen her from a distance, so he is familiar only with her outer appearance. He also knows that she is not married or engaged, because he is a member of the same social set, the aristocracy of the city of Messina. He also knows that Beatrice is Hero's cousin, and that Benedick and Beatrice are old friends/enemies. In a sense, his declaration of intention to Benedick can be seen as a first, informal step toward a formal declaration.

His next step is to state his intentions to his commander in the army, Don Pedro, a Prince, asking Don Pedro if he would be willing to arrange the marriage. Don Pedro agrees to do so. Don Pedro loses no time in his task; he first tells Hero, and with her assent, then Hero's father of Claudio's wish. The match is made quick as a wink, with no words passing between the two lovers.

The manner that the marriage was arranged, with the lovers not knowing each other, does not necessarily point to infatuation from afar. Arranged marriages were part of the cultural script of the time. Such arrangements could be made without infatuation, or indeed, without feelings of any kind. Claudio's words suggest however, that as well as following the cultural script, he also is infatuated.

Claudio is somewhat more verbal about his intended than with her. His words suggest that he idealizes Hero, and in a carefully controlled way, is infatuated with her. To Benedick, he says: "In mine eye she is the sweetest lady that ever I looked on," and a "jewel beyond price."

To Don Pedro, he discloses feelings toward her. Now that Claudio has put his thoughts of war and fighting behind him, in their place, he says,

> Come thronging soft and delicate desires
> All prompting me how fair young Hero is,
> Saying I liked her ere I went to wars. (ll. 296–298)

Calling Hero "the sweetest lady," "fair," and a "jewel beyond price" suggests idealization. The last line, in combination with words like "thronging," imply lengthy preoccupation and obsessive interest in a woman that Claudio had never met.

As the plot suggests, since he does not actually know her, Claudio's attraction to Hero is vulnerable to outside influences. In order to break up the marriage, the villain, Don John, insinuates to Claudio that Hero has had illicit relationships with men. To make this fabrication convincing, he arranges to have Claudio to see a woman he thinks is Hero conniving with men late at night outside Hero's window.

Even though Don John's charges are absurd, Claudio's attitude toward Hero immediately undergoes violent change. Without any investigation or attempt to question Hero herself, Claudio performs an instant about-face. From adoration without limit, his feelings change to intense hatred. He himself stages a scene at the wedding to humiliate and reject her.

Although the lightning-quick transformation in Claudio's feelings is somewhat melodramatic, it points to an important difference between infatuation and love. Love is more stable than infatuation because it is based on knowledge of the beloved. Knowing both good and bad, love leads to trust. Infatuation, on the other hand, involves little or no knowledge of the other. As in the case with Claudio's attraction to Hero, it is often based only on outer appearance. Lacking actual knowledge of the other, the infatuated one usually projects his or her own desires and longings on the beloved. The image of the loved one is almost entirely made up in the beholder's imagination. As Tennov (1979) has shown, strong long-term infatuation occurs in fans of movie and rock stars, persons completely unknown to the infatuated one.

Although the distinction I have made between love and infatuation seems obvious enough, it is not usually expressed in the literature on romantic attraction. In fact, infatuation is not treated as a serious concept in the human sciences. The psychoanalytic literature gives some attention to idealization, but virtually none to infatuation. The two standard studies dealing with idealization and infatuation are Person (1988) and Tennov (1979), already mentioned. Person discusses idealization, but does not even use the word infatuation. Tennov (1979) gives serious attention to neither concept. She went to the unusual length of inventing a word, "limerance," to avoid using the correct term, infatuation. Like the popular literature on love and romance, she actively obscures the distinction between love and infatuation. She uses infatuation only to mean a brief adolescent passion.

The distinction between love and infatuation is an extraordinarily important one, fraught with consequences both for individuals and societies. Love can be interpreted as a specific type of social solidarity, a strong bond based on deep knowledge and acceptance of the other. In another place, I have referred to persons with such knowledge of each other as being in a state of attunement (Scheff 1990). It is attunement that makes possible the rapid and flexible cooperation that is the foundation of a stable social order. From this point of view, relationships based on infatuation rather than love are extremely tenuous bonds disguised as strong ones. Such bonds are as confusing to the love object as to the lover. They may also be paralyzing for a relationship, and for a society in which there are many such relationships.

My argument concerning infatuation points toward a new approach to the phenomenon of charisma. Infatuation casts an irresistible aura over its target, whether a lover or a political leader. To the uninfatuated eye, the individual may seem an ordinary mortal, but to the infatuated, the most glamorous, accomplished or righteous one that has ever lived. In this view, it is not love that is blind, but infatuation. To suggest that it is love is blind is to confound it with infatuation, which is what infatuated persons feel compelled to do.

The argument here is that charisma exists largely in the eye of the beholder. It further suggests that charisma is for the most part produced by alienated societies; lacking secure bonds, its members seek pseudo-bonds with rock and movie stars, and more ominously, political leaders. If this is the case, an analysis of charisma requires a theory of social integration, of alienation and solidarity, that is applicable both to interpersonal and societal relationships. Such a theory must trace the nature of social bonds, with particular attention to the management of emotions.

The rudiments of such a theory are implied by Braithwaite's (1989) theory of crime and crime control. If his theory is generalized to apply to social institutions in addition to crime, it suggests that reintegrative forms of social control produce solidarity, repressive forms, alienation. Chapter 4 outlined some of the elements of a general theory of integration, and how it can be applied to relationships between individuals and those between nations. In this scheme, infatuation becomes an important element in conflict between persons and between groups.

Conclusion

In Shakespeare's plays, outside intervention often is necessary to clear away the obstacles between lovers. Indeed, to be effective, supernatural intervention is frequently required. In *A Midsummer Night's Dream*, Oberon, the fairy king, practices upon the lovers with a magic love-juice. In *Measure for Measure*, Vincentio, the Duke with god-like powers, removes the impediments which stand between Claudio and Juliet , and between himself and Isabella. The *Tempest* is the exemplary case. For Miranda and Ferdinand, the young lovers, the war is over; there are no impediments. However, all has been arranged by Prospero, the mighty magician. Like a God, he has brought them together in spite of storm and strife.

The reference to the need for god-like powers occurs even in *Much Ado*, despite the otherwise realistic nature of the play. Don Pedro, the architect of the scheme to match the two antagonists, ends his instructions to his co-conspirators on this note: "If we can do this (bring the lovers together) Cupid is no longer an archer; his glory shall be ours, for we are the only love-gods" (II.i). The need for supernatural assistance in affairs of the heart has a tragic resonance. In *King Lear*, Albany says

> If that the heavens do not their visible spirits
> Send quickly down to tame these vile offences,
> It will come,
> Humanity must perforce prey on itself,
> Like monsters of the deep.

Even in comedy, Shakespeare intimates a deadlock in the relationship between men and women. Given the discussion in this chapter, we may see that the feud between Beatrice and Benedick is kin not only to the comedic treatments of this theme, as in the verbal battles between Rosaline and Biron, and the physical fights between Katherina and Petruchio. It is also related to his tragic lovers.

Perhaps the closest relative to *Much Ado* is not *The Taming of the Shrew*, but *Troilus and Cressida*, a story set in the Trojan war. In this latter play, the interplay between infatuation and war, which is only hinted at in *Much Ado*, is made explicit. The main plot concerns the infatuation of Troilus for Cressida; in this relationship, the obsession of a Greek soldier with a Trojan woman he hardly knows leads only to personal anguish. But the play also traces, by implication, the parallel course of Paris's infatuation with Helen, the greatest beauty in the world, whom he has never met. Paris's obsession, because it becomes the cause of his nation, leads not only to personal anguish, but to war and destruction.

In both comedies and tragedies, the plays seem to say that infatuated romantic love between men and women, and perhaps hero worship between men and men, is not destined for cooperation, but for collision. This course is not inevitable, however. Even the most vicious deeds may be redeemed. In *The Winter's Tale*, sixteen years of suffering teaches Leontes a lesson. Even though he has lost his son, his wife and daughter are returned to him, partly through chance, but partly also, because he himself changes. His deep contrition over his misdeeds has increased not only his tolerance, but also his knowledge of himself. His unjustified jealous anger toward his queen can be interpreted in terms of shame dynamics: rather than acknowledging his own shame, whatever its source, he masked it with anger projected on to his innocent wife.

When Leonte's daughter is returned to him after sixteen years' absence, the queen's loyal retainer, Paulina, stages a viewing of a "statue" of his supposedly dead queen. Actually it is the queen herself; she has vowed to remain in hiding until the lost daughter is found. When Leontes first sees the supposed statue, he is quick to acknowledge his feelings:

> I am ashamed: does not the stone rebuke me
> For being more stone than it?

Perhaps acknowledging our own shame might be a first step away from war, toward peace. It might not decrease the intensity of human suffering, not a hair, but it might decrease its duration. If shame and anger are related to love, as has been argued here, then understanding of these emotions might help break the deadlock in the war between the sexes.

CHAPTER 7

Microanalysis of discourse: the case of Martha Johnson and her therapist

This chapter connects the small parts of discourse, the words, gestures, thoughts and emotions to the larger whole of the relationship. I describe a model of attunement, the process through which interactants achieve (or fail to achieve) joint attention and feeling, and a methodology appropriate for studying it. Two separate but interrelated systems are involved, a system of communication which can lead to joint attention, and a system of deference which can lead to the sharing of feeling, processes which occur both *between* and *within* interactants.

Through prospective–retrospective and counterfactual methods, interactants appear to use the resources of an entire society in each encounter. Their ability to understand any given moment in reference to the *extended context* in which it occurs provides the link between the individual and social structure. Society is based on the minute and unexplicated events which make up the *micro-world* underlying ordinary discourse. Research on human action involves reference to this world, and requires methods similar to those the interactants use, part/whole methods, as well as systematic, analytic methods.

Social action and natural language

How are the actions of individuals translated into recurring patterns of collective behavior? How is social structure realized in the actions of individuals? These questions pose an obvious conceptual problem for the social sciences, since they involve the basic model of social behavior. Less obviously, also implicated is the methodology of social science. All empirical research implies a model of social action, since it is ultimately dependent on observations of individual behavior. In the absence of an explicit theory, each researcher is forced to improvise a theory for the case at hand.

In this chapter I outline a rudimentary theory of social action, and a

This chapter is a slightly revised version of Scheff 1986a.

methodology appropriate to it. In order to do so, I bridge levels that are usually kept separate: micro and macro worlds, inner and outer, thought and feeling. I claim that the basic human *bond* involves mental and emotional connectedness, that social organization requires what Stern (1981) has called *attunement* between individuals, the sharing of thoughts and feelings. Society is possible to the extent that its members are able to connect with each other in this way. Society is endangered by anarchy to the extent that interacting members fail to find attunement, lack connectedness, as in the excerpt below. I illustrate this model with findings from recent research, and with a concrete episode of social interaction.

My starting point is an empirical finding from work on artificial intelligence. In the last twenty years an important discovery has been made by attempts at automated interlanguage translation. No algorithm has been found that is sophisticated enough to translate sentences from one natural language to another. To put it in a slightly different way, computers have been unable to understand natural language sentences, and are unlikely to do so in the foreseeable future (Winograd 1984.)

As indicated earlier, common words in natural languages have more than one meaning. Consider the sentence:

The box is in the pen.

Is pen to be understood as an enclosure or as a writing instrument? The computer faced with this decision has recourse only to a dictionary. The native speaker has encyclopedic knowledge of the meaning of pen, and also recourse to contextual knowledge of the sentence involved. Considerations of the usual sizes, shapes, and uses of pens and boxes might lead the native speaker to prefer enclosure as the meaning in this case. Even though this is a relatively simple problem (compared with highly metaphorical sentences) it would be extremely tedious to make the speaker's decision process explicit for just this one sentence.

Even at this elementary level, verbal sentences appear to involve *open*, rather than *closed* domains. As already indicated, the latter involve a finite number of objects, choices, and rules, each of which is uniquely defined. The game of tic-tac-toe provides a simple example: there are only two objects, x and o, and, on the first move, 9 choices. The rules are uniquely defined so that there is no possibility of ambiguity. Most branches of mathematics involve closed domains (e.g., algebra, calculus).

An open domain involves a very large number of objects and rules, none of which is uniquely defined. The ability to function in an open domain like natural language now appears to be based on extraordinarily complex skills, which are executed with lightning-like rapidity. If we move from the arena of sentences composed of words to those that are spoken, with their accompaniment of non-verbal gestures, we may appreciate the complexity. The amount of information carried by digital language is small compared with that carried by gestures both seen and heard. These gestures are not digital, but continuous; they signal vastly more information.

Recent findings from conversation and discourse analysis demonstrate the importance of non-verbal gestures in social interaction (Sacks et al. 1974; Atkinson and Heritage 1984). To summarize many studies, and extrapolate to expected future findings: it would appear that every sentence uttered contains sequencing signals which allow the listener to determine whether the speaker will continue to speak, or stop at the end of the sentence. Although some of this information is conveyed verbally, most is non-verbal. Particularly important is the intonation contour of the sentence: the relative speed, loudness and pitch of the syllables which make it up.

Sequencing signals allow for rapid and seemingly effortless coordination of speech between speakers, a turn-taking system. This finding may constitute the first universal, pan-cultural regularity in language use. Turn-taking also appears to occur virtually at birth in the interaction between care-taker and infant (Stern 1984; Tronic 1982.) For this reason it is plausible that the motive and some of the ability to take turns is genetically inherited.

It would appear that sequencing signals are only a minute part of the socially relevant information packed into a spoken sentence. Turn-taking makes up only one small aspect of the *deference/emotion system*. Coordinating turns at speaking is a mechanical problem of avoiding interruption only in part. It also involves a moral issue, the signaling of status.

In order to show respect, the listener must not only avoid speaking before the speaker has finished. There must be a decent pause (perhaps one or two seconds) before the listener begins, showing that speech has been registered, considered. Even if the listener's response has no overlap with the last sentence spoken, the absence of the requisite pause will usually be heard as disrespectful.

The listener must also avoid too lengthy a pause. A silence of more than three or four seconds will usually be heard as implying disagreement or confusion, and therefore as being possibly disrespectful. The rhythm of spoken speech is freighted with deference signals. Speaker and listener must both be involved.

In the role of listener, the interactant must take care to detect and honor sequencing signals. In the role of speaker, the signaling task is much greater. Not only must sequencing be signalled, but also the status of the speaker and the listener(s). For example, speaking too rapidly and/or with too little intonation may be understood as signaling lack of interest or respect. Similarly, speaking too slowly and with too much emphasis and gesticulation may also be taken as disrespectful of the listener's ability to understand.

The rhythm of speech is only one of many avenues for awarding or withholding deference. As already indicated, Goffman (1967) proposed that every sentence, its words, paralanguage and gestures, imply an evaluation of the social and interpersonal status of the interactants.

> The human tendency to use signs and symbols means that evidence of social worth and of mutual evaluations will be conveyed by very minor things, and these things will be witnessed, as will the fact that they have been witnessed. An unguarded glance, a momentary change in tone of voice, an ecological position taken or not taken, can drench a talk with judgmental significance. Therefore, just as there is no occasion of talk in which improper impressions could not intentionally or unintentionally arise, so there is no occasion of talk so trivial as not to require each participant to show serious concern with the way in which he handles himself and the others present. (1967, 33)

Goffman argued, furthermore, that all interactants are exquisitely sensitive to the exact amount of deference they are being awarded. If they believe they are receiving too much, or, much more frequently, too little, they will be *embarrassed*. His argument concerning embarrassment introduces us into the *realm of feeling*. Before discussing this realm, I once again refer to a second system with which the deference system is entangled.

Goffman's analysis of social interaction also implies another extremely intricate system, the system of communication which enables interactacts to understand one another. Although misunderstanding also occurs, it is also clear that interactants, at times, can understand each other. We are certain that we have understood another when we learn that we have correctly predicted their intentions, and they ours.

For example, an appointment is set up on one occasion for dinner on a later one. When our partner arrives at the right time and place, dressed as expected, and in the expected frame of mind, it is clear that interpretive understanding jointly occurred on the earlier occasion. One has correctly understood the other's intent, an inner phenomenon, by noting outer markers. One has understood not only the spoken words, but the inner intent to which the words referred; as expected, the other was not lying or joking. As shown in the analysis of the excerpt below, the same process of prediction and confirmation can also take place continuously within any given episode.

Although interpretive understanding is so frequent that we take it for granted, it is by no means clear how one "reads another's mind." Goffman carefully describes the conditions under which successful mind-reading is most likely to occur:

> An understanding will prevail as to when and where it will be permissible to initiate talk, among whom, and by means of what topics of conversation. A set of significant gestures is employed to initiate a spate of communication and as a means for the persons concerned to accredit each other as *legitimate* participants. When this process of *reciprocal ratification* occurs, the persons so ratified are in what might be called "a state of talk" – that is, they have declared themselves officially open to one another for purposes of spoken communication and guarantee together to maintain a flow of words . . . A *single focus of thought and visual attention*, and a single flow of talk, tends to be maintained and to be legitimated as officially representative of the encounter. (1967, 34; emphasis added)

This is a detailed description of the situation in which the "mystic union" of successful communication is likely to occur. The concept of legitimacy which Goffman introduces in this passage serves to bridge the two different systems, deference and communication. Communication occurs most effectively if the interactants "reciprocally ratify" each other as legitimate partners in the communication enterprise. Such ratification is signalled by the virtually continuous awarding and registering of markers of deference. (In his analysis of the child's acquisition of language, Bruner (1983) treats the communication system in a way very similar to Goffman, as the achievement of joint attention, but makes no reference to the deference system.)

It would appear that each uttered sentence is a dynamic package, loaded with an extraordinary amount of information. It may be considered to be analogous to the cell in a living organism, the smallest system. As Goethe suggested in his discussion of morphogenesis, it may be necessary to understand the structure of the cell in order to understand the organism, and the structure of the organism in order to understand the cell. In the proposed model, society exists to the extent that its members are able to achieve attunement, the sharing of meanings and feelings.

Example of interaction ritual: the opening exchange in a conversation

Goffman's analysis is so dense and abstract that it is difficult to know whether we understand his meaning. In this section I show, in a concrete example, the markers of deference and communication which suggest the existence of two distinct but interrelated systems. The analysis of this example will be used to describe exchanges of feeling, and the methods interactants (and researchers) use when they are interpreting events.

The passage comes from a widely known psychiatric interview (Gill et al. 1954). It was the basis for a subsequent study (Pittenger et al. 1960). Because the original work was accompanied by a long-playing record, Pittenger and his colleagues were able to conduct a microscopic study of the verbal and non-verbal events in the first five minutes of the interview. My analysis of the opening exchange is based upon, and further develops that of Pittenger et al. In particular, I use techniques implied in their work, and that of Labov and Fanshel (1977), and Lewis (1971) to interpret the *message stack*. That is, I utilize the words in the transcript and the nonverbal sounds in the LP recording to infer the unstated implications (the *implicature*) and *feelings* which underlay the dialogue.

> P1: (*Sits down*)
>
> T2: (*Closes doors*) What brings you here? (*Sits down*)
>
> P2: (*Sighs*) Everything's wrong I guess. Irritable, tense, depressed. (*Sighs*) Jus' . . . just everything and everybody gets on my nerves.
>
> T3: Nyeah.
>
> P3: I don't feel like talking right now.
>
> T4: You don't? (*Short pause*) Do you sometimes?
>
> P4: That's the trouble. I get too wound up. If I get started I'm all right.
>
> T5: Nyeah? Well perhaps you will.

A close reading of this passage unearths several puzzles. For example, a pause of *eight seconds* occurs in T4. As already noted, a pause of more than two seconds is likely to make interactants uncomfortable. In seeking to understand why the patient did not respond to the first part of T4, we notice her preceding comment (P3): "I don't feel like talking right now." Why would the patient not feel like talking when *less than a minute* has elapsed in the interview? Finding an answer to this question will illustrate Pittenger et al.'s methods and findings, and my elaboration of them.

Pittenger et al.'s analysis of the language and paralanguage in this passage suggests that failure of attunement occurred during the first three exchanges, resulting in a crisis after T4a. This crisis seems rectified after T4b. Their analysis of the rest of the first five minutes, however, and mine of the rest of the interview, shows that the crisis was averted only temporarily; the interactants are inadequately attuned for most of the interview. My analysis will be used to illustrate the interdependence of the systems of communication and deference. In this instance, the crisis involved both misunderstanding and an exchange of painful feelings.

Pittenger et al. say that a misunderstanding occurred at T4a because of T's choice of words and intonations in his first three utterances. Almost all of the words chosen are "pronominals," blank checks, and the intonations are "opaque," i.e. flat. P must have heard these utterances, they say, as indicative of detachment, boredom, and disinterest: *"Here we go again! How many times have I heard this kind of thing!"Although unstated, these sentences are implied by the choice of words and intonations, part of the structure of communication which I refer to as implicature.

The authors go on to argue that P has misunderstood at least T's intent, if not his actual behavior. They say that he did not intend to signal detachment, but neutrality: *"You can tell me anything without fear of condemnation." The authors argue that during the silence after T4a, T must have realized that P had heard him as cold and detached, because in T4b, for the first time, he uses "normal" intonations, i.e. he signals warmth and interest. (Perhaps he also leans forward slightly in his chair, and for the first time, smiles.)

T's understanding of P's mental state is apparently confirmed by P4: she resumes talking. To appreciate the significance of P4, it will be necessary to refer again to the rhythm of turn-taking. P responds to T4 ("You don't?") with an 8–second silence. She does not say *"No, I don't," or its equivalent, signaling that she is still involved. Her silence suggests, rather, that she has withdrawn. Conversation is like a ping-pong game. P has put her paddle down on the table, seated herself, and folded her arms. *"If you want me to play this game, Buster, you better show me something different than what I have seen so far."

In T4b, T gets the message, and is rewarded with P4. In T5a, however, "Nyeah?," he seems to forget what he just learned, since it is delivered without intonation. This time, however, a silence from P of only 1.8 seconds is necessary to remind him: T5b is delivered with normal intonation.

Another confirmation of the authors' interpretation is suggested by their analysis of the paralanguage of P3 and P4. They say that P seems upset in P3, but not upset in P4. Since the issue of emotional upset will be crucial for my argument, I review and elaborate upon their comments.

Embarrassment and anger: the feeling trap of shame-anger

Pittenger et al. interpret the paralanguage of P3 as indicative of *embarrassment* on the patient's part:

> This is a momentary withdrawal of P from the situation into embarrassment with overtones of childishness . . . [as signaled by] the slight oversoft, the breathiness, the sloppiness of articulation, and the incipient embarrassed giggle on the first syllable of *talking*. (1960, 30)

Pittenger et al. frequently infer embarrassment in P's utterances, as well as irritation, annoyance or exasperation. As was the case with the therapist, however, these phenomena do not figure prominently in their concerns, but are only mentioned in passing. The same thing is true of the analysis of emotion that occurs in Labov and Fanshel (1977), even though their analysis is much more sophisticated; for example, they note signs of the compound emotion "helpless anger" appear very frequently in the patient's paralanguage. Since no explicit theory of the role of emotions in behavior was available to them, these authors made little use of their findings concerning the emotional states of their subjects.

In my analysis, however, their references to emotional states will play a central role. The basic human bond involves both communication and deference, exchanges of thoughts and feelings. It will encompass understanding and misunderstanding, on the one hand, and love and hatred, on the other.

Interpretive understanding (*verstehen*) involves a process between and within interactants which was referred to by G. H. Mead (1934) as "role-taking," as indicated in earlier chapters. He indicated that each party can, under ideal conditions, come very close to sharing the inner experience of the other party. By cycling between *observing* the outer behavior of the other, and *imagining* the other's inner experience, a process of successive approximation, intersubjective understanding can occur. As already stated, Peirce used the term "abduction" when describing a similar process in scientists. Scientific discovery, he argued, involves not induction alone (observation), nor deduction alone (imagination), but a very rapid shuttling between the two.

Like Goffman's analysis, the formulations concerning *verstehen* by Dilthey, Mead, Peirce and others have been so abstract and dense that it is difficult to find out if they are useful or not. Because they offer no applications to concrete episodes, their ideas have remained somewhat mysterious.

Bruner's (1983) work on the acquisition of language is much more concrete. He does not invoke the concept of *verstehen*, but refers rather to "joint attention." His examples of instances in which the mother teaches the baby the meaning of a word points to the origins of intersubjectivity. The mother places an object (such as a doll) in the baby's line of gaze, shakes it to make sure of the baby's attention, and says "See the pretty *dolly*." The mother intends only to teach the name of the doll, but in doing so, she also teaches the baby shared attention. I will illustrate shared attention with the incident already cited. Before doing so, it is necessary to outline a model of exchanges of feeling.

Goffman's analysis of interaction ritual suggests that embarrassment and anticipation of embarrassment are pervasive in social interaction, and particularly, that they are exchanged *between* the interactants. Lewis's analysis outlines the process of *inner* sequences, how one may be ashamed of being angry, and angry that one is ashamed, for example.

Recent studies of infant-caretaker interaction, particularly that of Stern (1984), provide a picture of the elemental love relationship. Beginning very early in the infant's life, perhaps even on the first day, the infant and caretaker begin a process which might be described as falling in love. It seems to begin with taking turns at gazing into the other's eyes. This process rapidly leads to mutual eye gaze, mutual smiling, and what Stern calls mutual delight. Love can be visualized as occurring between and within the mother and child, involving meshed intrachain sequences. The perception of the mother's smile causes the baby to feel delight, which leads it to smile, which causes the mother to feel delight, which leads to a further smile, and so on, a virtuous circle.

The hate relationship can also be delineated, by using Lewis's concept of the feeling trap. A combination of anger and shame snowballs between and within the interactants, leading to extraordinarily intense and/or long-term relationship of hatred. In the kind of hatred that occurs between avowed enemies, the shame component in the exchange of feelings is not acknowledged, but the anger is overt. The vendetta provides a model for this kind of bond, involving insult to honor (shaming), vengeance in order to remove the stain on honor, and mutual hatred and interminable conflict, as explained in the last chapter. As in the love relationship, there is a snowballing of emotional reactions between and within the antagonists: an action of one party that is perceived as hostile by the other leads that other to feel angry and ashamed, which leads to a hostile action which causes the same cycle in the other party, and so on, a vicious circle. In relationships between intimates, elements of both love and hate often seem to be involved, as implied by Bowlby's studies of attachment (see chapter 3). To point out some of the ingredients of this mixture, I return to the exchange which was discussed above.

In this interview there are several instances of attunement between the therapist and the patient. As already indicated, even though they got off to a bad start, between T4b and the end of T5b one such moment occurred. The therapist, in the silence after T4a, seems to have correctly sensed the cause of P's embarrassed withdrawal, and corrected for it. In T4b he offers the sympathy and respect missing from his initial manner. The patient responds appreciatively, relieved of her embarrassment. Such moments recur in the interview, but infrequently. For the most part, the interview is characterized by misunderstandings and feelings like those in the initial crisis at T3–T4a. Since there is little direct hostility or anger expressed, the interview is not an open quarrel, but involves many impasses.

The causes of impasse can be inferred from Pittenger et al.'s analysis. They do not attempt to characterize the mood of the interview as a whole, but they point to recurring elements in the manner of the two interactants. They repeatedly remark on the therapist's tone: "cold, remote, and detached." They also point repeatedly to the emotionality of the patient. For example, about P6, "I'm a nurse, but my husband won't let me work." they say: "The narrowed register, overlow, scattered squeeze, and the rasp on 'work', together with the (lack of) intonation on the last phrase, mark P6 as a real complaint, invested with *real annoyance, misery, and resentment* (Pittenger et al. 50–51, emphasis added)."

Pittenger et al. also note frequent instances of embarrassment in the patient's manner (e.g., 70, 101b). Finally, they note several instances of what they call "whining," "fishwifely raucousness," (82, 83b) or a "fishwifely whine" (158) (these particular comments seem to slur the patient's gender, social class and emotionality). In summarizing the therapist's tactics, the authors suggest that one of the therapist's primary goals is to get the patient to reduce her level of emotionality in the session.

The paralanguage which the authors say accompanies the patient's "annoyance," "resentment," "raucousness," and "whining" is very similar to what Labov and Fanshel (1977) take to be the signs of "helpless anger" i.e. shame-anger. At the beginning of the interview, the patient is surprised, puzzled and very soon insulted by the therapist's manner. Although there are moments of reprieve, the patient seems to remain in that state for most of the interview. Since neither the patient nor the therapist acknowledge her emotional state, the interview turns into a polite but nevertheless baffling impasse, a mixture of understanding and misunderstanding, acceptance and rejection, love and hate.

So far the excerpt from the interview has been used to show the entanglement of communication and deference systems, how in this case, misunderstanding and exchanges of embarrassment and anger go hand in hand. The next step is to show how attunement of thought and feeling, or its absence, is related to social structure.

Interpretation and context

Before continuing with the example, it is necessary to outline what I consider to be innovative aspects of Pittenger et al.'s methodology.

1. The emphasis on paralanguage;
2. The separation of inferences from observations;
3. The prospective-retrospective method of understanding;
4. The use of counterfactual variants (hypotheticals).

The decision of the authors to attempt a virtually complete phonemic and phonetic analysis of every word of a text represents a marked departure from not only the practice of everyday life, but also from the practice of research on human behavior. The intensity of their description of the characteristics of the utterances, and of their analysis and interpretation of these characteristics gives their work a microscopic quality. They deal not just with the nuances of communication, but with the nuances of nuances.

The intensity of their analysis in itself results in a somewhat unexpected finding: if one forces oneself to pay as much attention to the paralanguage of a message as to the language, the extraordinary richness and complexity of human actions springs into life off the printed page. The sensation of reading the author's descriptions and interpretations is like looking at a drop of water under a microscope: one is shocked by the seemingly infinite variety of life that suddenly appears below the smooth surface of ordinary experience.

The authors' method of intensive, rather than extensive investigation may hold a lesson for contemporary social science and psychology. Perhaps we have put too much emphasis on generalization, on extensive knowledge, without also understanding a single instance very well. Perhaps the single case, sufficiently understood, could generate hypotheses that would be worth testing. As William Blake said: "To see a world in a grain of sand."

The second of the authors' methods concerns strict separation between their *observations* of utterances, and the *inferences* they make on the basis of these observations. This principle is made explicit by the authors: they strongly urge research discipline. The researcher must be continually aware, and wary, that interpretations are inferential, only, and therefore have a different status than observations, raw facts in the recorded transaction.

At first glance, this method does not seem at all innovative: it merely repeats one of the accepted tenets of science. However, their attempt to honor this tenet turned out to be fruitful, because they were unable to carry it out completely. By considering their analysis to be part of the text that I am investigating (along with the recorded transcript) I make deductions about the *authors'* process of understanding, the process that enabled them to arrive at many of their interpretations.

The authors show varying degrees of tentativeness or confidence in their interpretations. The most tentative are those made at the beginning of their analysis. In their first interpretation of the therapist's utterances, T2 and T3, they use the device of reporting the response of only one of the authors, how these two utterances were heard as cold and detached. This is their most cautious mode. Later, with respect to T16, they provide an interpretation that is less tentative, but still restrained, when they state that by this point, all three of the authors "came to have the feeling" that although there was some variation in T's style, it was basically "cold, detached, and remote."

This latter statement is typical of their usual style of interpretation. The implication is that they are only reporting an inference which could easily be in error. With conventional scientific caution, these statements invite the reader to make his or her own interpetations for the sake of comparison.

There is another style which the authors occasionally use, however, which seems to be a lapse from scientific prudence. These are the occasions in which they state that some matter is obvious, clear, or in one instance, "unmistakable." These matters are almost always inferences about what one of the interactants understands or intends. Although the authors do not acknowledge it, they are implying, with complete confidence, that they have been able to penetrate into the minds of the persons whose speech they have studied.

In order to illustrate these lapses from their stated rule, here is the evidence they cite for their most unguarded imputation:

> P2*b* shows unmistakable signs of "rehearsal." In anticipating the interview. P has planned certain things that she is going to say, and now simply reads this one off from memory. (Many therapists put a premium on spontaneity of patient's response during therapy; we must therefore make it clear that in the present context we imply no adverse judgment of P.) The pause with glottal closure after *so*, and

then the spacing-out of the three adjectives, the first two with non final intonations and the third with a distinctly final one, are reminiscent of "dramatic reading," and not characteristic of ordinary informal conversation. The wording–particularly the non-use of * *and* between the second and third adjectives–also contributes to the impression.

A sort of pedantic itemization, of which P's rehearsed statement is reminiscent, is customary in schools and in certain other situations where a student or junior is addressing a teacher or other senior. This style is perhaps especially emphasized by doctors. We learn later that P is a nurse. Her experience as a nurse may have reinforced earlier school experience to supply the basis for the pedantic itemizing style; one need only think of a nurse delivering a report on a patient, partly from written notes (* *The patient was sleepless, uncomfortable, . . .*). P knows, and has known in advance, that this interview is with a doctor, and knows from experience that the "nurse's report" style is one of the appropriate ways to address a doctor.

Is this evidence strong enough to warrant the authors' disregard for their own methodological principle? After listening to P2b several times, I found their argument compelling. However, the reader is not required to accept my judgment on faith. Since the record of this interview is available in most university libraries (Gill et al 1957), the interested reader can make their own judgment. For this reason, all of the authors' inferences are directly falsifiable, which gives their study a unique evidential status. Perhaps the raw data can serve as a warrant for the *validity* of the findings. The ready availability of the raw data stands in stark contrast to quantitative studies. I return to this issue below, when I consider an appropriate methodology for testing the theory that is offered here.

If we accept the authors' assertion about this utterance, then we are confronting an important issue. The authors are claiming that not only are they are able to share the conscious experience of the person being studied, as they do many times in their analysis, but in this instant, they are able to understand what the patient was thinking before she even arrived on the scene. They attribute to her what Mead called "imaginative rehearsal." Moreover, they are so confident of the validity of their imputation that they seem to forget their own rule, of rigorously separating inference from observation.

Another example of their unguarded style of inference occurs in their analysis of T4: "In either case, *it is clear that P does not understand T*, and the only obvious factor that may possibly be responsible is his intended opaque intonation." (Emphasis added in this and the following passage.) In the next sentence they also make an impetuous inference with respect to T's experience: "After a silence of eight seconds (which is quite a long time), this [the authors are referring to

P not understanding T3] *becomes obvious to T,* and he tries again." In an unself-conscious way, the authors infer, with great confidence, the inner experience of the interactants at this moment in the session.

Except for these and a few similar lapses, the book is a model of scientific rigor and probity. How can the lapse be explained? To understand the source of these errors, it will be necessary to consider the two further methods that the authors used to interpret the text they studied.

The third of the authors' methods is the prospective–retrospective method of understanding (Schutz 1962). In interpreting the significance of the utterance being considered, the authors do not limit themselves to the immediate context, but range far and wide, backward and forward.

For example, in their analysis of P2, quoted above, the inference that it is rehearsed is based on their knowledge that later in the interview P reveals that she is a nurse. The authors use this piece of information, which is prospective, in a retrospective way: she may have been accustomed, as a nurse, to reporting to doctors in the "pedantic" style they hear in P2. Thus the rehearsal inference is based not merely on the authors' knowledge of events in the text, but also their imagination of the P's experiences even before she began this transaction. In interaction, as well as in research on interaction, to understand the significance of an utterance, one must consider not only what is happening at the moment, but also what has happened before, and what might happen in the future.

Although the authors never mention this method, it is a vital element in their analysis. They use it in all of their more extensive interpretations. I have just described one of their many uses to infer a moment of the patient's inner experience. They also use it, again only implicitly, to explain the basis of their own understanding of the text.

For example, they state that by the therapist's sixteenth utterance, they all three "came to have the feeling" that T's manner to this point in the text was usually "cold, detached, and remote." They explain that it was only at this point in the analysis "that we finally realized that all of us had been registering a certain reaction to T's speech." In retrospect, they had understood they had been having a similar reaction to most of his earlier utterances that they were having to T16. Although not mentioned, their knowledge of T's manner after T16 was probably also involved. The interpretation of T's intonation in T16 utilized, it would seem, the prospective-retrospective method.

They also use this method with their analysis of T16 in a much more wide-ranging way. They state that their "impression of relative coldness is based on a comparison of his interview style with styles of everyday conversation. Perhaps relative to the interview styles of other therapists, T's manner in this interview would be felt as warm" (134). In the first sentence they seem to be saying that they each actually carried out, in their own mind, a comparision of T's style with what each thought of as the style of intonation of the average everyday conversation. In the second sentence they say that they did not actually carry out a comparison of T's style with the other therapists that they have known, but if they had, his might have turned out warmer.

Although it is only implicit, I believe that the authors used these two inferences throughout their analysis, in imputing understandings to the two interactants. That is, they used the first inference to imply that the patient must also have heard T's intonations as cold and detached, since her standard of comparison would be not other therapists, but ordinary conversations. (We learn toward the end of the interview that P had seen a psychiatrist only once before the present interview.) They use the second inference to imply that T, on the contrary, might have been hearing his intonation relative to other therapists. This point is hinted at in the authors' analysis of T3 and of T16 ("the special sub-culture of the psychiatric interview").

One might consider these two inferences to be couched in the authors' most completely guarded style of inferential statements, since they are never actually stated (my single jest in these sober pages!). Nevertheless, these inferences overshadow the authors' whole analysis: the two interactants have a misunderstanding about the meaning of T's intonations, since they bring to the transaction two different sets of earlier experiences. The method of prospective-retrospective understanding can be seen to be a powerful tool for reaching interpretive understandings.

The fourth and final of the authors' methods they refer to as the "Working Principle of Reasonable Alternatives." I prefer to call it the method of *counterfactual variants*, in order to relate it to earlier developments in philosophy and social theory. Counterfactuality concerns what might have happened in a given instance, but did not. In human experience, the imagination of what might have happened often seems to be at least as important as what actually happened.

Although Mead (1934) did not use this term, his theory provides a disciplined analysis of the origins of counterfactual imagination in the development of the self, and its importance in social interaction. The movement from the *game stage* to the stage of the *generalized other* is the basis for the human ability to escape from outer stimuli. It lays the foundation for the ability to construct imaginary standpoints, which is necessary for reflective intelligence and the construction of a self.

Vaihinger's philosophy of "as if" (1924) explores some of the implications of the ability to live in worlds which are subjunctive, contingent, or conditional.

By far the most comprehensive exploration of this issue can be
found in the work of George Steiner, in his magnum opus, *After Babel*
(1975). Although focused on the problems involved in translation
from one language to another, Steiner's book also establishes that *all
understanding involves translation, translation from one mind to another.*
Every understanding involves "translation" from the personal idiom
and cultural background of one person, to the personal idiom and
cultural background of another, from one imagined world to another.
His discussion of the all but insuperable impediments to communication between men and women, ethnic groups, and social classes
exactly parallels his illustrations of the limitless chances for error in
interlingual translation.

Counterfactuality is also of fundamental importance in physical
and social science, but is virtually undiscussed. Peirce's concept of
abduction implies the critical importance of counterfactuals. Pierce
seems to be saying that if the scientist is to come up with an original
and important hypothesis, he or she must be just as aware of what is
not occurring as what is. One does not observe events passively, but
within a framework, a framework which includes counterfactual
conditions or expectations.

The prevailing mood in modern science is inductive: one makes
discoveries by passively observing nature. According to this view,
systematic observation gives rise to generalizations about recurring
sequences of events. As suggested, Mead and other theorists of
counterfactuality indicated that all human understanding, including
scientific understanding, depends upon the imagination, as well as on
accurate observations. Pittenger and his colleagues not only reacted to
the actual utterances they could hear on the tape, they seem to have
understood what was said by placing it in the context of what could
have been said but was not. A brief and somewhat begrudging
acknowledgement of the importance of counterfactuality in physical
science can be found in Hofstadter. (1975, 634–640, 641–644.)

Pittenger et al. frequently employed the method of counterfactual
variants. As already indicated, in their first analysis of an utterance by
T (T2), they note that three of the four words in "What brings you
here?" are "substitutes," words with no actual reference. In order to
understand the significance of T2 as uttered, they contrast it with five
alternatives which were not uttered: "what *troubles, what *problems,
what *difficulties," and, instead of "here," T might have said *"to a
psychiatrist" or *"to this clinic." Similarly, in my own comparison of

what the authors might have done had they noticed that most of the words in T1 were also substitutes, they might have tried out the sentence "Will you please sit there, Mrs. Johnson, where it will be convenient and comfortable for you?" as a counterfactual alternative to T1. (This is an actual initial sentence used by another therapist, FD2's therapist in Lewis 1971.)

As they did the prospective–retrospective method, the authors use the method of counterfactual variants in every one of their major interpretations at least once. In the case of T2, they use it twice. The first use, quoted above, was to try alternatives involving words which were not substitutes. The second use of the method on T2 was much more elaborate, trying out 5 variant stress patterns in the sentence, with the greatest stress on "What" for the first variant, on "brings" for the second, and so on. Since T's actual utterance contained a complex pattern of stresses, with ties between two words, and a crucial change in stress from the beginning of the last word to its end, the authors could have tried out many more than five variants.

At first glance it might seem that the method of counterfactual variants, as used by the authors, is laborious beyond any conceivable value it might have. Since I am going to claim that if anything, the authors were too timid, rather than too bold, I will draw some of the implications of their analysis of T2 (and of mine of T1) for an understanding of the emotional exchange between T and P during the first moments of the session.

With respect to T2, the authors make the case that the words used are mostly substitutes, and that they have an opaque intonation. Later in their analysis, they imply that P has misunderstood the meaning that T intended for his intonations, as part of their interpretation of the impact of T's style on P throughout the first five minutes. This is the only use they make of their lengthy analysis of T2. They never refer to the significance of T's use of substitutes at all.

If we wish to understand the emotional components of the ex-changes between T and P, we can make further use of the authors' analysis of T2, if we join it with my comments on the similarity between the words used in T1 and T2; most of the words in both sentences were substitutes. Suppose we extend the method of counter-factual variants beyond its uses at the hands of the authors. They limit themselves to imagining words or sentences alternative to those that were used by the therapist (who I will call Dr. Noland) and the patient, who I have already referred to as Mrs. Johnson.

Suppose that instead of Mrs. Frank Johnson, the patient had been Mrs. Lyndon Johnson. Is it conceivable that T could have greeted her with these two blankcheck sentences? ("Will you sit there?" and

"What brings you here?") We know that the second sentence was intoned opaquely. Even if we allow that the intonation of T1 might have been more normal than T2, since Gill, et al. tell us that it was spoken softly, the conclusion still seems inescapable, to take on the authors' most impetuous style of inferential statement. Mrs. Lyndon Johnson would have found these two utterances insufferably rude, and would probably have said so, and perhaps even bid Dr. Noland a heated farewell. The counterfactual of Mrs. Lyndon Johnson implies that Mrs. Martha Johnson may also have been insulted by T's manner.

I have drawn upon the authors' analysis of the verbal and non-verbal elements in the early parts of the session to solve the problem of the patient's withdrawal at P3, and the therapist's response to her withdrawal. Their analysis, and my extension of it, indicates that P heard the therapist's first two utterances as cold and detached, to the point of rudeness. She became confused and hurt by this treatment, to the point of withdrawing.

Turning now to their analysis of the therapist's experience of P3, and P's silence after T4a, the authors infer that he must have understood her hearing of his initial utterances as detached, because he changes his manner of intonation in T4b ("Do you sometimes?") it becomes much more evocative of interest and concern, as in ordinary, as opposed to therapy conversations. Furthermore, they argue, the patient's response in P4 seems to confirm these inferences; she ends her withdrawal, resuming her part in the conversation. Using the authors' analysis and my own, it has been possible to arrive at an understanding of a crisis and its resolution.

It should be noted that the last two of the four methods used by the authors differ in character from the first two. The prospective–retrospective and counterfactual methods are intuitive and freewheeling; they draw upon the resources of the entire culture. In order to understand a particular utterance, Pittenger et al. do not limit themselves to the immediate context, but range far and wide in their imagination, over what could have happened before, during, or after the utterance.

The first two methods, the exhaustive analysis of the text and the separation of observation and inference, are, by contrast, not intuitive but analytical. These methods are used to control and discipline the flight of the imagination. The continuous shuttling back and forth between imaginative and analytic methods, between intuition and observation implied in their narrative, illustrates what Peirce meant by the method of abduction. If one interprets a text that is publically available, as Peirce did not, the interpretation may be as verifiable as in any other method in science.

Implicature, context and social structure

In this section I outline a model of the process which links individual behavior to social structure, using the Pittenger et al. study as an example. Since their narrative provides a report not only of their methods and findings but of their inner experiences, it can be used to envision the complex process of social action. The key concepts in the proposed model are the *message stack*, on the one hand, and the *extended context*, on the other.

The authors understood the intentions of the interactants because they did not limit themselves to observing their actual utterances, but also imagined their inner experiences. In order to accomplish this feat, the authors referred not only to the interactants' words and non-verbal gestures, but also to their feelings and to the "implicature," the unstated implications of their words and gestures.

An example of implicature is the authors' comments on the therapist's choice of pronominals in T3, and the flatness of intonation. *"Here we go again! How many times have I heard this kind of thing before!" This sentence was never actually uttered. It is the meaning which the authors imagine the patient attributed to the words and gestures in T3. The authors constructed this counterfactual implication by shuttling back and forth between the words and gestures they observed before, during, and after this moment, imagining what these words and gestures might have implied to the patient. This is the informal process of testing inferences about inner experience by checking their implications against observable outer signs, the process of role-taking.

Although the authors are extremely energetic in pursuit of the unstated implications of the words and gestures, they are much less so with respect to the fourth component of the message stack, the feelings. Like Labov and Fanshel (1977), they limit themselves to the inductive method with respect to feelings. They note the occurrence of signs of anger and embarrassment, but do not construct complex inferences with respect to them, as they do with the implicature. Because no theories of emotional process were available to them, both sets of authors emphasize the cognitive components of the interaction they observed.

Lewis's work on feeling traps provides a way of integrating all four components of the message stack. The observables, the words and gestures, provide data for making inferences about the inner experiences of the interactants, the thoughts and feelings.

The method of inferring implicature plays a crucial role, since it serves as a bridge between observables and inner feelings on the other. If the interactants *stated* the implications of their actual words and gestures, rather than being silent about them, they could probably understand why such intense emotions are aroused by them. Since the interactants do not state them, however, and seldom investigate them, they ignore or are puzzled by the intense *feelings* engendered.

My analysis of the components of the message stack in the interview suggests that the therapist and the patient are seldom attuned because they are enmeshed in a feeling trap. Mutual resentment, puzzlement, and misunderstanding occur because of chain reactions of shame and anger within and between them. The signs of a shame-anger spiral are clear in the patient, her embarrassment and exasperation. They are less obvious in the therapist, however. To clarify this point, it is necessary to return to the distinction between bypassed and overt, undifferentiated emotion.

My interpretation of the patient's emotional state is that from T3 onwards, she is frequently involved in a spiral of *overt*, undifferentiated shame and anger. She is grossly insulted by the therapist's manner. Although she tries to hide her feelings, they can be inferred from her words and gestures, as Pittenger et al. show.

Bypassed emotion does not cause disruption of behavior and speech, as the overt, undifferentiated type does. Rather it disrupts the fine-tuning of thought necessary for effective action in problematic situations. Since one's inner resources are given over to emotional arousal and to the attempt to hide it, one can not devote full attention to problem-solving. At best, while obsessing because of unacknowledged shame and anger, one can go into a holding pattern, repeating stereotyped behavior sequences.

In the present instance, the therapist does not respond constructively to the impasse between him and the patient. As Pittenger et al. indicate, his agenda appears to be to discourage the patient from her repeated emotional complaints about her husband. Like the patient, he simply repeats the same sequence over and over, even though it is ineffective. He does not attempt to negotiate about their respective agendas: *"I notice that you keep complaining about your husband. Could you get away from him awhile, and talk more about yourself?" Similarly, the patient does not say *"I notice that every time I express emotion, you respond by ignoring it and asking me a question about some irrelevant fact. I am puzzled and offended, because you seem to be condemning my feelings just like my husband does. What are you doing?" Since their conflicting agendas are never discussed, they butt heads for the entire interview.

It is possible that the therapist is ineffective because the patient's behavior touches off his own shame–anger sequence. He may have experienced the patient's balking and emotionality as insulting to his authority, or, more subtly, to his competence as a therapist. In order to test this hypothesis, it would be necessary to investigate this same therapist's behavior in a different setting, one in which he was acting effectively, to highlight the subtle signs of bypassed shame and rage in the present interview.

The inference of enmeshment of the two interactants leads to the last issue to be discussed. In what way are the exchanges of feeling and innuendo that are discussed here related to social structure? The spontaneous use of prospective-retrospective and counterfactual methods by the interactants, and by Pittenger et al., and by Labov and Fanshel, who use very similar methods in their study, suggest an answer to this question.

These methods imply that in order to understand the meaning of even a single utterance, it may be necessary to invoke not just the immediate *context*, but what might be called the *extended context*, i.e. all that has happened before or after, retrospectively and prospectively, and all that might have happened instead, counterfactually. Each interpretation of meaning presupposes not only the history of the whole relationship, but also the history of the whole society, in so far as it is known to the interactants. Effective communication implies a social structure shared between the interactants. In so far as interaction takes place in an open domain such as natural language, and in so far as the interactants are experts in that domain, then each exchange depends upon, and helps maintain the social structure.

I have argued that there is a micro-world underlying all social interaction. This micro-world connects individuals in shared meanings and feelings, and also connects them to the social structure of their society. I have given an example of analysis of the micro-world involved in a single brief exchange between a therapist and his patient. In this example, following Pittenger et al., I examined the message stack of words, gestures, implicature and feelings that occurred at several particular moments during the exchange. By interpreting these stacks, we can come to understand the thoughts and feelings of the interactants.

According to the theory outlined here, social interaction involves an open domain. In order to understand any given utterance, the interactants must have access to the extended context of the utterance, all events which took place or could have taken place before, during, and after the particular moment. The micro-momentary actions of the interactants in relating the moment to the extended context connect them with the social structure. Paradoxically, understanding social structure involves examination of the minute events in the micro-world.

The methodology appropriate to testing such a theory requires painstaking analysis of recorded instances of social interaction: the repeated playing of film or audiotape allows the researcher to use the same intuitive interpretation of the message stack that is used by the interactants. I have argued, in another place, that the reporting of this kind of study would require that the recorded text be appended, so that the readers could also use their own intuitive expertise in assessing the validity of the findings (Scheff 1986). A method like this would bridge the present gap between the proponents of objective measurement and those who uphold intuitive methods, perhaps helping to resolve what are usually thought of as irreconcilable differences.

Social status and respect

One question that Pittenger et al. did not consider was the social status of P relative to T. and a closely related question, the amount and type of courtesy that P felt was due her from T. These questions, in turn, will lead us to a discussion of what Goffman (1967) referred to as ritual aspects of the interaction between T. and P. and particularly, the amount of deference or respect that P thought she was entitled to from T, and the amount that she actually got. These questions, as I will argue below, are crucial for an understanding of the emotional components of the transaction being considered.

For the moment, suffice it to say that the method of hypothetical alternatives as the authors have used it, and as I have extended it, has led to a set of new hypotheses:

1. T accords P less deference than is normative for a therapist in relation to a patient in our society.
2. The deficit in the amount of deference T shows to P, in combination with his usual stance of therapeutic detachment, not only confuses her, but also "hurts her feelings", to use the vernacular phrase. Translating these vernacular terms into more precise concepts of emotional reponse, T's manner toward P arouses in her the affects of surprise, shame (humiliation) and anger.
3. Since these affects are never dispelled in the interview, or even acknowledged, they are disruptive. T1 through T3 may be thought of as a trauma from which the interview never recovers. P's level of symptomatic behavior, as evidenced by the content and pattern of her utterances, rises and falls somewhat during the interview, but

shows no improvement, on the average, throughout the whole course of the interview.

Note that the validity of the second hypothesis is not dependent on the validity of the first. Whether or not the first hypothesis is true, the second depends only on P's perceptions, and her emotional responses to them. If P felt that she was getting less respect from T than was her due, the rest of this hypothesis and the next should follow. This is fortunate, because the first hypothesis might be difficult (but probably not impossible) to prove.

Here I will concentrate on evaluating the second hypothesis, that P was surprised, insulted, and angered by T's manner. The evaluation of the third hypothesis, on the effects of P's emotional state on the interview, since it concerns the entire interview and not just the first five minutes, was attempted in an earlier article (Scheff 1985a). Suffice it to say here that this hypothesis is congruent with the theoretical and empirical work of Lewis (1971;1981) on shame and anger dynamics, and the empirical studies by Retzinger (1985a; 1985b).

With respect to the first hypothesis, I will not attempt to test it, but only offer some scattered evidence that supports its plausibility. The absence of the standard courtesies from T1 and T2, the use of the patient's name, for example, along with a respectul status label ("Mrs. Johnson", or much less courteously, but still more courteous than the omission of the name, Martha,") seems to me more appropriate for use with a child or servant than with a patient.

It is true that T1 is not completely devoid of courtesy. It is phrased as a question, rather than as a command ("Sit there" would have been unambiguously insulting) and, as already indicated, it was spoken softly. However, the use of substitute words, in conjunction with the same usage in T2, and the non-use of the patient's name would at least raise a question in P's mind whether she was being treated with adequate courtesy. If this question was raised by T1, T2 very likely provided the answer. T2 is absolutely bare of courtesy. It is brief, packed with pronominal forms that give it a very abstract and impersonal tone (like the omission of the patient's name in T1), and intoned in a way, as already indicated, that P was very likely to hear as cold, aloof, and detached.

The situation could still have been saved if T had used P's name in this utterance. I have tried different stress renderings of the four-word question with P's name added to the end: "What brings you here, Mrs. Johnson?" It seemed to me that the addition of her name made it very difficult for me not to give the question a nearly normal pattern of stresses, with the highest stress on the end of the word "here", rather than the opaque intonation which T actually used.

Since T's failure to call P by name seems so troublesome, I will give some consideration to the scene that might have happened immediately before the transcript begins. It is important to note that just as T does not address P by name, she does not use his name either. This raises the question of how they were able to identify each other as the persons that each wished to meet. Suppose that prior to the meeting, P identified herself to the receptionist, and the receptionist, in turn, introduced P to T. which would be one of the customary ways in which this type of meeting is arranged. If the introduction were managed in this way, T and P would have probably had only a very minimal exchange before the transcript begins, possibly only a "How do you do?" by each of them.

It seems unlikely that any exchange preliminary to the beginning of the transcript could have softened the brusqueness of T's initial utterances T1–3, unless it was rather extensive. If the exchange were very brief, even a very solicitous and courteous manner would not have helped, since P would have been even more surprised and perhaps shocked by the contrast presented by T1–3. It is conceivable, however, that T might have been very cordial in the reception room. Then, during their walk to the interviewing room (Gill et al. tell us that they entered together), he might have explained the meaning of his manner: "Look, Mrs. Johnson. We haven't much time, considering what we have to accomplish, so I am going to waive the usual chitchat and get right down to business. Is that alright with you?" The approach of explaining his intentions to P before trying to carry them out would probably have enlisted her cooperation, and have changed of the interview.

Given what actually happened in the interview, however, this scenario seems unlikely. At no point in the interview does T explain any of his intentions. His pattern of behavior, as far as it can be known from the transcript, gives us no basis for imagining that he would have acted any differently beforehand. Moreover, P's responses in the beginning of the interview, especially P3, implies that she had not been prepared for T's manner; she seems to be surprised, puzzled, and hurt. The most likely scenario is that T's manner beforehand was much like it was in T1–3, curt to the point of rudeness, with perhaps the addition of a brief and faint social smile at the moment of introduction, which would not have added much warmth to his appearance. Under these conditions, the two would have proceeded together into the interviewing room in a faintly embarrassed, and for P, ominous silence.

The question remains as to why T might have accorded P less deference that is normative, and less then she felt entitled to from him. The text provides some hints in this matter, and in a somewhat indirect way, the authors' comments on several of P's utterances. My comments will mainly concern P's social status relative to T's along the dimensions of gender, age, and social class. In addition, I will briefly address the issue of P's personal appearance also.

The first and probably the most important status difference between T and P is their gender. The Gill et al. volume was published in 1954; this interview was recorded in the early 1950s, some twenty years before the beginning of women's liberation. The patient is a thirty-year-old nurse, whose husband, as we learn later in the interview, is a truckdriver, giving us grounds to believe that P is from the working class, rather than the middle class. There are two bits of evidence which run counter to this supposition. First of all, she says, in answer to one of T's questions, that her religion is "Protestant Episcopal," rather than Catholic, as T seems to have expected. (He asked her what her religion was after she had indicated, in P23, tha she was opposed to divorce.) This religious denomination reflects middle-, rather working-class status.

The second bit of evidence which at first glance, at least, is indicative of middle-class status is the absence, in P's speech, of strong markers of social class. Given the acknowledgements in the preface of the Gill volume, it would seem that this interview took place in New Haven, Connecticut. The working-class dialect of New England, which is strongest perhaps in Boston, is not consistently present in P's speech. Since I am not a specialist in this area, I am unable to make the kind of definitive assessment of this issue that someone like Labov could.

What is most needed for my analysis, however, is not an assessment of P's absolute social class, which might turn out to be a rather complex matter, but only her status relative to T. This issue seems much simpler to me. From listening to the interview as a whole, I am reasonably confident that P's class status is lower than T's. There are some indications of working class, rather than middle-class pronunciation in several of P's utterance which seem strong even to me. For example, her articulation of the phrase "candy bars" the first time she says it in P14, with the "a" in "candy" flattened and rasped, is indicative of the working-class patois of New England. It is of some interest to note that she repeats this phrase, "Candy bars," for no readily apparent reason.

Why is this particular phrase repeated? This question leads into the detailed particulars of P's social class position. I looked at the authors' phonemic analysis to see if there was any difference between her first pronunciation of this phrase and her second. They show none, rendering both as "kehndiy". But when I listened to the tape, I could hear a difference between the way she articulated the vowel. The second time she said the word there was less flattening and less rasp. I believe that she heard what was to her an undesirable articulation in her first pronunciation, and she corrected it in her second. A similar sequence occurs in P153. The first time she used the phrase " a hue and cry" she actually said "a hue and a cry."Two sentences later, ending the utterance, she uses the phrase again, but this time correctly, "a hue and cry. " Apparently she was monitoring her own speech, at least in these two instances, in order to correct errors. (She does not catch them all, however. In P40, tearfully, she states that she is so depressed that she has wanted to turn on the gas and jump out of the window.) The way in which she corrects her errors of pronunciation and phrasing in P14 and 153 implies that P is of working-class origins, but aspires to enter the middle class, at least in her manner of speaking. The fact that she is taking more classes toward college graduation (P31) provides some support for this possibility also.

Although it is only a conjecture, this line of reasoning about P's class aspirations also might be used to explain her answer to T's question about her religion. Like many persons who aspire to a higher class position, she might have joined a church of higher status that that of her parents. At this time I have no way of checking this idea.

There is one more bit of evidence for the supposition that P had a working class background in a comment that the authors make about one of her utterances. About the second half of P8b ("I'm in a constant stew."), when she is complaining about her husband, the authors state that this utterance sounds as though she were beginning a "fishwifely whine"–that is, to be stewing. Thus she is acting out what she is describing." What the authors seem to be alluding to is the emotional quality of this utterance. However, instead of trying to define the nature of the emotional components involved, they resort instead to an unfortunate epithet: "fishwifely whine."

It seems to me that there are three different types of disparagment in the phrase "fishwifely whine." The authors are male members of the middle class, referring to the emotionality of a woman who is probably lower in class status. The term "fishwife" carries connotations of disparagement based both on gender and class distinctions, and the word "whine" has some connotation of disparagement of what seems to be perceived as unpleasant or improper emotionality. The authors inadvertent use of a gender-class epithet suggests that they heard P8b, at least, as indicative of a working-class quality in P's speech.

I heard several other indications of working-class pronunciation in P's speech (one of them, the absence on any final "r" in "November" in P14, was much stronger than her pronunciation of "candy bars.'). I heard no such indications in any of T's speech in the course of the entire interview. His speech seems to me devoid of class or regional speech markers, which is probably itself a marker of upper middle class speech. His occupation makes him a member of the middle-class. His speech indicates middle, rather than working-class origins. For this reason, and the reasons already discussed with respect to P's speech, I feel confident that T's class position is higher than P's.

Although I have no way of ascertaining T's exact age, I am also confident that he is older than P. The sound of his voice is not that of a young man. The breezy, almost brazen self-assurance with which he treats P suggests that he has had considerable experience at his job; there is very little tentativeness in his manner anywhere in the interview. What is most convincing with respect to his being consider-ably experienced at his work is the great skill with which he carries out what I consider to be his standard agenda for a first interview. I am far from saying that this skill was helpful to the patient. Rather I would say that he shows that he is quite skillful in carrying through what probably was the standard psychotherapeutic agenda for the time and place in which the interview took place, parrying what he sensed to be patients' projections in order to help them resolve what he thought to be their neurotic patterns. For the reasons given, I would guess T to be in his early or middle forties.

Given the evidence adduced above, it would seem that T and P differed in status in terms of their gender, age, and social class. T would seem to have been a middle-class man who was older than P, a working-class woman. There are two more considerations to be discussed which might be relevant to T's manner toward P, as it seemed to be manifested in the beginning of the interview, and , as it would appear, throughout its entire course.

The first concerns the occupations of the two interactants, an issue which the authors themselves allude to. They say, in their analysis of P3, with reference to what they call its "pedantic itemizing style": P knows, and has known in advance, that this interview is with a doctor, and knows from experience that the 'nurse's report' is one of the appropriate ways to address a doctor. Because of their respective occupations, P is an enlisted soldier in an army in which T is an officer. Although he might not have known this at the beginning of the interview (this would depend on whether there was an appli-cation form that he had seen), her manner or bearing might have suggested it to him. This would seem to be a matter of distinctions of rank, which might be considered to be closely related to class distinctions.

The usual manner of most doctors toward nurses even today is still peremptory, if not completely authoritarian. They are treated as subordinates, and at times, almost like servants. If T had some foreknowledge of P's occupation, or if he merely responded to clues from her manner or appearance, that would explain most or all of the lack of deference with which he treats her. The authors' comment about P3 cited above suggests the possibility, for example, that P might have inadvertently and unconsciously manifested a subservient attitude toward T from the beginning, since he is an older male doctor, which gives him not just one, but three markers of status higher than hers. Just as these markers might have called out in P her habitual manner of subservience toward doctors, his reaction to her might have been in his habitual mode toward nurses, peremptory.

There is one more matter to be considered, which concerns T's reaction to P's appearance. If T had found P to be quite attractive when he met her, this reaction could have overridden all of the status differences that have been discussed. At this time there is no way of directly evaluating this issue. There is some indirect evidence however, in several comments the authors make about P's manner early in the interview. They use the term "kittenish" several times to try to convey the manner of several of her utterances. This term bears a faint intimation of heterosexual maneuvering on P's part. The authors report no trace of such activity on T's part, however, nor do I note any in the course of the whole interview. This discussion implies that T is not particularly attracted to P, and does not reject the possibility that he finds her unattractive.

The discussion above, of the evidence suggesting that T showed less than the normative amount of deference toward P, completes my re-analysis of the interview which Pittenger et al. studied. I have argued that his rudeness toward her, when coupled with his aloof style as a therapist, dealt the patient's self-esteem a blow from which she was unable to recover during the course of the interview. My analysis of ritual interaction between therapist and patient, and of the emotional effects of this interaction on the patient, has put the interview in a very different light than it was seen by Gill et al., and Pittenger et al. , because it explicates the social structural effects in the interview.

Summary and conclusions

In this chapter I have analyzed an audiotape of a psychiatric inter-view, and Pittenger et al.'s analysis of the first five minutes of that interview. By focusing on very short spans of time in the interview, and by adding an analysis of the patient's emotional responses, I have extended the authors' findings concerning this interview, and formulated some testable hypotheses concerning symptom formation in relationship to the interaction between patient and therapist. I have also called attention to some innovations in the authors' methods which may be useful in future research. Given these advances, it is conceivable that the general problem of understanding between persons, and the special version of this problem for the social and behavioral sciences, the implementation of a verstehende soziologie, may be solvable.

CHAPTER 8

Conflict in family systems

This chapter uses the topic of conflict in families to show how the family is a system in which each relationship is part of the family whole. What are the origins of quarrels which are unending? Even a casual glance at current newspapers assures that such conflicts constitute a vast human problem. Scientific and scholarly reports suggest the same conclusion. There is a specific type of escalating conflict which has proved extremely difficult to understand, not only for the participants, but for researchers as well. In this type of conflict, the initial sources of conflict may be trivial. In any case, once in conflict, the disputants may forget its origins. More important, conflict often continues even when it is clear that even the winner faces ruin if fighting does not stop. What are such fights about?

This chapter builds upon the previous discussions of the origins of interminable conflict in emotion dynamics and alienation. I suggest that some of the origins may be found threates to the bond, and in emotions that are so disguised from self and others as to be almost invisible. The hypothesis proposed here derives from the work of Lewis (1971) on unacknowledged shame. In my formulation, interminable conflicts are caused by alienation and the hidden shame which accompanies it.

This chapter once again uses part/whole morphology. In the present day human sciences, there is a vast gap between qualitative and quantitative approaches. Here I explore a method that might help fill this void. I apply the new approach to a specific problem, sequences of shame and anger in alienated family interaction.

If shame is evoked but goes unacknowledged, the result may be a repetitive cycle of insult and revenge. Unacknowledged shame in party A can lead to A's anger or further shame, which can then lead to A's hostility toward or withdrawal from party B. If A's hostility or withdrawal leads to unacknowledged shame in B, then B may repeat

This chapter is based on Scheff 1995.

the same cycle as A. When this is the case, the two parties become trapped in an interminable quarrel (hostility–hostility) or impasse (withdrawal–withdrawal).

In my theory, shame is treated as both an individual and a social phenomena. It is both a genetically determined emotion within individuals and equally a signal of the state of a social relationship, revealing the degree of alienation (separation or engulfment) of the participants. Shame cues signal alienation in social interaction; too great or too little exposure of one's position can disrupt the relationship. (Too much exposure may feel like suffocation or violation, too little, invisibility or rejection).

By treating shame as part of a transpersonal system, this chapter bridges two hitherto disparate literatures, the individual and social psychology of shame. I articulate the components of a complex system: the degree of attunement in social relationships (the mix between solidarity and alienation), sequences of emotions, and, finally, the degree of awareness of the participants of their level of alienation and of their emotions.

The principal literature on interminable conflicts is found in the anthropology of duels, feuds, and vendettas. These reports show that unending conflicts between individuals and groups is a universal feature of the human condition, to be found in virtually all historical eras and cultural contexts. This literature is particularly useful in teaching us that such conflicts can transcend individuals, handed down from one generation to another.

Descriptions of never-ending conflicts can also be found in reports on family systems, although this literature is less clearly defined. The linguistic analysis of family discourse by Labov and Fanshel (1977) is a well-known example in this genre. In this study, the researchers conducted an extremely detailed analysis of both verbal and non-verbal behavior, second by second, in the discourse of a family of an anorexic woman. They were surprised to find that virtually every word and gesture used by family members was conflictual, and that the family members themselves were almost completely unaware of their own contributions to the conflict.

Many clinical accounts make the same point less explicitly: unending conflict between family members is quite common, even though in many of the cases the participants themselves seem unaware, or only partially aware of their own hostility and aggression, and that of the other members. Although the studies of group and family conflict are helpful in framing the problem of interminable quarrels, most of them provide little or no explanation of its sources, being descriptive rather than explanatory. The anthropological studies, particularly, limit themselves to describing the patterns of behavior, with no attempt at causal explanations.

Most of the studies of family conflict are also descriptive. However, there is a tradition of studies of family communications and family systems which powerfully advances our understanding. Summarizing this tradition, Watzlawick, Beavin and Jackson (1967) carefully define interminable conflict and review earlier studies of family conflict. These studies focus upon defective communication practices that lead to conflict. In this same tradition is the work of Bowen (1978), who calls attention to specific types of conflict-producing communication patterns.

The family systems approach has been extremely important in increasing our understanding of quarrels and impasses. The present study is based in part on these earlier studies. It is probably true that interminable conflict is caused by dysfunctional communication patterns, but what causes these patterns? Like most theories of human behavior, even those studies which attempt explanations content themselves to emphasizing a single link in what may be a long causal chain.

Other examples of partial approaches can be found in the literature of experimental social psychology and in marital communication studies. For brevity, I will comment on only one study, since it is representative of the approach. Brockner and Rubin (1985) review a series of laboratory experiments concerning entrapment in and escalation of conflict. These experiments all involve a single causal variable (for example, individual differences in "self-justifying commitments to past actions"). Although most of the results are statistically significant, the amount of variation explained is always extremely small, suggesting that many other variables not included in the study are much more important causes than those included.

Another limitation of the experimental literature is that it virtually excludes contextual cues of the kind that are necessary for detecting unacknowledged shame. Laboratory experiments seek to *verify* rather *generate* theory. For this reason, they use settings and instruments which provide little biographic and interactional information. But emotions cues are embedded in this kind of information. Context plays a significant role in the kinds of interpretations that are central to my analysis of conflict systems in families.

It is significant that the adherents of the various approaches to conflict seldom cite approaches other than their own, or seem to be even aware their existence. Experimental social psychologists, for example, do not cite family systems literature, and vice versa. It is my belief that in order to make progress, we must utilize the insights available in the various approaches, integrating them into a complete theory of conflict. In this chapter, I draw upon several approaches, particularly family systems theory, sociolinguistics, and sociology of emotions, seeking to generate, rather than verify, a theory of interminable conflict (for a justification of this approach, see Glaser and Strauss 1967).

A useful theory should do more than explain the relation between two aspects of conflict. It should clearly spell out the whole system which results in conflict. That is, it should provide both conceptual and operational definitions of the concepts that are needed to explain the conflict, and the *causal links* between these components. At least in the early stages of theory development, the complexity of such a system makes attempts at verification premature. The theory first needs to be stated clearly enough so that it can ultimately be tested.

This approach focuses on an issue seldom broached in the human sciences literature, the huge gap between qualitative and quantitative methods. Qualitative methods are used to describe human behavior and to generate theory. But these types of studies have many limitations from a scientific point of view. Typically, there is little attention to falsifiability, the concept that lies at the heart of all science. Qualitative workers claim that their work is more *valid* than that of quantitative workers, but they provide little or no documentation to back up this claim. Furthermore, studies of this kind pay no attention whatever to *reliability*, the repeatability of methods and techniques. Both shortcomings limit the credibility and more importantly, the usefulness of qualitative findings.

Most quantitative studies have strengths and limitations that are just the opposite of those of qualitative studies. Quantitative methods stress reliability, but give little attention to validity. As already indicated, most of these studies also avoid testing general, comprehensive theories, and delete from their data the kinds of evidence that would allow the assessment of context.

One way of bridging the gap between the two standard approaches is to blend the strongest elements of each, with a comprehensive metatheory. Here I combine elements of flexibility and intuition which underlie effective qualitative methods, with the explicitness and direct orientation to empirical data which underlie effective quantitative methods. Because of lack of space, this chapter must gloss over many details of the new approach. Once more I draw on the explicit coding system for shame and anger described by Retzinger (see Appendix).

An approach to the methods I use here was earlier suggested by

Campbell and Fiske (1959), the idea that concepts and theories might be validated by a multi-trait, multi-method orientation. However, in my judgment, they did not carry their suggestion far enough. In particular, they did not include elements of qualitative technique; all of the methods they suggest are quantitative.

The great advantage of the qualitative approach is that it allows the researcher to get quite close to the original events from which data are generated. By looking closely enough at discourse, the researcher is able to detect contextual clues to meaning, as already indicated, and also to observe unambiguous temporal relationships. This latter advantage is a powerful tool for generating causal theories. Combining the advantages of qualitative and quantitative approaches, I use concepts that are at least partly explicated, and show causal sequences of behavior in discourse.

Here I further develop a theory of conflict by closely examining discourse in families. My method follows that used by Labov and Fanshel (1977), but is more detailed and has a broader scope than theirs. In particular, I do not limit my analysis to cognition and behavior, as they did, but give equal attention to emotions and emotion cues. I outline the interrelations between thoughts, emotions and behavior as these components occur in social interaction.

Method

In my university classes I investigated family systems by having students role-play brief exchanges with their parents. On the first day of class, students were told this would be a requirement of the class (some students always left the class at this point). Through role-playing I taught students to examine their own contributions to the family status quo, as well as those of the other members. Initially most students were unaware of their own part in family problems. Although other kinds of exchanges were also touched upon, the most useful place to start seems to be conflictful exchanges, brief excerpts from quarrels of the kind that are discussed below.

At first sight it might seem misleading to try to understand a whole relationship, much less a whole family, on the basis of excerpts from conversations. I propose, however, that because of the complexity of human communication, every exchange is a microcosm, representing many of the elements of the larger relationship of which it is a part. Each exchange is like the smallest functioning unit of the relationship, standing to the whole as a cell does to the living organism of which it is a part. One cannot understand everything about the host organism from the cell. But, on the other hand, knowledge of the cell is of considerable help in understanding the larger system of which it is part.

Human communication is so complex and ambiguous that in order to understand it, participants must constantly be shuttling back and forth between the smallest moving parts, the words and gestures, and the largest wholes: not only the whole conversation of which the exchange is a part, but the whole relationship, family, society, and civilization out of which each utterance has grown. If the excerpt is the smallest cell, the civilization is the host organism. Human communication is an open system, incredibly charged with both meaning and ambiguity. Correctly deciphering human expressions requires skill, agility, and perseverance in the participants. In particular, there is a skill at improvisation that seems necessary in order to understand dialogue.

Researchers must be no less diligent and inventive than participants, if we are to understand human behavior. In this chapter, I employ the same kind of part/whole analysis of utterances that participants seem to use. I apply this kind of analysis to a set of verbatim texts. My interpretation of some of the dialogue also uses my own eyewitness observation, as in the case of the role-plays of the three student dialogues in this chapter, and conversations with students in my office.

Direct observation allows one access not only to the words but to the paralanguage, the manner of talk, as well as its verbal content. Like the thicket of gestures in which dialogue is enclosed, these facts provide a backdrop for a part/whole analysis, in order to ground verbal texts in their larger matrix of meaning. Specifically, I rate recurring communication patterns, which are directly observable, and hidden emotions, which can only be inferred from verbal and non-verbal cues.

My approach to the analysis of meaning in discourse has two advantages over being an actual participant. First, I can make explicit my assumptions and observations, describing in great detail how I have come to make my interpretation, and the facts upon which it is based. Actual participants are usually too immersed in their activity to have the luxury of such explicitness. The second advantage is closely related to the first. Unlike the participant, the researcher is able to replay an event as many times as necessary before making a decision. These two advantages suggest a resolution to the problem of meaning in human relationships, the problem that Geertz (1973) has described as "thick description" (Scheff 1986a).

One way to make one's assumptions explicit is to use a formal theory. My theory concerns communication patterns, the emotion of shame, and the relationship between the two. Personal relationships are based on communication, on dialogue. My basic hypothesis is that *interminable conflict is generated by dysfunctional communication patterns and by unacknowledged shame.* I will first discuss communication patterns.

Effective cooperative relationships involve more than a little *leveling* (Satir 1972). That is, it is possible to voice one's immediate thoughts, feelings and needs to others without injuring or insulting them, so long as one's *manner* is respectful.

Leveling is an important idea, since we often assume that in our relationship to a particular person, some topics are automatically dangerous, others completely safe. As it turns out, this is not the case; we can get into trouble with safe topics, and escape trouble with dangerous ones, depending not only on *what* we say, but *how* we say it. In close relationships, nonverbal elements like tempo, loudness, facial expression and other bodily gestures are often as important as words. Offense, insult, and humiliation, i.e. shame, usually arises out of manner; if one is respectful, any topic can be discussed, any criticism can be made. In interminable conflicts, the *manner* of the disputants is always disrespectful, which evokes shame.

Continued escalation may be caused not by conflicts of interests, but by disrespectful words and manner, and by shame which is not acknowledged. In the absence of shame, or if shame is acknowledged, disputing parties can always find a compromise which provides maximum reward or at least minimum punishment to the parties. In other words, it is hidden shame leading to insult and retaliation that interferes with rational compromise.

Communication tactics involve not only manner, but also a wide variety of styles which are seldom noticed. Most of these styles are ways of avoiding leveling, and do not result, at best, in the growth of a relationship, and may actually damage it. As already indicated, Satir (1972) called attention to several of these styles: *blaming, placating, distracting,* and *computing* are some of her categories.

Another maneuver for avoiding leveling has been called *"triangling"* (Bowen 1978). Instead of revealing their own immediate thoughts, feelings and needs, one or both parties can resort to talking about a third party, not present. This device not only excludes the absent party, but also interferes with the relationship between the speakers, since it substitutes for revealing self and learning about other.

Given these concepts, it is possible to discern a type of alienation that usually goes unnoticed, what Bowen (1978) has called *engulfment*. The style of alienation that Bowen calls *isolation* is obvious enough; one or both parties place the self over and above the relationship, resulting in distance and separation. Computing, blaming, and open conflict usually occur in this mode.

Engulfment is the opposite mode of alienation, in which one or both parties place the relationship over and above self. One or both give up significant parts of the self in order to be loyal. Placating and distracting are usually in this mode. Since the participants in engulfed relationships usually think of themselves as close and supportive, considerable self-deception is also involved. Engulfment is a pervasive mode in normal families, since it involves the appearance of solidarity and closeness.

Family discourse

The dialogues reported here are taken from a larger study of family systems. A total of forty-one protocols were available to me, as well as fourteen role plays in either classroom or my office. I report here on several typical protocols. The student in the first set of excerpts, Becky, sees her mother as her enemy in two different ways, one direct, one indirect. She believes that her mother is hostile and critical toward her, and that she also interferes with her (Becky's) relationship with her father, by nagging him about her. Becky illustrates both points with dialogue concerning her car.

1. Father–daughter dialogue

> Father: Your mom's really bugging me to do something about your car, so if you don't deal with it, I'm selling it. And I mean it this time.
> Becky: Okay, Dad. I'll do something. I want my car.

2. Mother–daughter dialogue

> Mother: Its the same thing with your car. You don't want to deal with it. What's it gonna take?
> Becky: Why is my car always brought up? It happened a year ago. I'm sorry. It wasn't on purpose.

It may be that Becky's understanding of these dialogues with her parents is faulty, as is her understanding of her relationships with her parents as a whole. The texts of the dialogues indicate that she is idealizing her father and vilifying her mother. Furthermore, they show that all three relationships in the triangle are alienated, and that none of the participants are aware of the depth of the alienation.

Becky's comments about her mother suggest a third dialogue between the father and mother.

3. Father-mother dialogue* (Once again, this asterisk is the conventional symbol for a counterfactual text, imagined dialogue):

Mother: Why are you so lenient with Becky about the car? She is
being completely irresponsible. You have got to come down on her.
Father: Yes, dear, you're right. I'll take care of it.

Although I imagined this third dialogue, Becky confirmed that it was
similar to an exchange she had overheard (but on another topic than
the car).

Family systems theory points to dysfunctional communication
patterns in all three of these dialogues. One of the faulty tactics
appears in two of the conversations, what Bowen (1978) called
"triangling." In each case, one of the participants brings in an absent
person, rather than revealing their own position.

In dialogue 1, Dad makes a threat: if Becky does not take care of her
car, he'll sell it. However, he does not take responsibility for the threat
himself: rather he blames it on his wife. This tactic illustrates Bowen's
concept of triangling: instead of revealing something about himself (in
this case, his desires about Becky's car) he invokes an absent third
party.

The daughter is also implicated in Dad's maneuver, since she does
not complain: *"Never mind what Mom wants, Dad, what do you
want?" Since the daughter does not complain, she is colluding with
Dad in blaming Mom. She allows Dad to maintain the fiction that he
is the good person, and that Mom is the bad person. In this respect, he
is probably not only deceiving Becky, but also himself. He is ensnared
in his own communication tactics.

In Bowen's theory, this type of alienation is referred to as engulfment,
a type of false solidarity. Both parties are withholding thoughts and
feelings, which gives each a false sense of security. However, both
parties are giving up parts of self to maintain this pretence. Dad might
be quite angry at Becky, but denies his anger, at least he does not
acknowledge it explicitly. The threat and the abruptness of his language
implies anger that is being denied. Just as he was probably unaware of
his desire in the case of Becky's car, he is probably also unaware that he
is angry at Becky, and, as will be explained below, at Mom also.

Becky's evasiveness is more subtle than Dad's. First, in allowing
him to blame Mom for the threat he is making, she is giving up the
opportunity to come to know Dad better. What does he actually want
her to do, and more indirectly, how does he feel about Mom's
nagging? Secondly, by colluding in blaming Mom, she is setting up
obstacles to resolving her own differences with her mother.

Dialogue 2, Becky and Mom, also indicates alienation, but a
different type than with Dad. If Becky and her father are engulfed,
then she and her mother are isolated, to use Bowen's term. In this
case, Mom is openly critical and disrespectful toward Becky, and there

are signs of anger on both sides. Mom implies that not only is Becky irresponsible, but that she is grossly unresponsive to her, the mother ("What's it gonna take *[to get you to respond to my request, an earthquake]?", the language of insult).

Becky responds in kind, with a counter-insult. "Why is my car always brought up? It happened a year ago." Just as mother implies that Becky is unresponsive, Becky, in turn, implies that Mom is unreasonable, that she is a nag. Immediately after insulting Mom, however, Becky retreats by apologizing in a half-hearted way, and then, again half-heartedly, attempts to justify herself ("It wasn't on purpose.") If the style of interaction between Becky and Dad is one of false (exaggerated) solidarity, the style between Becky and Mom is one of open conflict.

Dialogue 3, between Mom and Dad, shows many of the same characteristics as the other two exchanges. As in the first dialogue, the two participants are triangling against a third who is not present: Mom is complaining about Becky; Dad does not object to her practice. Mom is also critical of Dad, but in a somewhat indirect way. Rather than stating her criticism of him directly (*"You are too lenient with Becky"), she asks a question "Why are you so lenient . . . ?" which implies a criticism of Dad. However, she is direct about criticizing Becky, who is not present, in the second sentence. In the third sentence, she issues a command, "You have to come down on her."

Although Dad has indicated to Becky in dialogue 1 that it is not he but Mom that is critical of Becky, he does an about-face in his exchange with Mom. That is, he makes no effort to defend Becky, siding instead with Mom's criticism of her with a blanket agreement ("Yes, dear, you're right . . . "). Mom and Dad collude in vilifying Becky.

There is evidence in this dialogue that Mom is angry at Dad, but is not expressing it directly. She is indirectly critical of Dad, demanding, and uses a word in describing Becky ("completely") that indicates not only that she may be angry at Becky, but in a state of anger at the time of this dialogue. (Words like completely, never, always, etc. are called "extenders" in the analysis of emotions in discourse. Since they are exaggerations, they imply hidden anger (Retzinger 1991). Mom is in an angry blaming mode.

Since Mom is critical and demanding toward Dad, we might expect that he might be angry in return. However, the words show no evidence of anger; they are placating. However, some of his comments in dialogue 1 suggest in an indirect way that he may be angry at Mom. He tells Becky that Mom is "really bugging me" in regard to Becky's car. This phrase may have a double meaning, that Mom is pressing him, but also that she is making him angry.

The three dialogues can be used to derive a style of communication tactics and emotion management for each of the family members. There is no leveling in any of the dialogues; no one is direct in a respectful way. All three are indirect both about their needs and their feelings. Mom is an angry blamer and critic with Becky, and critical and blaming in an indirect way with Dad. Dad is completely placating with Mom, but threatening and indirectly blaming with Becky. Becky, finally, is placating with Dad, and first blaming, then placating with Mom. The three exchanges illustrate a system of dysfunctional communication in this family; instead of leveling, all three dialogues are in the blaming–blaming or blaming–placation mode.

The exchanges shown above supply only verbal information, no non-verbal information was included. In the role-playing exercises with Becky, however, she provided non-verbal gestures as well, her own, and in mime, she portrayed those of Dad and Mom. Based on both the verbal and non-verbal information, a classification of the styles of emotion management can be made, with emphasis on the management of shame and anger.

Mom is the most overt with anger; she shows anger in her words and gestures directed at Becky, and in a less overt way, toward Dad. Becky is next most overt; she shows some overt anger toward Mom, but quickly takes it back. She show none at all toward Dad. Dad is the least overt; he shows no anger at all toward Mom in her presence, and only covert signs of anger toward her in her absence. In Becky's presence his words and gestures imply covert anger.

The indications of shame in this family are much more subtle than those of anger. One indication of shame is how indirect all three members are with each other, when in their presence. The indirection of anger is particularly indicative that each person is ashamed of their anger. Another indication is that all three dialogues are entirely oriented toward a topic, the car; no one comments on relationship issues. For example, no one complains directly about the other's manner toward them, although respect is clearly an issue in the dialogue between Becky and Mom, and indirectly, between Mom and Dad. To understand the shame dynamics in this family, it will help to discuss how the three relationships might effect each other over time.

I have argued that Becky and Dad idealize themselves and each other, and collude in vilifying Mom. Becky and Mom engage in overt, angry conflict. Mom shows covert anger toward Dad, but he placates in return. One place to start to understand the interactions between each of the subsystems is to visualize what would happen if Dad tried to level with Mom.

Suppose that in the dialogue with Mom, instead of his blanket endorsement of her criticism of him, her criticism of Becky, and her demand that he take action against her, he said:

> *Father: I'd prefer that together you and I talk about this issue directly with Becky, rather than behind her back.

Although Mom might experience this line as an attack, she might also feel relieved that the issue was finally out in the open: how does Dad himself feel on this (and other) issues? Mom might experience the placation in his actual response as somewhat false; there is a monotony and flatness to his four affirmations of her position inside of two short sentences. She also might have a sense that Becky's defiance of her wishes could mean that Dad is covertly backing Becky, and defying Mom. The combination of Dad's bland compliance toward her (Mom), and the sense of a secret alliance between Dad and Becky could generate feelings of confusion, powerlessness, rejection and anger in Mom, a situational paranoia.

This counterfactual was used to illustrate the abstract idea of the dynamic interaction between the three relationships. To start arbitrarily with one of the relationships, without implying that it is the cause: to the extent that Becky and Dad idealize themselves and each other and vilify Mom because she is so critical (angry), to that extent Mom will feel excluded, rejected and angry (critical) toward both of them. To the extent that Mom is critical and angry toward Dad, to that extent he will placate and withhold his own feelings. To the extent that he placates and withholds toward Mom and Becky, to that extent will the anger between Mom and Becky be increased, a perfect feedback loop around the three-way system.

Janie's family: a mother–daughter alliance

Another student's family system shows much the same patterns as Becky's, except that in this case the daughter and mother are allied against the father. The topic for Janie's dialogues was the father's TV habits:

1. Father–daughter
> Father: Sssh!!! I'M WATCHING THE NEWS!!!
> Janie: THAT'S ALL YOU EVER DO, WATCH TV. TV IS MORE IMPORTANT TO YOU THAN YOUR OWN DAUGHTER!!!

2. Mother–daughter
> Mother: Oh! I just don't understand your father. I just don't understand why he won't help with the housework.
> Janie: I don't know, Mom. I just don't know.

3. Father-mother* (Counterfactual)

Father: The roast is overcooked again.
Mother: Sorry. I didn't watch it because I was so busy cleaning the house.

Although this last dialogue is hypothetical, Janie confirmed that she had heard many such exchanges between her father and mother on various topics. As indicated, the communication patterns in this family are quite similar to those already reported in Becky's family. I will begin with the father–daughter exchange.

Janie has walked into the living room where her father is watching TV. Rather than go all the way around him to get his attention, she speaks to him from behind, as she is walking toward him: "Dad, I have a question–." As indicated in the exchange above, he interrupts her by shushing her before she can finish her sentence. This exchange takes the form of an overt quarrel, with both father and daughter raising their voice angrily, and with no eye contact during the whole dialogue. The consequences are predictable: Janie left the room hurt and offended. Characteristically, instead of confronting the problem, she withdrew.

The father's response to Janie's request to talk is disrespectful; he commands her to keep quiet in a loud voice, and he does not turn away from the TV to face her. Without the courtesy necessary to turn down her request without offense, his words and manner are harsh, abrupt, and rejecting.

Although Janie was unaware of it at the time, her approach to her father was also disrespectful. Although she did not raise her voice in requesting his attention, she also was discourteous. A more respectful beginning would have been to avoid talking to the back of his head. Janie could have walked up to him from the side, seeking eye contact, but wait to speak until he turned toward her. This approach would have been a tacit admission that she was interrupting him. She might even have apologized for the interruption: *"Dad, I know you're busy, but I need to talk to you." If she had begun this way, perhaps the dialogue would have taken a different direction:

*Father: Can you wait ten minutes til the news is over?
Janie: Yes.

Like Becky, Janie was unaware of her own part in the ongoing quarrel with her dad. She became aware only in re-enacting it in class.

Students often had strong emotional reactions when they became aware of some new feature of their family relationships, but not always. Becky's emotional reactions were mild; she shed a few tears when she realized her role in excluding her mother. Janie's reactions were much stronger. At first, when she became aware of her part in excluding her father, she seemed a bit stunned. She also seemed excited to have discovered something new about herself and her family. Her emotional response to new knowledge about her relation with her mother was still stronger, as will be now discussed.

The exchange between Janie and her mother, like the one between Becky and her father, is an example of triangling. Instead of thrashing the issue of housekeeping duties out with the father, the mother complains about the father to Janie. Although the mother's statement is in the form of a question, it is not a real question, but a complaint. (Janie indicated that her mother had asked her the same question many times.) Like Becky, Janie also colludes with one parent against the other, since she does not object. Instead of suggesting to her mother that she complain directly to the father, Janie evades answering by stating that she does not know.

In the role-playing that took place during class, Janie became aware of the part she was playing in the ongoing quarrel with her father, but did not become aware of her role in the impasse with her mother. Awareness in this instance occurred later, in my office, when Janie and I were discussing her dialogue with her mother.

I questioned her about what she was feeling when her mother complained about her father to her. First she said that she felt proud that her mother was confiding in her. In response to my question about any other feelings, at first she said there were none. When I repeated the question, however, she began to cry, and became red in the face. When I asked her what she was feeling, she said that she felt anger at her mother for coming between her and her father. She cried deeply and for a considerable length of time. At the end of our talk, however, she was alight with enthusiasm. In response to my question about how she was feeling, she said she was hopeful, because now she saw that there was something that she herself could do to improve her relationships with both her parents.

I will present one exchange from the family system of a third student, Lyn, because it contains an element different than the two already discussed. Both Becky and Janie were involved in an overt quarrel with one of their parents: Becky with her mother, Janie, with her father. Lyn's relationship with one of her parents (her mother) was one of idealization and pseudo-solidarity, much like the relationship between Becky and her father, and Janie and her mother. However, Lyn's relationship with her father involved little or no quarreling. It involved instead a silent impasse: tension, distance, and the slow withdrawal of affection. Lyn's exchange with her father illustrates this kind of conflict:

Father: Do you have something in mind that you want to do tonight?

Daughter: No, nothing in particular.

The impasse in this situation is carefully disguised. Each participant seems to have been hiding their thoughts and feeling not only from each other, but even from themselves. The father's question came at the end of dinner. When he asked it, Lyn was expecting her father to suggest an activity that the two of them could do together, a game, perhaps, or watching a particular TV program. She was disappointed and somewhat stunned when instead he rose to go, saying "Well then, I have some work to do in my room."

Apparently Lyn and her father had played out similar exchanges many, many times before. Both seem hesitant to make the first step. Each does not want to intrude on the other's privacy. This kind of hesitancy and mutual misunderstanding is reminiscent of Harrington's (1989) study of romantic propositions: although both participants may want to date, each waits for the other to be the initiator. Apparently this kind of dance is not limited to romantic invitation, but can obtain in any kind of relationship, as in the case of the father–daughter situation in Lyn's exchange.

Lyn was quite surprised when she realized during role-play in my office that she was as responsible for the impasse as her father; she had been assigning all the responsibility to him. Lyn had a strong emotional reaction to her realization; she wept intensely. However, when she later role-played the exchange in class, she showed little emotion. She told me afterwards that she felt she needed to swallow her feelings in front of such a large group.

There was one other case, Richard, whose family system was somewhat different than any of the others. The exchanges he presented involved his mother and his step-father. Unlike the other students, he was combative and seemingly alienated from both parents. His exchange with his step-father was particularly intense, each forcefully criticizing the other's actions. However, I gathered from the way he role-played the exchanges that his bonds were probably more secure than most of the other students, since the conflict in his family was largely out in the open. Conflict does not necessarily lead to alienation; the crucial issue is the manner that the participants show in quarrels. If one's manner is respectful, then quarrels can have beneficial effects. Open conflict can lead to needed adjustments in relationships, as Simmel (1955) and others have argued.

My experience with the students in this class caused me to change my mind about gender issues in the family. Like most of the students, I had assumed that the traditional role of the father, the hard-driving, somewhat distant breadwinner, was one of the fundamental causes of the high levels of alienation in modern families. In the student's families, the father was more often cast in the role of the distant or vilified parent, by a ratio of almost two to one. However, after seeing the same faulty communication patterns repeated by all three participants, it seems to me that gender is not a central component in the problem: in all of the families systems we examined, all three family members, father, mother, and offspring, seemed equally implicated in causing and maintaining the status quo.

When the father is the odd man out, his exclusion is more noticeable than the mother's; his isolation is more visible than the mother–child engulfment, to use Bowen's (1978) terms. In our society, the male role is correlated with the isolated style of alienation, and the female role with engulfed style. Judging from the students' family systems, however, these differences are only superficial; the emotional and communication patterns are equally dysfunctional and disruptive, no matter whether a relationship is isolated or engulfed. Janie's and Lyn's relationships with their mothers were as alienated as their relationships with their fathers, since they maintained them by ignoring key parts of their selves, such as their anger.

Awareness and emotion

In the class as a whole, there were variable reactions to the family system exercises. The students divided into three roughly equal groups. About a third did not seem to gain any new awareness of their own family system. (Even though virtually all students claimed that they understood family systems better in the abstract.) Another third obviously gained awareness, but had little or no emotional reaction, like Becky. The last third, finally, reacted like Janie and Lyn: they seemed to grow in awareness, and had strong emotional reactions.

Judging from their later comments, I would guess few of the students in the first group will undergo change as a result of the class. In the second group, perhaps half or less might change. In the last group, virtually all will probably change. This is to say that I believe that new awareness is unlikely to result in personal growth unless it is accompanied by strong emotional responses.

One reason for students' resistance to awareness, emotion and change was that they were all enmeshed, in varying degrees, with their own family systems. How can such a self-perpetuating system change? Perhaps by changes in the communication tactics and acknowledgement and discharge of emotions by one or more of the participants. If Dad levels with Mom, instead of withholding, or levels with Becky instead of colluding with her against Mom, the whole system must change.

There are three key dimensions of the system under consideration: solidarity-alienation, communication tactics, and emotion management. Solidarity in my usage involves attunement: each party understands self and other both cognitively and emotionally. Alienation involves misunderstanding or lack of understanding. Solidarity promotes trust and effective cooperation, alienation promotes suspicion and conflict. The relationships between these three dimensions are depicted in figure 8.1.

Solidarity reflects and generates effective communication tactics, some form of respectful leveling. These tactics involve both truthfulness towards others and self-knowledge. Dad is not intentionally deceptive with Mom and Becky; his deceptiveness, and the deceptiveness of the other two family members as well, arises out of self-deception. He is not aware of many of his own desires and emotions.

Alienation from self and others reflects and generates dysfunctional communication tactics. Blaming flows from idealization of self and one's allies, vilification of one's opponents. Blaming the other party may generate placating, distraction, or computing, but it can also generate counter-blaming, as in the exchange between Becky and Mom. This analysis shows that because of the interactions between the relationships in a system, a blaming-placation relationship (peace) in one part or phase of a system can generate an interminable blaming-counter-blaming relationship (war) in another part of the system.

Triangling would seem to be a crucial tactic leading to interminable conflicts. Two or more parties in the system communicate secretly concerning a third party. These two parties usually become engulfed in a mutual admiration society, which conspires against the third party. This engulfment may be quite ineffective in the long run, however, because the parties become zealots, yes-persons because they overconform, idealizing themselves and each other, and undervaluing the opponent.

Bowen (1978) defines triangling strictly in terms of two parties communicating about a third party, rather than about revealing themselves. However, there is another type of faulty communication tactic which involves a triangle, but with objects or topics, rather than another party. In dysfunctional family systems, communication is usually locked into topics (money, sex, education, ideas, etc) in a way that relationship issues are avoided.

In such systems, parties do not reveal or even reflect on their own

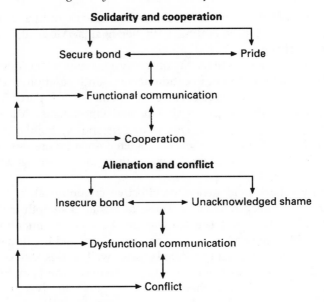

Figure 8.1 The proposed relationships resulting in (and created by) solidarity and cooperation on the one hand, and alienation and conflict on the other.

positions; instead they triangle on to other parties or topics. For this reason, there is considerable misunderstanding or ignorance of one's own position and that of the other members, a state of alienation. As students in the larger study sometimes remarked, one or both of their parents were strangers, even though they had lived with them their whole life.

It is of great interest and concern that in the large class from which this case was taken, transfer of knowledge to the student's own family system from knowledge of another student's seemed to take place only very slowly. That is, students watched case after case of role-playing which revealed the alienation underlying the appearance of solidarity and/or topic-related conflict to the student involved, and to the class as a whole. Students could correctly apply concepts such as engulfment and isolation to other's dialogues, but most seemed to find it difficult to see the same patterns in their own.

When students role-played their own family system they could become aware of its dynamics. It appeared that their awareness was blocked by intense emotions which they were unable to countenance on their own. In the safety of the class setting, or, more likely, my office, they seemed able to deal with these emotions; then they could apply what they had learned abstractly in the class to their own case.

Since I have not role-played dialogue with all forty of the students, it is possible that there are exceptions, students who correctly understood their own family system on their own. Even so, it seems to me that for the majority, abstract, dispassionate knowledge is not enough. Contact with their own painful emotions is a precondition for increased self-awareness.

Summary

The family systems of my students, the three described here, as well as the others in the class that I have not included in this chapter, share several patterns in common. In the great majority of cases (all but one) communication among family members seemed to be extraordinarily indirect. The evasiveness and indirectness of communication suggests that shame is a pervasive presence in these families, even though it is usually denied. Family members seem ashamed of the thoughts and feelings, especially shame and anger, that are inevitable in close relationships.

In the theory proposed here, shame is both cause and effect of protracted conflict. It is a signal of the alienation in these families, i.e. the lack of understanding and misunderstanding between the members, but a signal that is uniformly ignored and denied. It is not shame that causes interminable conflict, but its denial. Continuing shame is also a consequence of unending conflict: family members cycle through disrespectful words and gestures, shame and anger, which leads to further disrespectful gestures, and so on around the loop.

Whether openly conflictful or bypassed, family members in most of the dialogues did not seem to understand each other, or misunderstood each other, or, in most cases, a mixture of both. Denial of shame is both cause and effect of a continuing cycle of deception and self-deception about thoughts and feelings. Judging from some of the students' comments, the system of relationships in each family was static, having existed for as long as the students could remember, and showed virtually no change or variation over time.

Most students seemed completely unaware of basic features of their family systems. Typically students idealized one parent and vilified or misunderstood the other. In every case students seemed unaware of their own contributions to maintaining the system. They saw their family conflicts as exterior and constraining, to use Durkheim's (1915) phrase. That is, by denying their own part in producing unresolved quarrels and impasses, they experienced them as coming from others (exterior), and controlling and limiting their own behavior (constraining).

As already indicated, students were always surprised and often stunned or shocked when they discovered their own role in maintaining their family system. This effect stood out particularly in the students who showed understanding of other's family systems; even though they had gained abstract understanding of alienation and faulty communication tactics, they had been unable to apply these ideas to their own families.

I summarize these findings in order to suggest that they may also apply not only to families, but also to societies. Durkheim (1915) proposed that social facts, permanent, institutionalized patterns of collective behavior, are experienced by individuals as exterior and constraining, coming from outside themselves. By this definition, the quarrels and impasses described above were social facts.

It follows from my discussion that interminable conflicts in families are social facts, stable patterns of behavior that are experienced by the participants as exterior and constraining. My analysis suggests that such patterns are not inevitable, as most social scientists believe, but are results of the types of relationships, communication patterns and emotion management that obtain in our historical era. (For a brilliant analysis of the role of shame in our civilization, see Elias 1978). If my theory proves to be true, it might be possible to decrease the level of conflict in our civilization by changing our relationships, communication patterns and patterns of emotion management.

The next and last chapter pulls together the various strands discussed in this book, and suggests paths toward integrating the human sciences.

CHAPTER 9

Conclusion: integrating the human sciences

This book proposes a new approach to the human sciences, one that encompasses levels, disciplines, and subdisciplines which are usually kept rigidly separate. Why change the game of the normal science that is practiced in the disciplines and subdisciplines when most researchers are happy with it? Because it does not appear to be a winning game. The procedures of normal science can provide a mopping up operation after a breakthrough has occurred. Why has no breakthrough occurred in the human sciences?

The approach outlined in these chapters, part/whole morphology, suggests a way of approaching a crucial problem for the human sciences: how can we observe ourselves and our societies objectively, when our very lives are constituted by the very structures and processes that we need to study? This is not a simple problem. Alas, even making it explicit is a taxing maneuver.

In every society there is an "attitude of everyday life," a life world, which most of its members assume, indeed, take for granted, most of the time. This world goes without saying to the point that it is invisible under most conditions. Elias and Bordieu referred to it when they spoke of the *habitus*, our second nature, the mass of conventions, beliefs and attitudes which each member of a society shares with every other member. The habitus is not the whole culture, but that part which is so taken for granted as to be virtually invisible to its members. As Geertz suggested, to be discussed below, for the members of a society, the habitus is just "commonsense."

Oddly enough, social and behavioral scientists also share most of the habitus, most of the time. For the most part, we also take for granted, both in our work and in our lives, the same assumptions about what is reasonable, possible and decent that the lay members of our society also take for granted. Indeed, most of us share a double set of conventions, not only those of our society, but also those of our discipline or sub-discipline. Most economists, for example, share the assumption that their discipline consider only mathematical models or quantitative data, just as most academic psychologists insist that research use quantitative methods and experiments. The great majority of researchers in all disciplines in the human sciences are entrapped within this double set of conventions. But these are the very conventions that we need to study; the habitus, by and large, determines the shape of our lives and our societies.

The core methods of the human sciences, such as the experiment and the survey, assume that human behavior is determined by isolated individuals, individuals who think clearly, are conscious of their own motives and those of others, and who mean what they say and say what they mean. This highly idealized image is virtually ubiquitous. Occasionally it is even made explicit, as in the concept of "the reasonable man [person]," in law, and of rational choice in the social sciences. This assumption is realized in a whole set of conventions which in the short run make large scale studies easy to do, but in the long run make them ineffectual. Heilbroner (1995) has complained about modern economics that its conventions eliminate all important problems. But the same thing could be said about the other human sciences. The disciplines were each founded by one or more creative geniuses. But the charisma of these founders has been all but completely routinized, to use Max Weber's phrase.

The late Richard Feynman, a Nobel laureate physicist was referring to this kind of routinization in his essay "Cargo Cult Science" (1986). The natives of the islands in the South Seas where the US military had dropped largesse from the skies during the Second World War, felt deprived when the military left after the end of the war. To try to bring back the largesse, the natives formed cults which imitated the military airfields, setting up simple runways with improvised lights, hoping the planes would return. In the course of talking to his colleagues in the psychology department at Cornell, he came to the conclusion that the scientific methods in use in academic psychology were simple imitations of natural science that missed the point of research, since the imitations concentrated entirely on procedures, rather than the relationship of the procedures to the underlying logic of free inquiry. Although I certainly agree with Feynman's point about psychology, it's too bad that he did not realize that it applied not only to psychology but to all of the human sciences.

I have already mentioned the way that the initial insights of economics and psychology have been routinized, to the point that innovation is hardly possible. Another example is psychoanalysis. Following Freud's pioneering effort, there have been many brilliant analysts, often struggling not only against the societal habitus, but also against the orthodox conventions of the psychoanalytic establishment. But in current psychoanalysis, the creative elements in Freud's work, and in those of the innovators who came after him, have been all but lost in the plethora of beliefs and practices that govern the minds of today's analysts. Like the academic disciplines, it has been bureaucratized.

The notion of habitus was a central theme in the work of the great nineteenth century novelists like Tolstoy, as in this description of one of the characters in *Anna Karenina*: "Stepan A. chose neither his attitudes nor his opinions . . . [they] came to him on their own, just as he chose neither the style of his hats or his coats but got what people were wearing." This idea is presented clearly in Kundera's (1995) comments about a central theme in the work of the novelist Thomas Mann: "we think we act, we think we think, but it is another or others who think and act in us; that is to say, timeless habits, archetypes, which . . . carry an enormous seductive power and control us (says Mann) from 'the well of the past.'"

Perhaps the clearest evocation of the cultural habitus of the mind is that of Geertz (1983), which he refers to as "commonsense."[1] The main impediment to describing systems of commonsense, he notes, is their virtual invisibility. The problem is becoming aware that they exist, and that they may be described and commented upon: "There is something . . . of the purloined-letter effect in commonsense, it lies so artlessly before our eyes it is almost impossible to see" (p. 92) His essay begins with one of Wittgenstein's comments about the difference between invented and natural languages:

> [Chemistry, calculus and similar invented languages] are suburbs of our language. And how many houses or streets does it take before a town begins to be a town? Our language can be seen as an old city: a maze of little streets and squares, of old and new houses, and of houses with additions from various periods; and this surrounded by a multitude of modern sections with straight regular streets and uniform houses.

The old city and the modern suburbs, a striking image. Geertz provides another, natural language as "ancient tangle": "the ancient tangle of received practices, accepted beliefs, habitual judgments, and untaught emotions . . ." Unlike the modern suburb, the old city is not systematized, even though as much as calculus, it is a functioning system. That is to say that unlike calculus, commonsense is unselfconscious: "Religion rests its case on revelation, science on method, ideology on moral passion; but commonsense rests its case on the assertion that it is not a case at all, just life in a nutshell. The world is its authority" (p. 75). Commonsense, Geertz says, is the system made

[1] The next five pages are based in part on chapter 8 of Scheff (1990).

up of whatever the members of a group take to be *self-evident*, of what is taken for granted, of what goes without saying, and in fact, had better not be said or talked about. To talk about it is to undercut it, to challenge its status as completely self-evident. In a functioning social group, commonsense is seen as untouchable, and as complete. In his words (p. 84):

> As a frame for thought, and a species of it, commonsense is as totalizing as any other: no religion is more dogmatic, no science more ambitious, no philosophy more general. Its tonalities are different, and so are the arguments to which it appeals, but like them – and like art and like ideology – it pretends to reach past illusion to truth, to, as we say, things as they are.

Geertz's essay enlarges upon and extends Schutz's idea of "the attitude of everyday life" considerably, because he considers not just the commonsense attitude, but its components, "the ancient tangle" of practices, beliefs, judgments and emotions, as together making up a working system.

Geertz attempts to describe the attitudes toward reality common to all cultures. Acknowledging the difficulty, he tries five "quasi-qualities"; in systems of commonsense, reality is seen as *natural, practical, thin, accessible,* and *immethodical.* (For reasons that will be discussed below, I have changed Geertz's order by putting immethodical last.) Of these qualities, Geertz thinks that *naturalness* is the most fundamental (p. 85):

> Common sense represents matters – that is, certain matters and not others – as being what they are in the simple nature of the case. An air of "of-courseness," a sense of "it figures" is cast over things – again, some selected, underscored things. They are depicted as inherent in the situation, intrinsic aspects of reality, the way things go.

Geertz's description of *practicalness* is droll (p. 87):

> What we most often mean when we say an individual, an action, or a project displays a want of common sense is that they are impractical. The individual is in for some rude awakenings, the action is conducing toward its own defeat, the project won't float. But, simply because it seems so more readily apparent, it is also more susceptible to misconstruction. For it is not "practicalness" in the narrowly pragmatical sense of the useful but in the broader, folk-philosophical sense of sagacity that is involved. To tell someone, "be sensible," is less to tell him to cling to the utilitarian than to tell him, as we say, to wise up: to be prudent, levelheaded, keep his eye on the ball, not buy any wooden nickels, stay away from slow horses and fast women, let the dead bury the dead.

There is also comedy underlying his description of the third quality, *thinness* (p. 89):

The third of the quasi-qualities common sense attributes to reality, "thinness," is, like modesty in cheese, rather hard to formulate in more explicit terms. "Simpleness," or even "literalness," might serve as well or better, for what is involved is the tendency for common-sense views of this matter or that to represent them as being precisely what they seem to be, neither more nor less . . . "everything is what it is and not another thing"– expresses this quality perfectly. The world is what the wide-awake, uncomplicated person takes it to be. Sobriety, not subtlety, realism, not imagination, are the keys to wisdom; the really important facts of life lie scattered openly along its surface, not cunningly secreted in its depths. There is no need, indeed it is a fatal mistake, to deny, as poets, intellectuals, priests, and other professional complicators of the world so often do, the obviousness of the obvious.

It is not unusual to see others' system of commonsense as comical. Geertz's description, however, seems to suggest the humor in one's own. It is important to realize, however, that even though systems of commonsense can be easily seen as absurd, they are, at the same time, vastly powerful, since they function as general problem-solvers. Although unsystematic and non-reflexive, common sense functions in the intuitive mode, utilizing the vast resources of natural language. For this reason, as pointed out in earlier chapters, commonsense is incredibly swift, broad and flexible, in comparison with expert systems. I return to this issue in the discussion below.

The fourth and last of the qualities which seem to me to be similar is *accessibleness*:

the assumption, in fact the insistence, that any person with faculties reasonably intact can grasp common-sense conclusions, and indeed, once they are unequivocally enough stated, will not only grasp but embrace them . . . Common sense, to put it another way, represents the world as a familiar world, one everyone can, and should, recognize, and within which everyone stands, or should, on his own feet. (p. 91)

These first four qualities overlap considerably, with accessibleness especially similar to thinness (note the similarity of the last sentence above to the passage [p. 89] defining thinness). I return to this issue after discussing the last quality, *immethodicalness*, which seems quite distinct from the first four.

In systems of commonsense knowledge, Geertz says, reality is represented as inconsistent and possessing an "intractable diversity" (p. 90): "Commonsense wisdom is shamelessly and unapologetically *ad hoc*. It comes in epigrams, proverbs, *obiter dicta*, jokes, anecdotes, *contes morals* – a clatter of gnomic utterances – not in formal doctrines, axiomized theories, or architectonic dogmas." The *ad hoc*ness that Geertz attributes to commonsense reality returns him to his initial quote from Wittgenstein about the old city, as against the systematized suburbs. It also relates to my discussion of *ad hoc*ing and total association in chapter 4, as I indicate below. First, however, it is necessary to return to the underlying similarity between the first four qualities.

The first four qualities of commonsense reality that Geertz names – naturalness, practicalness, thinness, and accessibleness – seem insufficiently distinct from one another. The four might be subsumed by a more abstract concept: cultural systems of commonsense are *non-reflexive*.

The system of commonsense operates outside of awareness. An outsider can reflect and comment on it, but an insider cannot; it is not just that the insider *does* not consider its operation, but unless he or she is willing to start at square one, the insider *can* not.

The insider feels that to consider any single item of commonsense would require starting over, from scratch, considering everything in the universe. The commitments have come too early, they are too deep, they are too vast. Rather than examine one's own commitments, they are projected on to the outside world: it is not me that is committed, it's just the way things are: "Like its naturalness, the practicalness of commonsense is a quality it bestows upon things, not one that things bestow on it" (p. 88). This is to say that a cultural system of common sense is a collective mechanism of defense, an intensely defended individual and collective projection of inner commitments onto the outside world.

This explanation of the non-reflexiveness of commonsense in terms of collective psychodynamics parallels Freud's (1927) analysis of religion in traditional societies. He had the temerity to argue, in a society that was still sufficiently traditional that he might have been lynched, that religion functioned as a mechanism of defense. The belief in an after-life, particularly, is a defense against the fear of dying. In modern societies, religion has lost much of its sacredness, but commonsense has not. As Geertz (p. 84) suggests, when insiders consider something real, they "damn well mean it," and no fooling around, as we say.

In Mannheim's (1936) terms, a cultural system of commonsense imposes a traditional *ideological* order upon reality. The true outsider's vision is *utopian*, it shatters what is felt to be the natural order of things, everything that is possible, natural, and decent. It is a tribute to Geertz's good sense and the charm of his prose that he can lead us to reflect upon our own system of commonsense without insulting us. We are programmed to be unaware of the operation of our own system, and to be indignant when it is brought to our attention.

Although human beings, both as individuals and collectively, have the capacity for instant reflexive awareness about many things, one's own system of common sense is not one of them. It is clear from Mannheim's treatment of the beliefs of sectarian religious sects that utopian views are fanatically held: the status quo is reviled because of belief in an idealized world. But ideological views are just as rigidly held. The members of mainstream society believe in their common-sense world just as fanatically as the utopians believe in theirs. The two worlds are antagonistic and mutually exclusive.

The discussion in chapter 5 of the state of mind in Europe which helped precipitate the First World War is an example of the fanaticism of the mainstream. Although there were no major differences between the antagonist nations, the overwhelming majority believed that war was necessary, which helped make the war happen. It was a shared delusion. Even the greatest of the intellectuals were caught up in it. Both Max Weber and Freud thought that the war would be a cleansing experience. In this respect they were both ideologues, rather than what Mannheim was later to call free-floating intellectuals. Maude Gonne was not caught up in the delusion because she was a utopian, living in the worlds of Irish nationalism, feminism, and mysticism. For this reason, she could see the war much more clearly than Weber, Freud and the normally more sane intellectuals. In this matter, she was much more sane than the "commonsense" reigning in Europe.

Returning to Geertz's discussion of commonsense, I consider the quality that Geertz calls "immethodicalness" last because it seems to point to an aspect of systems of common sense different than the first four qualities. This last quality points to the elusive quality of human thought which is usually referred to as intuitiveness: the ability to understand a complex issue without any obvious attempt or labor, almost instantaneously.

The intuitive capacity is distinct from, yet closely related to natural language. Intuition, or mother-wit as it is sometimes called, depends upon our mother-tongue. I think that this is the import of another of Wittgenstein's quotes (Geertz, p. 92): "In the actual use of expressions we make detours, we go by side roads. We see the straight highway before us, but of course we cannot use it, because it is permanently closed." Geertz quotes an African proverb which makes the same point: "Wisdom comes out of an ant heap" (p. 91).

Is there any way of escaping from the entrapment of the common-sense of one's culture and one's discipline? The idea of "bisociation" originated by Arthur Koestler (1964) suggests a possible route for obtaining escape velocity. Bisociation means experiencing a problem from two contradictory viewpoints simultaneously. Koestler notes that successful jokes, that is, those that produce spontaneous laughter, are those that set up the conditions for bisociation; "getting" the climax of the joke or pun means that by experiencing it from two contradictory points of view, one is able to resolve the contradiction.

Koestler goes on to say that bisociation is the key to all creative art and science. Discoveries are made when the artist or scientist is able to experience the problem from two contradictory points of view. This is a key issue for the human sciences; we need the vast intuitive power of commonsense, but also to escape from it using an analytic approach. How can one induce a condition of marginality, so that by participating in both the world of commonsense and the analytical world, one can use the strengths of both, and resolve the conflicts between them?

In anthropology, the traditional requirement that the doctoral candidate pursue her research in an alien culture might be interpreted as an attempt to induce marginality, and therefore discovery, not only in the alien culture, but also in her own culture. Similarly in psychoanalysis, the requirement that a candidate be required to undergo her own analysis might also produce marginality and bisociation. Extended participation in a strange culture, or in the strangeness of a detailed review of one's own life, might be expected to produce estrangement from one's culture or one's life, and therefore foster creativity.

On the whole, however, this expectation appears to be seldom met. Most anthropologists appear no less free of their twin habitus than the members of any other discipline, nor do psychoanalysts. What appears to usually happen is that both anthropologists and psychoanalysts compartmentalize the strange experiences from their lives and in their work. Like Tolstoy's Stepan A., most of them usually wear the same clothes that others wear, and think the same thoughts. Most academics, like Stepan A., are ideologues, accepting most of the status quo without reservation or awareness. But even the utopians among us are also in a similar state, except that their habitus rejects the status quo unconditionally, but rigidly. Is there any way out?

The rule of disciplinary habitus in the human sciences

I have mentioned already the way in which the discipline of economics is ruled by the convention that research be quantitative and if possible be expressed by mathematical models. Another ruling convention is the assumptions that a free market is the answer to all economic problems. The assumption is having tragic results in what was the Eastern Bloc in Europe. Russia and many of the other countries that were part of this bloc are now in social, political, and economic upheaval, at least partly because advice they received from Western economists, "shock therapy," was taken. Economists universally advised these countries that privatization would automatically take them through the transition from communism to capitalism. There was little advice given to the contrary, and when it was given, it was ignored.

One example of very good advice that was ignored, because it contradicted the habitus of the discipline of economics, was offered by the sociologist Etzioni, on the basis of what he called socio-economic analysis (Etzioni 1991). In a letter to the *New York Times* (Etzioni 1990), well before any changes had been made, he argued that eastern bloc countries lack, for the most part, the social/political/economic infrastructure that allows capitalism to function in Western democracies. For this reason, he proposed a gradual transition from a planned economy to a free market. If the transition was to be made cold turkey, without an interregnum, he predicted the very types of upheaval that we are witnessing today: a surge in crime rates and criminal economic activity, inflation and deprivation of the lower classes, and the possibility of a return to totalitarian rule.

In his letter Etzioni was referring specially to the case of Poland. As it happens, his predictions were only partly fulfilled there, because Poland has more of the infra-structure of the West than Russia. In Russia, however, Etzioni's predictions have been amply fulfilled. But Etzioni's advice was ignored by economists, since it is based on an analysis of institutions that falls outside of their habitus.

Another example of disciplinary habitus concerns studies of the causes of war. Although there are several surveys of studies of warfare, I will single out the one by Vasquez (1993), because it seems to be the most precise and comprehensive. It references almost 400 studies, most of which are empirical investigations of actual wars. From these studies, the author generates close to 100 propositions about the causes of war. Here is an example: "7. More interstate wars will occur between contiguous states than non-contiguous states (Vasquez 1993, p. 310)." All of the propositions cite several studies which provide supporting evidence. The list of propositions is broken down into several sections, such as Territorial Contiguity (from which no. 7 above was selected), Rivalry, Alliances, Arms Races, Crises, and Domestic Politics. The style of reasoning is atheoretical, that is, inductive and correlational (no. 7 implies only a correlation between warfare and contiguity of the opponents). But the large number of studies which use one or more of the section headings suggests a view of causation that is part of the habitus of the political scientists and others who study war. That is to say, they believe that territorial contiguity, rivalry, alliances, arms races, crises and domestic politics are causes of wars.

The massive number of studies tell us little about the causation of war because they are low-level generalizations, perilously close to being truisms. They are too abstract to include any of the ambient details in the social and psychological process that leads to war. But it may be these very details which are needed to develop a useful theory. Does one need careful empirical studies to find that wars are more frequent between states that are contiguous, or rivalrous? Or that arms races, crises, and domestic politics figure in the instigation of war? These "findings" can be seen as another variation of the cargo cult science that Feynman complained about. The investigators have developed a habitus which insists on a single procedure and set of categories, even though this direction has not produced significant results.

The only direction not flirting with truism are the fifteen propositions about the types of alliances which precede wars, as against the types of alliances which do not precede wars. But even these propositions are stated in vernacular, rather than theoretical terms, and tell us little about causal process: "15b. When the global institutional context limits unilateral acts through the establishment of rules of the game, alliances tend not to be followed by war." Once again, this proposition is only correlational, and does not furnish any information about the step-by-step process which leads to war.

Few studies that would provide step-by-step details are included in Vasquez's study, since he favors generalizing studies over case studies. Kennan's brilliant study (1984) of the political process which led to the formation of what he called "the fateful alliance" between France and Russia just prior to the First World War is not referenced. The idea of nationalism, which Kennan and many others have named as a powerful cause of war, is mentioned only once in the proposition section of Vasquez's book. Nationalism is not actually involved in any of the 100 propositions; it is mentioned in a query following 44c, and then only along with several other factors. It appears that the idea of nationalism as a powerful force for war is not part of the habitus of the political scientists of warfare.

What seems to be lacking from the studies of the causation of war in political science is the kind of theory and the kind of details that would allow us to understand the human behavior that leads to war. Historical studies of single cases also lack theory, but do provide the details of process, as in Kennan's study. But intimate knowledge of the details is needed to untangle the complex web of truth-telling, half-truths, lies, deception, and self-deception that make up the road to war. The case studies provide these details, but without comparative study, do not foster general theories. The comparative studies could generate theory, but need to be supplemented with the details of process. The method of part/whole morphology outlined in this book could be used in a way that would combine the two seemingly disparate approaches.

Another example of disciplinary habitus is provided by the best of the quantitative studies of marriage, by Gottman (1994), who has been studying marital interaction for many years. Once again, this work is inductive and atheoretical, citing only similar studies. The potent sources of hypotheses about marriage relationships, such as psychoanalysis, and particularly, family systems theory, are ignored. One particularly damaging omission can be found in Gottman's selection of emotions that he studied in marital interaction. Following the atheoretical, inductive classification of emotions by Ekman and Friesen (1978), Gottman determined the correlations of anger, sadness, fear, contempt, and so on with marital satisfaction and divorce, but not shame humiliation, or embarrassment, because these crucial emotions are not included in the Ekman and Friesen scheme.

Like most other quantitative studies of emotions, Gottman ignored the work by Lewis (1971), Retzinger (1991), myself (1994) and others, suggesting that shame/anger spirals are a central source of interminable conflict. (An exception is to work of Tangney (1992), whose experiments support the shame/anger hypothesis.) Like all the other human sciences, quantitative social psychologists are laboring under a mistaken conception of science. As Peirce and many others have suggested, scientific inquiry is not merely inductive, but also deductive, a mixture of imagination and observation, as discussed in chapter 1.

Regaining intellectual autonomy

Part/whole morphology may offer a way out of entrapment in the habitus. If there is any reality to the habitus, it must show up in social interaction. By applying part/whole analysis to verbatim transcripts of interaction, perhaps the analyst can become aware of the habitus, and describe it, rather than being ruled by it.

As indicated in chapter 1, Elias's study (1978) of books of etiquette over 500 years suggested some features of the European habitus; the growth of self-control, increasing shame, and decreasing awareness of shame. Although central features of European culture, Elias's analysis implies that these changes occurred almost entirely outside of awareness, as befitting the concept of the habitus. Elias's study suggests that the analysis of verbatim texts may be a way of grounding investigations of habitus in empirical data. This method might save the study of habitus from the fate of earlier studies of national character, which lacked sufficient empirical reference.

There is also a suggestion of the linguistic study of habitus in a well-known work on Mexico, by Paz (1985). He suggests that the verb *chingar* (a crude translation into English is *to violate*) carries a complex but important emotional weight in the language of Mexico, a weight that is necessary to understand if we are to understand Mexican people:

> In our daily language there is a group of words that are prohibited, secret, without clear meanings. We confide the expression of our most brutal or subtle emotions and reactions to their magical ambiguities . . . They are the bad words, the only living language in a world of anemic vocables . . . (pp. 73–74)

Note that Paz, much more explicitly than Elias, evokes the unconsciousness of the habitus. There is no exact equivalent to *chingar* in English. The closest analogue is the word *fuck*, when it is used to be mean violate or "fuck over." But the Mexican usage is much broader, since it is used frequently in a non-sexual sense.

Paz locates a central feature of Mexican culture in a single phrase: "All of our anxious tensions express themselves in a phrase we use when anger, joy or enthusiasm cause us to exalt our conditions as Mexicans: 'Viva Mexico, *hijos de la chingada*! (p. 74).'" He compares this phrase to a frequently used phrase in Spain, *hijo de puta* (son of a whore). In the Spanish usage, the sexual act resulting in birth is voluntary, but in the Mexican usage, it is involuntary. This idea is linked to the conquest and subjugation of Mexican by Spain. In this usage, all Mexicans see themselves as children of Dona Malinche, the mistress of Cortez. During his conquest of Mexico, Cortes used his mistress both sexually and politically; she was his translator of the Indian languages. But Cortez discarded her when he had no further need of her (pp. 86–88).

It is possible that the analysis of curse words will reveal some of the central emotional themes of a culture, as Paz suggests. The people of the United States never have had the experience of defeat, conquest, subjugation, and enslavement. This historical fact probably plays a part in the excessive self-confidence of North Americans, their cocksureness. Similarly the Mexican historical experience probably plays a role in the passiveness and lack of self-confidence that seem to be part of the Mexican culture. Perhaps a comparative analysis of words that are our nearest equivalent to *chingar* (fuck, in everyday profane usage, son-of-a-bitch) might yield up some knowledge of our habitus as compared to the Mexican one. Notice that the nearest equivalent to *hijos de la chingada* in American English is "son of a bitch." Stating that one's mother is a dog is an insult, but it lacks the freight of a history of defeat and subjugation of the Mexican term.

Elias (1996) has implied a somewhat parallel idea about the German habitus, that the German people suffered a series of defeats and humiliations historically, and were unable to deal with their emotions peacefully. Translated into emotion dynamics, these ideas suggest that the German reaction to humiliation was shame/anger spirals, which lead to aggression, and the Mexican reaction was shame/shame spirals, which lead to passivity and withdrawal. If ideas like these were taken as hypotheses, they could lead to a systematic study of habitus, which could be an important ingredient in all human behavior.

Microanalysis of interaction, when it is related to the part/whole ladder, estranges the analyst from her own culture. By getting beneath the smooth surface of behavior, it exposes the invisible process and structure that give order and meaning. Estrangement is most obvious in my analysis of the message stack in verbatim texts. My literary friends have not appreciated the portrait of the relationship between Beatrice and Benedick (chapter 6) that emerged from my analysis of the conflict in their relationship. The analysis suggests that this relationship is based more on neurosis, hidden chains of shame and anger, than on love. But the conventions of literary studies exclude this kind of analysis, just as the conventions of social science exclude this kind of data. The study falls into a no-person's land, a territory not recognized by existing disciplines, as do most of the important problems of human existence.

The methods used in this book, especially those concerned with the determination of meaning, estrange the researcher from the text in a way that can create bisociation. The component tools of part/whole morphology, such as analyzing the message stack using the prospective–retrospective method of understanding, and the use of hypotheticals, leads toward those meanings which exist outside of the consciousness of the actors. The researcher who belongs to the culture in which the discourse took place, can participate in both sets of meanings simultaneously, seeing the text both from the point of view of the untutored commonsense of the actors, and from the point of view of the meanings uncovered by microanalysis.

The present situation of the disciplines is little more than tribal: "Each tribe has a name and a territory, settles its own affairs, goes to war with the others, has a distinct language or at least a distinct dialect and a variety of ways of demonstrating its apartness from others" (Bailey 1977). The solution for the human sciences would mean integration of the disciplines.

> The problem of integration of cultural life becomes one of making it possible for people inhabiting different worlds to have a genuine, and reciprocal impact upon one another . . . the first step is surely to accept the depth of the differences; the second to understand what these differences are; and the third is to construct some sort of *vocabulary* in which they can be publically formulated. (Geertz 1983; emphasis added)

Part/whole analysis may provide the common vocabulary that is needed. How could we begin to insinuate part/whole morphology into the human sciences?

One direction would be to require a binocular approach to theses and dissertations, one that would encompass more than one discipline and/or level in its approach. Although this would be only a small step, if it resulted in a sense of mastery and advance in the researchers and their advisors, it might begin a long process of reawakening in the human science disciplines.

Cues for shame and anger

From Retzinger 1991; 1995.

Verbal markers

Shame:

alienated: rejected, dumped, deserted, rebuff, abandoned, estranged, deserted, isolated, separate, alone, disconnected, disassociated, detached, withdrawn, inhibited, distant, remote, split, divorced, polarized.

confused: stunned, dazed, blank, empty, hollow, spaced giddy, lost, vapid, hesitant, aloof.

ridiculous: foolish, silly, funny, absurd, idiotic, asinine, simple-minded, stupid, curious, weird, bizarre, odd peculiar, strange, different, stupid.

inadequate: helpless, powerless, defenseless, weak, insecure, uncertain, shy, deficient, worse off, small, failure, ineffectual, inferior, unworthy, worthless, flawed, trivial, meaningless, insufficient, unsure, dependent, exposed, inadequate, incapable, vulnerable, unable, inept, unfit, impotent, oppressed.

uncomfortable: restless, fidgety, jittery, tense, anxious, nervous, uneasy, antsy, jumpy, hyperactive.

hurt: offended, upset, wounded, injured, tortured, ruined, sensitive, sore spot, buttons pushed, dejected, intimidated, defeated.

Anger

cranky, cross, hot-tempered, ireful, quick-tempered, short fuse, enraged, fuming, agitated, furious, irritable, incensed, indignant, irate, annoyed, mad, pissed, pissed off, teed-off, upset, furious, aggravated, bothered, resentful, bitter, spiteful, grudge (the last four words imply shame–anger compounds).

Other verbal markers

Shame

Mitigation (to make appear less severe or painful); oblique, suppressed reference, e. g. "they," "it," "you"; vagueness; denial; defensiveness; verbal withdrawal (lack of response); indifference (Acting "cool" in an emotionally arousing context).

Anger:

interruption; challenge; sarcasm; blame
Shame-anger: Temporal expansion/condensation or generalization ("you always . . .," "you never . . ."). Triangulation (bringing up an irrelevant third party or object).

Paralinguistic markers

Shame

(vocal withdrawal/hiding behaviors, disorganization of thought): over-soft; rhythm irregular; hesitation; self interruption (censorship); filled pauses (-uh-); long pauses ( ); silences; stammer; fragmented speech; rapid speech; condensed words; mumble; breathiness; incoherence (lax articulation); laughed words; monotone.

Anger:

staccato (distinct breaks between successive tones); loud; heavy stress on certain words; sing-song pattern (ridicule); straining; harsh voice qualifiers.
Shame–anger: whine; glottalization (rasp or buzz); choking; tempo up/down; pitch up/down.

Visual markers

Shame:

(1) Hiding behavior: (a) the hand covering all or parts of the face, (b) gaze aversion, eyes lowered or averted. (2) Blushing (3) Control: (a) turning in, biting, or licking the lips, biting the tongue, (b) forehead wrinkled vertically or transversely, (c) false smiling (Ekman and Freisen 1982); or other masking behaviors.

Anger:

(1) brows lowered and drawn together, vertical lines appear between them. (2) The eyelids are narrowed and tense in a hard fixed stare and may have a bulging appearance. (3) Lips pressed together, the corners straight or down, or open but tense and square. (4) Hard direct glaring (5) Lean forward toward other in challenging stance (6) Clenched fists, wave fists, hitting motions

Like all human expressions (including words), the meaning of these markers are context-related; that is, their relevance depends on the relationship between self and other. Look for constellation of markers in context; the more markers from each category, the stronger the evidence.

References

Adler, A. 1956. *The Individual Psychology of Alfred Adler*. New York: Basic Books.

Ainsworth, M., M. Blehar, E. Waters, and S. Wall. 1978. *Patterns of Attachment*. Hillsdale: Erlbaum.

Albertini, Luigi. 1952–57. *The Origins of the War of 1914*. London: Oxford University Press.

Amrine, F., F. Zucker, and H. Wheeler. 1987. *Goethe and the Sciences: A Reappraisal*. Boston: D. Reidel.

Atkinson, M., and Heritage, J. 1984. *Structures of Social Action*. Cambridge: Cambridge University Press.

Ayers, Ian, and John Braithwaite. 1992. *Responsive Regulation*. New York: Oxford University Press.

Bailey, F. G. 1977. *Morality and Expediency*. Oxford: Blackwell.

Barnes, Harry E. 1928. *In Quest of Truth and Justice*. Chicago: National Historical Society.

Baudrillard, J. 1976. *L'echange symbolique et la mort*. Paris: Gallimard.

Berghahn, V. R. 1973. *Germany and the Approach of War in 1914*. New York: St. Martins.

Blainey, Geoffrey. 1988. *The Causes of War*. London: Macmillan.

Bloor, D. 1983. *Wittgenstein: A Social Theory of Knowledge*. London: Macmillan.

Bok, Sissela. 1983. *Secrets*. New York: Vintage.

Bosworth, Richard. 1983. *Italy and the Approach of the First World War*. New York: St. Martins.

Boudon, R. 1979. *La logique du social*. Paris: Hachette.

Bowen, M. 1978. *Family Therapy in Clinical Practice*. New York: J. Aronson.

Bowen, M. and M. Kerr. 1988. *Family Evaluation*. New York: Norton.

Braithwaite, J. 1989. *Crime, Shame and Reintegration*. Cambridge: Cambridge University Press.

Brockner, J. and J. Rubin. 1985. *Entrapment in Escalating Conflicts*. New York: Spring-Verlag.

Bruner, J. 1983. *Child's Talk*. New York: Norton.

Buber, M. 1958. *I–Thou*. New York: Scribners.

Campbell, D. T. and D. W. Fiske. 1959. Convergent and Discriminant Validation by the Multi-trait, Multi-method Matrix. *Psychological Bulletin* 56: 81–105.

Chomsky, N. 1965. *Syntactic Structures*. The Hague: Mouton.

Cicourel, Aaron. 1964. *Method and Measurement in Sociology*. New York: Free Press.

1974. *Cognitive Sociology*. New York: Free Press.

1977. Cognitive and Linguistic Aspects of Social Structure. *Communication and Cognition* 10: 25–31.

1980. Three Models of Discourse Analysis: The Role of Social Structure. *Discourse Processes* 3: 101–131.

1981. *Advances in Sociological Theory and Methodology: Toward an Integration of Micro and Macro Sociologies.* Boston: Routledge.

1981. The Role of Cognitive-Linguistic Concepts in Understanding Everyday Social Interactions. *Annual Review of Sociology* 7: 87–106.

1985. Text and Discourse. *Annual Review of Anthropology.* 14: 159–185.

Coopersmith, S. 1967. *The Antecedents of Self-Esteem.* San Francisco: W. H. Freeman.

Cottle, Thomas. 1980. *Children's Secrets.* New York: Anchor

Denzin, Norman, and Yvonne Lincoln. 1994. *Handbook of Qualitative Methods.* Newbury Park: Sage.

Doi. T. 1971. *The Anatomy of Dependence.* Tokyo: Kodansha International.

Dreyfuss, H. and S. Dreyfuss. 1986. *Mind over Machine.* New York: Free Press.

Durkheim, Emile. 1895. *Rules of Sociological Method.* London: Macmillan (1982).

1902–1911. *Education and Sociology.* Glencoe: Free Press (1956).

1903. Sociology and the Social Sciences. In *The Rules of Sociological Method and Selected Texts*, ed. Steven Lukes. New York: Free Press.

1905. *Suicide.* London: Routledge (1952).

1915. *Elementary Forms of the Religious Life.* Glencoe, Ill.: Free Press (1965).

Ecksteins, Modris. 1989. *The Rites of Spring.* Boston: Houghton Mifflin.

Ekman, P. and W. Friesen. 1978. *Facial Action Coding System.* Palo Alto: Consulting Psychologists Press.

Elias, Norbert. 1972. *What is Sociology?* London: Hutchison.

1978. *The History of Manners.* New York: Pantheon.

1982. *Power and Civility.* New York: Pantheon.

1987. *Involvement and Detachment.* Oxford: Blackwell.

1996. *The Germans: Power Struggles and the Development of Habitus in the Nineteenth and Twentieth Centuries.* Oxford: Blackwell.

Etzioni, Amitai. 1991. *Socio-Economics.* Armonk, NY: M. E. Sharpe.

1990. Is Poland getting Bad Advice? *New York Times* 139: June 17, Sec.3, F13.

Evans, R. J. and H. P. von Strandmann. 1988. *The Coming of the First World War.* Oxford: Clarendon.

Fay, Sidney. B. 1930. *The Origins of the World War.* New York: Free Press (1966).

Fearon, David. 1994. The Bond Threat Sequence: Discourse Evidence for the Interdependence of Shame and Social Relationships. Unpublished MA thesis, Dept of Sociology, UCSB.

Ferguson, B. 1988. *The Anthropology of War.* New York: Occasional Paper of the Herman Guggenheim Foundation.

Ferraroti, F. 1984. *Une théologie pour athées.* Paris: Meridiens.

Feuer, Lewis. 1982. *Einstein and the Generations of Science.* New Brunswick, NJ: Transaction Press.

Feynman, Richard. 1986. Cargo Cult Science. In *Surely You're Joking, Mr. Feynman.* New York: Bantam, pp. 308–318.

Fischer, Fritz. 1967. *Germany's Aims in the First World War.* New York: Norton.

1975. *War of Illusions: German Policies from 1911 to 1914.* New York: Norton.

Fleming, D. F. 1968. *The Origins and Legacies of World War I.* Garden City, NY: Doubleday.

Freeman, Derek. 1983. *Margaret Mead and Samoa: The Making and Unmaking of an Anthropological Myth*. Cambridge: Harvard University Press.

Freud, Sigmund. 1927. *The Future of an Illusion*. London: Hogarth.

Gaylin, Willard. 1984. *The Rage Within*. New York: Simon and Schuster.

Geertz, Clifford. 1973. *The Interpretation of Cultures*. New York: Basic Books.

1983. *Local Knowledge*. New York: Basic Books.

Giddens, A. 1984. *The Constitution of Society*. Berkeley: University of California Press.

Gill, M., R. Newman, and F. Redlich. 1954. *The Initial Interview in Psychiatric Practice*. New York: Norton.

Glaser, Barney, and Anselm Strauss. 1967. *The Discovery of Grounded Theory*. Chicago: Aldine.

Goethe, Johann Wolfgang. 1790. The Metamorphosis of Plants. quoted in B. Fairley (1963, 195) *A Study of Goethe*. Oxford: Clarendon Press.

Goffman, Erving. 1967. *Interaction Ritual*. New York: Anchor

1974. *Frame Analysis*. New York: Harper.

Goodspeed, D. J. 1977. *The German Wars*. Boston: Houghton Miflin.

Goodwin, M. 1990. *He-Said-She-Said*. Bloomington: Indiana University Press.

Gottman, J. 1994. *What Predicts Divorce?* Hillsdale, NJ: Lawrence Erlbaum Associates.

Gottschalk, L., C. Winget, and G. Gleser. 1969. *Manual for Using the Gottschalk-Gleser Content Analysis Scales*. Berkeley: University of California Press.

Haas, J. 1990. *The Anthropology of War*. Cambridge: Cambridge University Press.

Habermas, J. 1988. *Theory of Communicative Action*. Cambridge: Polity.

Hardy, J. 1984. *Jane Austen's Heroines*. London: Routledge.

Harrington, C. Lee. 1992. Talk about Embarrassment: Exploring the Taboo-Denial-Repression Hypothesis. *Symbolic Interaction* 15: 203–225.

Hays, Janice. 1980. Those "Soft and Delicate Desires": *Much Ado* and the Distrust of Women. In C. R. Lenz, G. Greene, and C. T. Neely (eds.), *The Woman's Part*. Urbana: University of Illinois Press.

Heilbroner, Robert. 1995. *The Crisis of Vision in Modern Economic Thought*. Cambridge: Cambridge University Press.

Hentig, Ruth. 1989. *The Origins of the First World War*. London: Routledge.

Hofstadter, D. 1975. *Goedel, Escher, Bach*. New York: Vintage.

Hooley, Jill. 1986. Expressed Emotion and Depression: Interactions between Patients and High vs. Low-Expressed Emotion Spouses. *Journal of Abnormal Psychology* 95: 237–246.

Hughes, Judith. 1983. *Emotion and High Politics*. Berkeley: University of California Press.

Jackson, M. 1984. *Self-Esteem and Meaning*. Albany: SUNY Press.

Jervis, R., N. Lebow, and J. Stein. 1985. *Psychology and Deterrence*. Baltimore: Johns Hopkins University Press.

Joll, J. 1984. *The Origins of the First World War*. London: Longmans.

Keiger, John. 1983. *France and the Origins of the First World War*. London: Macmillan.

Kennan, George. 1979. *The Decline of Bismarck's European Order*. Princeton: Princeton University Press.

1984. *The Fateful Alliance: France, Russia, and the Coming of the First World War*. New York: Pantheon.

Koch, H. W. (ed). 1972. *The Origins of the First World War*. London: Macmillan.

Koestler, Arthur. 1967. *The Act of Creation*. New York: Dell.

Kohut, Heinz. 1979. *The Restoration of the Self*. New York: International Universities Press.

Komarovsky, M. 1967. *Blue Collar Marriage*. Oxford: Oxford University Press.

Krieger, Suzan. 1991. *Social Science and the Self*. New Brunswick: Rutgers University Press.

Kuhn, Thomas. 1961. *The Structure of Scientific Revolutions*. Chicago: University of Chicago Press.

Kundera, Milan. 1995. *Testaments Betrayed*. New York: Harper-Collins.

Kurz, Demie. 1991. Corporal Punishment and Adult Use of Violence: A Critique of "Discipline and Deviance." *Social Problems* 38: 155–161.

Labov, W. and D. Fanshel. 1977. *Therapeutic Discourse*. New York: Academic Press.

Lacqueur, Walter, and George Mosse, (eds.). 1966. *1914: the Coming of the First World War*. New York: Harper and Row.

Lafore, Laurence D. 1965. *The Long Fuse*. Philadelphia: Lippencott.

Lampert, Jay. 1989. Husserl's Theory of Parts and Wholes. *Research in Phenomenology* 19: 195–212.

Lee, Dwight. 1963. *The Outbreak of the First World War*. Boston: D. C. Heath.

Lerner, Daniel (ed.). 1963. *Parts and Wholes*. Cambridge: Harvard University Press.

Lévi-Strauss, Claude. 1963. *Structural Anthropology*. New York: Basic Books.

Levine, Donald. 1985. *The Flight from Ambiguity*. Chicago: University of Chicago Press.

Lewis, Helen. 1971. *Shame and Guilt in Neurosis*. New York: International Universities Press.

1977. *Psychic War in Men and Women*. New York: New York University Press.

1981. *Freud and Modern Psychology*. Vol.1. *The Emotional Basis of Mental Illness*. New York: Plenum.

1983. *Freud and Modern Psychology*. Vol.2. *The Emotional Basis of Human Behavior*. New York: Plenum.

Lievan, D. C. 1983. *Russia and the Origins of the First World War*. London: Macmillan.

Loseke, Donileen. 1991. Reply to Murray Straus: Readings on "Discipline and Deviance." *Social Problems* 38: 162–166.

Lynd, H. 1958. *Shame and the Search for Identity*. New York: Harcourt Brace.

McCord, Joan. 1991. Questioning the Value of Punishment. *Social Problems* 38: pp. 167–179.

Maher, Brendan. 1991. Deceptions, Rational Man, and Other Rocks on the Road to a Personality Psychology of Real People. In William Grove and Dante Cicchetti (eds.), *Thinking Clearly about Psychology*, vol. 2, pp. 72–88. Minneapolis: University of Minnesota Press.

Main, Mary, K. Kaplan, and J. Cassidy. 1985. Security in Infancy, Childhood and Adulthood: A Move to the Level of Representation. In *Growing Points of Attachment Theory and Research*. Monograph Social Research on Child Development, Dev. 50, Ser. # 209, pp. 66–104.

Mannheim, Karl. 1936. *Ideology and Utopia*. London: Routledge.

Markus, H. and S. Kitayama. 1991. Culture and the Self: Implications for Cognition, Emotion, and Motivation. *Psychological Review* 98: 224–253.

Mead, G. H. 1934. *Mind, Self and Society*. Chicago: University of Chicago Press.

Mills, C. Wright. 1959. *The Sociological Imagination*. Oxford: Oxford University Press.

Minsky, Marvin. 1985. *The Society of Mind*. New York: Simon and Schuster.

Monk, Ray. 1990. *Ludwig Wittgenstein The Duty of Genius*. New York: Free Press.

Morin, E. 1984. *Sociologie*. Paris: Fayard.

Moses, John A. 1975. *The Politics of Illusion*. New York: Harper and Row.

Nuttall, A. D. 1983. *A New Mimesis: Shakespeare and the Representation of Reality*. London: Methuen.

Oatley, Keith. 1996. Inference in Narrative and in Science. In D. R. Olson and N. Torrance (eds.), *Modes of Thought*, pp. 123–140. New York: Cambridge University Press

O'Connor, James. 1987. *The Meaning of Crisis*. London: Blackwell.

Parpal, Mary, and Eleanor Maccoby. 1985. Maternal Responsiveness and Subsequent Child Compliance. *Child Development* 56: 1,326–1,344.

Paz, Octavio. 1985. *The Labyrinth of Solitude*. New York: Grove.

Peirce, C. S. 1896–1908. Abduction and Induction. In *Philosophical Writings of Peirce*, ed. J. Buchler, pp. 150–156. New York: Dover. (1955).

Peristiany, J. 1966. *Honor and Shame in Mediterranean Societies*. Chicago: University of Chicago Press.

Person, Ethel S. 1988. *Dreams of Love and Fateful Encounters*. New York: Norton.

Pittenger, R., C. Hockett, and J. Danehy. 1967. *The First Five Minutes*. Ithaca, NY: Paul Martineau.

Remak, J. 1967. *The Origins of World War I*. New York: Holt, Rinehart and Winston.

Retzinger, Suzanne. 1991. *Violent Emotions: Shame and Rage in Marital Quarrels*. Newbury Park: Sage.

———. 1995. Identifying Shame and Anger in Discourse. *American Behavioral Scientist* 38, no. 8 (August): 1,104–1,113.

Riches, D. 1986. *The Anthropology of Violence*. Oxford: Blackwell.

Ryan, Michael. 1993. Shame and Expressed Emotion: A Case Study. *Sociological Perspectives* 36: 167–183.

Sachs, Harvy, Emanuel Schegloff, and Gail Jefferson. 1974. A Simplist Systematics for the Organization of Turn-Taking Conversation. *Language* 50: 696–735.

Sacksteder, W. 1991. Least Parts and Greatest Wholes: Variations on a Theme in Spinoza. *International Studies in Philosophy* 23, no. 1: 75–87.

Satir, V. 1972. *Peoplemaking*. Palo Alto: Science and Behavior.

Scheff, T. 1979. *Catharsis in Healing, Ritual and Drama*. Berkeley: University of California Press.

———. 1984. The Taboo on Coarse Emotions. *Review of Personality and Social Psychology* 5: 156–169.

———. 1986a. Toward Resolving the Controversy over "Thick Description." *Current Anthropology* 27: 408–409.

———. 1986b. Microlinguistics: A Theory of Social Action. *Sociological Theory*. 4, no. 1: 71–83.

———. 1987. The Shame–Rage Spiral: Case Study of an Interminable Quarrel. In H. B. Lewis (ed.), *The Role of Shame in Symptom Formation*. Hillsdale, NJ: LEA, 109–150.

———. 1989. Emotions & Understanding: Toward a Theory & Method. In S. Wapner (ed.), *Emotions in Ideal Human Development*. Hillsdale, NJ: Lawrence Erlbaum Associates, 101–134.

1990. *Microsociology: Discourse, Emotion, and Social Structure*. Chicago: University of Chicago Press.

1993. Toward a Social Psychological Theory of Mind and Consciousness. *Social Research* 60: 171–195.

Scheff, T. and D. Bushnell. 1985. A Theory of Catharsis. *Journal of Research in Personality* 18: 238–264.

Scheff, T. and S. Retzinger. 1994. Symposium. Reply to Reviews of *Emotions and Violence* by Candace Clark and Richard Felson. *Social Psychology Quarterly* 56: 310–312.

Scheff, T., and S. Retzinger. 1991. *Emotions and Violence: Shame and Rage in Destructive Conflicts*. Lexington: Lexington Books.

Scheff, T., S. Retzinger and M. Ryan. 1989. Crime, Violence and Self-Esteem. In A. Mecca, N. Smelser, and J. Vasconcellos (eds.), *The Social Importance of Self-Esteem*. Berkeley: University of California Press.

Schegloff, E. 1993. Reflections on Quantification in the Study of Conversation. *Research on Language and Social Interaction* 26: 99–128.

Schmitt, Bernadotte E. 1930. *The Coming of the War 1914*. New York: Scribners.

Schutz, A. 1962. *The Problem of Social Reality*. The Hague: M. Nijhoff.

Searle, John. 1994. Literary Theory and its Discontents. *New Literary Theory* 25: 637–667.

Seboek, T. and J. Umiker-Sebeok. 1983. "You know My Method." In U. Eco and T. Sebeok (eds.), *The Sign of Three: Dupin, Holmes, Pierce*. (11–54). Bloomington: Indiana University Press.

Seeman, Melvin. 1975. Alienation Studies. *Annual Review of Sociology* 1: 91–124.

Shakespeare, William. 1972. *Much Ado about Nothing*. New York: Harcourt Brace Jovanovich.

Shaver, P. and C. Clark. 1994. The Psychodynamics of Adult Romantic Attachment. In J. Masling and R. Bornstein (eds.), *Empirical Perspectives on Object Relations Theory*. Washington, DC: American Psychological Association.

Simmel, Georg. 1950. *The Sociology of Georg Simmel*. Glencoe: Free Press.

1955. *Conflict and the Web of Group Affiliations*. Glencoe: Free Press.

Smith, Barbara H. 1968. *Poetic Closure*. Chicago: University of Chicago Press.

Sontag, Raymond J. 1933. *European Diplomatic History*. New York: Appleton-Century.

Sperber, D. 1985. *On Anthropological Knowledge*. Cambridge: Cambridge University Press.

Stayton, Donelda, Robert Hogan, and Mary Ainsworth. 1971. Infant Obedience and Maternal Behavior: The Origins of Socialization Reconsidered. *Child Development* 42: 1,057–1,069.

Steiner, G. 1975. *After Babel*. London: Oxford University Press.

Steiner, Zara. 1977. *Britain and the Origins of the First World War*. London: Macmillan.

Stern, D., L. Hofer, W. Haft, and J. Dore. 1984. Affect Attunement: The Sharing of Feeling Starts Between Mother and Infant. In T . Field and N. Fox (eds.), *Social Perception in Early Infancy*. New York: Elsevier.

Stoessinger, John. 1990. *Why Nations Go to War*. London: St. Martin's.

Straus, Murray. 1991. Discipline and Deviance: Physical Punishment of Children and Violence and Other Crime in Adulthood. *Social Problems* 38: 133–154.

242   References

Tallis, Raymond. 1988. *Not Saussure: A Critique of Post-Saussurean Literary Theory.* New York: Macmillan.

Tangney, June, P. Wagner, C. Fletcher, and R. Gramzow. 1992. Shamed into Anger? The Relation of Shame and Guilt to Anger and Self-reported Aggression. *Journal of Personality and Social Psychology* 62: 669–675.

Tennov, Dorothy. 1979. *Love and Limerance: The Experience of being in Love.* Chelsea, MI: Scarborough House.

Tronick, E. Z., M. Ricks, and J. Cohn. 1982. Maternal and Infant Affect Exchange: Patterns of Adaption. In T. Field and A. Fogel (eds.), *Emotion and Early Interaction.* Hillsdale, NJ: Lawrence Erlbaum Associates, 83–100.

Turner, J. and A. Maryanski. 1979. *Functionalism.* Menlo Park, CA: Benjamin\-Cummings.

Turner, L. C. 1970. *Origins of the First World War.* New York: Norton.

Turner, P. and D. Pitt. 1989. *The Anthropology of War and Peace.* Granby, MA: Bergin and Garvey.

Turney-High, Harry H. 1949. *Primitive War.* Columbia: University of South Carolina Press.

Vaihinger, H. 1924. *The Philosophy of "As if".* London: Kegan Paul.

Vasquez, John. 1993. *The War Puzzle.* Cambridge: Cambridge University Press.

Watson, John. 1980. *The Double Helix.* New York: Norton.

Williamson, S. 1988. The Origins of World War I. In R. Rotberg and T. Rabb (eds.), *The Origins and Preventions of Major Wars.* Cambridge: Cambridge University Press, pp. 225–248.

Winograd, T. 1984 Computer Software for Working with Language. *Scientific American* 251: 130–145.

Index of authors

Index of topics

Studies in Emotion and Social Interaction

First Series
Editors: Paul Ekman and Klaus R. Scherer

8621